Corel DRAW!™
SPECIAL EFFECTS

Consulting Editor David Brickley

New Riders Publishing
Carmel, Indiana

CorelDRAW! Special Effects

Published by:
New Riders Publishing
11711 N. College Ave., Suite 140
Carmel, IN 46032 USA

Printed in the United States of America 1 2 3 4 5 6 7 8 9 0

Library of Congress Cataloging-in-Publication Data

CorelDRAW! Special Effects / David Brickley, consulting editor.
       p.   cm.
    Includes index.
    ISBN 1-56205-123-7 : #39.95
    1. Computer graphics. 2. CorelDRAW!   I. Brickley, David, 1954-
.
T385.C6654 1993
006.'869--dc20

Publisher
Lloyd J. Short

Associate Publisher
Tim Huddleston

Acquisitions Manager
Cheri Robinson

Acquisitions Editor
Rob Tidrow

Managing Editor
Matthew Morrill

Marketing Manager
Brad Koch

Acquisitions Coordinator
Stacey Beheler

Editorial Secretary
Karen Opal

Publishing Assistant
Melissa Keegan

Production Editor
Lisa Wilson

Editors
Patrice Hartmann
Peter Kuhns
Rob Lawson
Steve Weiss

Technical Editor
David Libby

Book Design
Roger Morgan

Production
Dennis Clay Hager
Juli Pavey
Michelle Self

Proofreaders
Terri Edwards
Mitzi Foster Gianakos
Howard Jones
John Kane
Tonya Simpson
Marcella Thompson
Dennis Wesner
Donna Winter
Phil Worthington

Indexed by
John Sleeva

About the Consulting Editor

David Brickley has been involved in art since he was a child. His professional career has carried him through advertising art direction and graphics design since 1975. He received a BFA in Computer Graphics from the Art Center College of Design in 1987. David currently is owner and operator of a computer graphics business in Moss Beach, California. His clients include many of the significant players in the personal computer industry.

Contributing Authors

Steve Arscott	Canada
Gary Bouton	USA
Wil Dawson	USA
Giuseppe DeBellis	USA
Joe Donnelly	Canada
Richard Feldman	USA
Joe Ferreira	USA
Mike Giles	USA
David Gronbeck-Jones	Canada
Shane Hunt	USA
David Libby	USA
Kevin Marshall	USA
Deborah Miller	USA
Dora Modly	USA
William Mogensen	USA
Chris Purcell	USA
William Schneider	USA
Gerry Wilson	USA
Lisa Windham	USA

Trademark Acknowledgments

New Riders Publishing has made every attempt to supply trademark information about company names, products, and services mentioned in this book. Trademarks indicated below were derived from various sources. New Riders Publishing cannot attest to the accuracy of this information.

Apple and Macintosh are registered trademarks of Apple Computer, Inc.

CompuServe is a registered trademark of H&R Block.

Corel is a registered trademark and CorelDRAW!, CorelPHOTO-PAINT!, and CorelTRACE! are trademarks of Corel Systems Corporation.

DeskJet, LaserJet, and PaintJet are registered trademarks and DeskJet is a trademark of Hewlett-Packard Co.

Gateway is a trademark of Gateway 2000, Inc.

IBM/PC/XT/AT are registered trademarks of the International Business Machines.

Northgate is a registered trademark of Northgate Computer Systems.

Panasonic is a registered trademark of Matsushita Electric Industrial Company, Ltd.

Phaser is a trademark of Tektronix, Inc.

PostScript is a registered trademark of Adobe Systems Incorporated.

Trademarks of other products mentioned in this book are held by the companies producing them.

Warning and Disclaimer

This book is designed to provide information about the CorelDRAW! computer program. Every effort has been made to make this book as complete and as accurate as possible, but no warranty or fitness is implied.

The information is provided on an "as is" basis. The author and New Riders Publishing shall have neither liability nor responsibility to any person or entity with respect to any loss or damages arising from the information contained in this book or from the use of the disks or programs that may accompany it.

Table of Contents

Introduction

I am pleased to present to you a collection of exceptional artwork created by the talents and ingenuity of a number of artists. I was very fortunate to have been asked by the publishers to help guide the selection of pieces included in this book. The publisher and I selected from work appearing in the *Corel Art Show 3* book, which showcased the winning entries. We also selected work from among entries to the 1993 CorelDRAW! World Design Contest.

The criteria for choosing work simply was that the piece displayed a valid use of a "special effect." *Special effect* is defined as an extraordinary visual quality created manually or by some feature of the software, such as blends. Allowances were also made for work that displayed overall effects qualities, such as mood and style.

In putting this book together, the publishers and I tried to ensure that it represented the best of what artists could do with CorelDRAW. You will be introduced to many artists and designers as they describe in detail how they created their work.

Artists who use CorelDRAW have become accustomed to using its amazing collection of effects tools. Regardless of all these capabilities, successful CorelDRAW artists use a measure of restraint when they apply special effects to their art. It was easy to find examples of art in which special effects took over and became the focus of the image.

Many fine pieces from the *1992 Corel Art Show 3* book were not chosen because either no special effect was apparent in the image, the artist elected not to participate, or time, distance, and language translations made their participation impractical.

Please do not construe this book as an endorsement for using special effects in your work. The objective is not to encourage the use of effects in art and design, but rather to show how well they work when used appropriately.

It is easy to understand how one can be swept away by the novelty of new effects, but as a designer or illustrator, you must carefully weigh the implications of using an effect in your work. Regardless of how "special" an effect may be, effects change the nature of your creation, and not always for the better. New Riders wants to provide you with the tools to create stunning special effects and to have fun creating these effects. We also want to show you how these effects can be used properly and at the right time.

How To Use this Book

You can benefit from exposure to this collection of artists and their work because you may come to rely on this book as a resource for ideas and approaches to solving problems. As you read through the artists' explanations and descriptions, you undoubtedly will see different levels of skill and sensibilities. One thing that most of these pieces have in common is that they solve a problem. Work is never more powerful than when it is an elegant solution to a problem. In that regard, we hope this book is of value to you.

Most of the art in this book is, or looks like, commercial illustration. *Commercial art* is produced to create a message for a business or enterprise. This type of artwork is created in response to a need or to solve a problem. One could say that commercial art is an expression of business. In contrast, fine art is a personal expression of the artist.

The Computer's Role in Art

As a relatively new form of art, computer graphics has captured the enthusiasm and imagination of many people, perhaps more than any other in history. What this means is that suddenly a lot of people who have little or no training or art education are now creating art. Personally, I see this as a good thing, even if it means more questionable work is floating about for a while.

Talent stems from desire. If this technology awakens a desire in people to create and express themselves, good! Each person who has the desire to create work is, at some point in their evolution, an artist or designer. That desire translates into a need for understanding and training. Perhaps this growing pressure for knowledge eventually will be felt by our schools. The educational system then, hopefully, will respond and actually begin to treat design and rendering as a standard part of basic education.

Sudden Interest in Computer-generated Art

Why are so many people suddenly interested in using a computer to create original artwork? It is my belief that the computer has become popular for artists and designers (trained or otherwise) because it is a risk-free environment in which to create work.

The computer allows you to change your mind: you can put a mark on the "paper," move it, change it, and then erase it without penalty. You can waffle to your heart's content. Unlike more traditional mediums, such as watercolor, there is no consequence for changing your mind or making a mistake. If an element in your drawing needs to be scaled or moved, you can do so without affecting or damaging the "paper" or having to start again.

One of the reasons desktop computers have become so popular is that software technology enables you to create interesting visual effects. Special effects began with a moving dot on a screen that represented a bouncing ball. It was created in "real time" by a room-sized computer created in 1950 that had only 2,048 bytes of memory.

Visual effects continued to be the domain of big computers for the next three decades. Then, in 1981, the personal computer industry exploded with the introduction of the IBM PC. Even though these computers had limited capabilities, a viable market suddenly developed, and the drive was on to create interesting software.

As more powerful processors and graphics hardware were introduced in 1984, more capable and interesting software was written. Simple paint programs were developed with the basic tools one needed to draw pictures. They also came with special effects features. You could easily "cycle" palettes, rubber stamp sections of your image, and fill areas with graded colors. Even in the very early graphics software programs, special effects found their place.

By the time interesting graphics programs emerged, an explosion of interest was taking place in personal computers. PC hardware not only made special effects possible to program, it also was the rationale companies needed to spend money developing software. Competition is what drives graphics software companies into developing innovative features and powerful special effects. The users, of course, are the winners.

The Introduction of CorelDRAW!

Since its launch in 1989, CorelDRAW has garnered a following of devoted users whose estimated numbers currently approach 700,000. The size of CorelDRAW's user base demonstrates the caliber of its technology. Extensive research and development paid off even from the first release. New users were attracted to features that were both powerful and easy to use. Even in the relatively primitive environment that was Windows 2.11, CorelDRAW quickly became the program to use if you wanted to create an image for PostScript output or other formats.

Types of Effects

Two types of effects can be created on the computer: traditional and technical. *Traditional effects* are created on the computer the same way artists have always created them—manually. This includes such things as rendering form, lighting, describing surface qualities, and blending colors and visual effects that help set a mood.

The other kind of effect is software dependent. Blends, envelopes, extrudes, graded or radial fills, and other similar functions are examples of *technical effects*. As an artist, I strongly encourage you to understand first how a visual effect can be created in a traditional way.

Traditional rendering is far more flexible than technical capabilities, enabling you to draw what you need the way you need it. If you rely entirely on your software for special effects, your choices are limited to its set of features. Moreover, some effects, such as smooth blends and graded fills, can create a "superficial" or "plastic" quality to otherwise good art.

Some special effects have become separate software products, such as type manipulation software, 3D rendering programs, and fractal image generators. The emphasis on special effects often seems to be overexaggerated, however, to help sell a product. Some artists who are still forming an understanding of their craft use special effects without any measure of restraint. A similar problem was evident when desktop publishing software first became popular: users tended to overload a document with several typefaces.

Evolution Effects

The desire for special effects was not born with the computer industry. You can trace its roots back to an earlier time in our culture. From the first moment technology helped us describe our thoughts visually, special effects were evident. Soon after photography was developed (no pun intended) in the mid-1800's, interesting effects were discovered.

These effects, such as blur, exposure time, double exposure, and depth focus, either were not apparent to the human eye or were only possible on film. Each of these effects soon became part of the tools that any competent photographer used. There was even an effect that became a form of parlor amusement—a stereoscopic viewer. People could use this device to see nearly identical, side-by-side photos that gave a hyper-real sense of depth. It seems to be in our nature to readily accept new visual expressions that expand our ability to communicate ideas.

Special effects as we know them today are an outgrowth of entertainment and the high-tech mass media that pummels us every day with sophisticated images. In the last 20 years, both the volume and production quality of these effects have increased at a phenomenal rate, thanks in large part to the computer. The media and entertainment industries have learned that images influence people—the more visually arresting, the better.

Incredible visual enhancements and effects have become an addiction these industries share. The competition among media and entertainment companies for your attention, opinions, money, or votes drives them to rely heavily on special effects. These industries are, in some measure, special effects "junkies"—having an escalating need for ever more powerful effects with no way out. This cycle is exasperated because today's "gee whiz" effects soon lose their novelty, and then quickly become passé.

The significance of how quickly special effects lose their novelty should not be understated. The more you rely on a glitzy special effect to communicate an idea, the sooner your idea will be dated. The effect of water rippling, for example, always is valid. Art that is created using extruded type with a graded fill or a calligraphic outline on a wavy path, however, is artificial and will be seen as no more than just another expression of a period. If you are interested in creating work that transcends time, special effects will not be helpful.

The result of this constant barrage of special effects on our culture is a de facto sensibility that seems to condone their excessive use. Special effects have developed a language all their own. Flying logo graphics on TV, for example, are an unspoken endorsement, as are computer wireframe animations of objects being "beamed down" in a shimmering light.

Special effects on television are also used as a presentation device. For example, glitzy video effects help weather and sports announcers hold our attention while they spew facts and figures. It's nearly impossible to watch any amount of TV without seeing examples of highly-charged special effects.

Living in a culture subjected to a large volume of slick media has an effect on the average user. The threshold that separates good work from bad is now much higher than it was. It is now harder to create work that will be received favorably. If you see a new ad that was produced using standards from 20 years ago, both the message and what it talks about will likely be passed off as "cheap." Work that is poorly produced is associated with risky products or shoddy service. We have become an increasingly sophisticated audience that expects a lot from those who ask for our time and attention.

The Creative Process

After someone spends money to buy a computer, learns how to use it, and then discovers how wonderful it is to create work in this "risk free" environment, he or she is faced with a hardened audience. This culture has learned to expect nothing but great work. Thus, the dilemma: with all these incredible tools at your disposal, why is it still so hard to create successful work?

The answer lies in the process used to create the original work. The creative process consists of two basic steps: decide what to do, then do what you decide. If you want to build a house, for example, your first step would be to design it. Before you nail one board to another, you must have blueprints in hand. That's the first half of the creation process—deciding what to do.

The computer, by nature, is best used for the last half of the creation process. The computer is like a hammer and a saw. It is a dumb tool. The computer must be told how to do everything it does at every level of its operation. You shouldn't depend on your software for design help. Software's real job is to make the computer do what you ask of it. Computers and software are not meant to help you make design decisions; that is your job. For this reason, you should design your work before you switch on your computer.

If you use the computer for design, you probably will find that your design decisions are being influenced by the features in the software. If you look at designs you created before you use a computer and compare them to designs you create on the computer, more than likely the software influenced your decisions. In some ways your decisions become an extension of and limited by the software you use.

A word to the wise: design with a pencil and scrap paper. Get technology out of the way. Only after you finish your thinking and concepts should you turn to the computer to begin experimenting and executing your work.

When you begin to use the computer in its proper role as a tool to execute your designs, you will see an improvement in the quality of your ideas and your productivity and have more confidence in the results. Although some special effects require experimentation before you are familiar with the way to create the idea, you should complete your design off-line before you start to execute it.

By sheer weight of numbers and diversity, it seems that special effects have found a place in our way of life. They have become the window dressing of our cultural identity. But they are best used to help us communicate and understand ideas rather than as a substitute for artistic and creative merit. Knowing this may help you avoid being swept along with the tide. Have fun creating special effects, but use them with restraint.

Conventions Used in this Book

This book uses three special icons, which help you identify certain parts of the text:

A note presents brief, additional information relating to the current topic. A note also can be used as a reminder or to clarify a point.

A tip is an added insight for your benefit.

A warning tells you when a procedure may be dangerous—that is, when you may run the risk of losing data, locking your system, or even damaging your hardware.

New Riders Publishing

The staff of New Riders Publishing is committed to bringing you the very best in computer reference material. Each New Riders book is the result of months of work by authors and staff, who research and refine the information contained within its covers.

As part of this commitment to you, the NRP reader, New Riders invites your input. Please let us know if you enjoy this book, if you have trouble with the information and examples presented, or if you have a suggestion for the next edition.

Please note, however, that the New Riders staff cannot serve as a technical resource for CorelDRAW or CorelDRAW application-related questions, including hardware- or software-related problems. Refer to the documentation that accompanies your CorelDRAW or CorelDRAW application package for help with specific problems.

If you have a question or comment about any New Riders book, please write to NRP at the following address. We will respond to as many readers as we can. Your name, address, or phone number will never become part of a mailing list or be used for any other purpose than to help us continue to bring you the best books possible.

> New Riders Publishing
> Paramount Publishing
> Attn: Associate Publisher
> 11711 N. College Avenue
> Carmel, IN 46032

If you prefer, you can FAX New Riders Publishing at the following number:

> (317) 571-3484

We welcome your electronic mail to our Compuserve ID:

> 70031,2231

Thank you for selecting *CorelDRAW! Special Effects.*

Light and Shadow Effects

"Painting is the nail to which I fasten my ideas."

—Georges Braque

Corelosaurus

by Giuseppe De Bellis

New Design Concepts
Fair Lawn, New Jersey

Equipment Used

486/50 computer system
16M of RAM
ATI video accelerator board

Output Equipment Used

400dpi CANON CLC500
Fiery image processing unit

Giuseppe De Bellis is an architect for the N.Y.C. Board of Education and a free-lance graphics designer.

He has used CorelDRAW, since its very first version, on a daily basis for both professions.

CorelDRAW and three months of work were needed to complete "Corelosaurus." The program was used to its fullest extent and capabilities.

A wide range of techniques and different modules offered by CorelDRAW were adopted for the completion of this artwork.

Procedure

1. Create a hand-drawn sketch of the dragon. Make sure that you apply pressure to the pencil as you draw so that all the lines are dark and well-defined.

2. Scan in the newly created drawing on a high-resolution scanner. A 600 dpi scanner is sufficient. Save the image as a TIFF or BMP file (see fig. 1.1).

3. Open CorelTRACE, then open the scanned image. From the CorelTRACE pull-down menu, select Tracing Options, and click on Edit option.

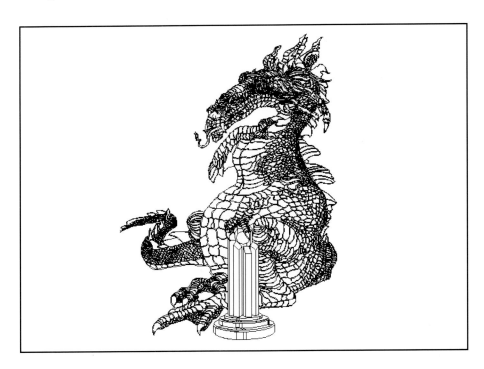

Figure 1.1:
The scanned drawing.

Now, in the Tracing Options dialog box, change the following options (see fig. 1.2):

Tracing Method	=	Follow Outline
Curve Length	=	Medium
Convert Long Lines	=	Medium
Outline Filtering	=	Mild
Fit Curve	=	Medium
Sample Rate	=	Fine

Begin the tracing process.

4. Start CorelDRAW, and open the newly traced image. Clean up all unwanted lines, dots, and marks.

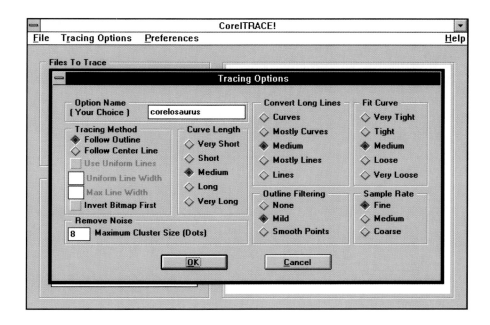

Figure 1.2:
The Tracing Options dialog box.

5. Connect all the nodes of the various objects that belong to the same path. Using the Node Edit tool, find all the "open" curve segment paths, and join the beginning of each open curve segment with the end of each open curve segment (see fig. 1.3).

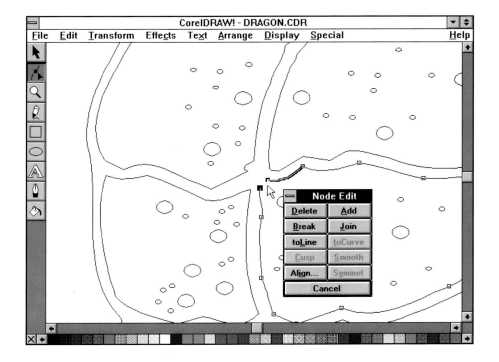

Figure 1.3:
Example of objects to be joined.

By joining the beginning and end of each "open" curve segment, you can later fill these single continuous curves with colors.

6. Make sure that all the horizontal and vertical lines in the trophy are straight. If the lines are not straight, use the Node Edit tool to select the first and last node of a line. Double-click on the line, and use the Al**i**gn option to align accordingly. Then click on OK (see fig. 1.4).

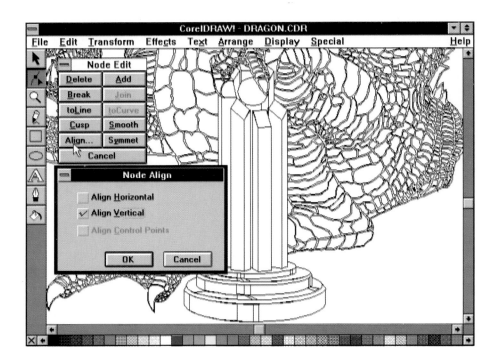

Figure 1.4:
The Node Align dialog box.

7. Start the painting process. Open the Fill roll-up window, and click on fountain fill. Choose the colors to be blended by clicking on the Start and End color buttons.

   Change the angle of the linear or radial fill by dragging the control in the Fill roll-up window's preview box. Make sure, prior to this operation, that an imaginary light source direction has been chosen so that all the other fills follow the light source of the drawing accordingly (see fig. 1.5).

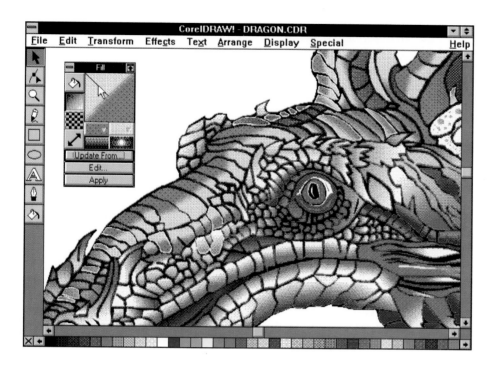

Figure 1.5:
The Fill roll-up window.

8. Repeat the preceding step for all the objects associated with the dragon.

9. Use the Blend feature to fill the nails, teeth, and center row of the scales located on the belly of the dragon.

To do so, first make a **D**uplicate of each object that you want to blend. Hold down the Shift key, and crop the object by dragging one of the side handles and pressing the right mouse button. Change the color of the newly created object to the shade you want. Select the two objects, and blend them together. Repeat this for all the objects in question (see fig. 1.6).

10. To create a rough look on the belly of the dragon, draw a random number of small circles on top of the scales. Make these circles a different color from the scales.

11. Now it is time to design the background. Assign the background a new layer.

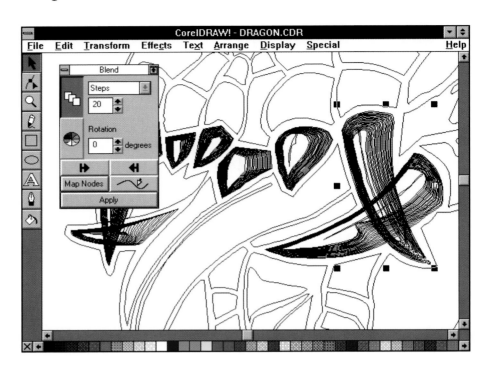

Figure 1.6:

The Blend roll-up window. The teeth are individually blended to create a round look.

 Assigning elements to different layers helps organize the drawing.

To assign the background a new layer, choose **L**ayers Roll-Up from the **A**rrange menu. The Layers window appears.

Click on the Layers roll-up window's arrow. Then click on New. The Layer Options dialog box appears. Make your selection, and click on OK.

In the Layer Options dialog box, double-click on the layer containing the dragon, and deselect the **V**isible option (see fig. 1.7).

12. Minimize CorelDRAW module, and open CorelPAINT. From CorelDRAW CD-ROM version, import CLOUDS2.TIF, located in the Library\phtpaint\textures subdirectory (see fig. 1.8). If the textures are not installed, use any suitable color bitmap for the background.

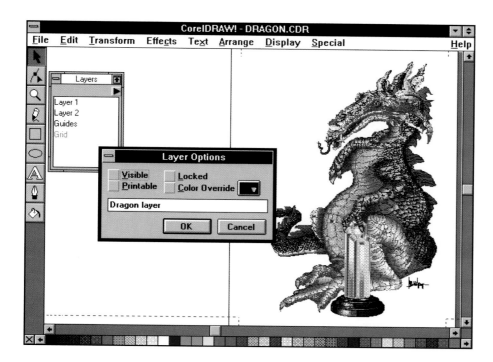

Figure 1.7:
The Layer Options dialog box.

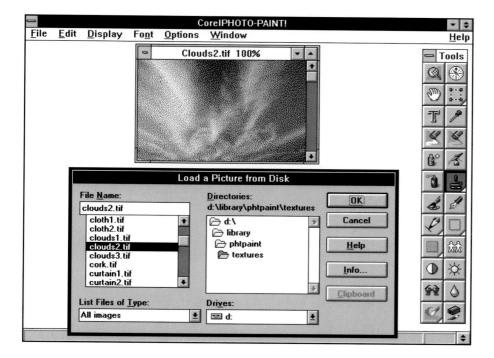

Figure 1.8:
The CorelPHOTO-PAINT screen showing the selected TIF image.

Make sure that the work is saved before you perform this operation. If you do not have enough free windows system resources,
the computer may crash!

13. Edit the image with the Filled Box tool by adding a one-
    inch strip of red to the bottom of the image.

14. Blend the newly created red strip with the rest of the image
    by using the Flood Fill and Airbrush tools.

15. Save the image. Then go back to CorelDRAW, and import
    the image. Use the Pick tool to size the image and reposi-
    tion it in the upper half of the drawing (see fig. 1.9).

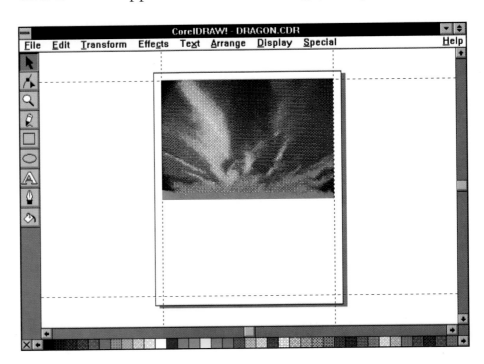

Figure 1.9:

*The correct position of the
newly created image.*

16. Use the Pencil tool to draw the cityscape. Make sure that
    the two ends of the cityscape contour are 2" long vertical
    lines and the bottom (of the contour or perimeter of the
    cityscape) is a horizontal line that connects the vertical
    lines to create a closed path. Fill the cityscape with 80-
    percent black and no outline.

17. Pick the newly created object, drag the upper middle handle down one inch, and make a copy of the object by pressing the right button mouse.

Change the fill to 40-percent black and no outline.

18. Select the two objects and blend them together. Figure 1.10 shows a wireframe and a preview example of the cityscape.

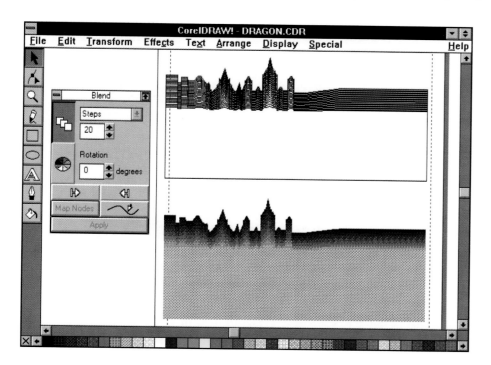

Figure 1.10:
The cityscape.

19. Position the cityscape on top of the red strip of the clouds, approximately in the middle of the page.

20. Draw the dunes using the procedures in step 15.

Make sure that the tallest dune is created first. Then create the other dunes, overlapping each one and gradually making them shorter.

Fill the dunes with a horizontal linear fill at 90 percent, using a lighter color on top and a darker color on the bottom. Do not apply any outline.

21. In the Dragon's layer, select the **V**isible option. Make sure that the Dragon's layer is on top of all the other layers.

22. Create a rectangle around the perimeter of the drawing. Do not fill it, but apply a thick white outline so that a sharp and clean border covers all the imperfections.

Figure 1.11 shows the completed artwork.

Figure 1.11:
The completed artwork.

Gerry Wilson
1991

Nantucket Lighthouse

by Gerry Wilson

Bay Ridge Graphics
Brooklyn, New York

Equipment Used

A Northgate 386/33
16M of RAM

Output Equipment Used

Iris 3024

Gerry Wilson is a self-employed computer graphics artist who specializes in historically accurate illustrations of military equipment. This award winning piece was developed as a change of pace from his daily routine and as an exercise in deep foreground and light background techniques.

Procedure

The Background

Create the background by following these steps:

1. Set up your page to letter size in landscape mode, and use guidelines to establish 1/2" margins.

   Use Snap To **G**uidelines throughout the process to ensure that all the objects align properly.

2. Draw a rectangle to fill most of the page within the margin guidelines. Leave a 1" space along the bottom so that when you apply a gradient fill it does not go to the bottom of the page.

3. Set the outline for this rectangle to None, and fill it with a linear gradient from red at the top to pale yellow at the bottom.

4. Draw a circle approximately 2" in diameter in the lower left area of the background. Set the outline for the circle to None, and fill the circle with a radial fill from yellow to pale yellow in the center.

5. **S**tretch & Mirror this circle by 50 percent both horizontally and vertically, and leave the original. Select all objects on this layer, and **G**roup them (see fig. 1.12).

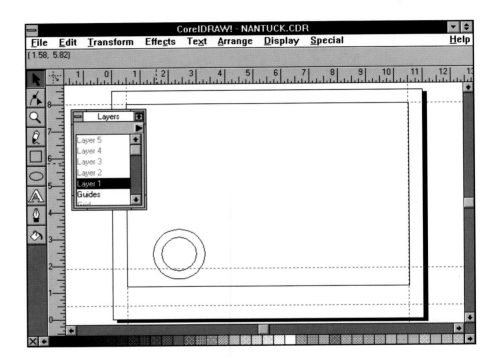

Figure 1.12:
Creating the background layer.

The Foreground

To create the foreground, follow these steps:

1. Draw a rectangle at the bottom of the page with no outline, and fill it with black. Then snap the rectangle to the lower guideline and the side guidelines.

2. Convert this rectangle to curves, and use the Node Edit tool to change the upper line of the rectangle to a curve.

3. Add as many nodes as you want to the top line of the rectangle, and shape the top line to the desired effect for the horizon.

4. Add some foliage by selecting the Plants Symbol Category and pasting four or five symbols into the image.

There is a wealth of interesting objects in the Symbols Library that comes with CorelDRAW. Symbols can be accessed by selecting the Text tool and pressing the mouse button to display the Symbols dialog box. This drawing makes use of the Plants Symbol Category, which contains 94 plants. Use any of the plants that you think will enhance your drawing. I used 41, 42, 43, and 44.

5. Set the size to .50". Then **D**uplicate the plant symbols, and place them along the horizon to break up the harsh line. Fill them with black.

It makes no difference whether the plant symbols are on top of the foreground or behind it as they are filled with solid black.

6. Using the Pencil tool's Bézier Mode, add some short lines and convert them to curves for grass.

Remember that you want to break up the horizon and add a little interesting detail so that the horizon is not a smooth line.

7. Select all objects on this layer, and **G**roup them as shown in figure 1.13.

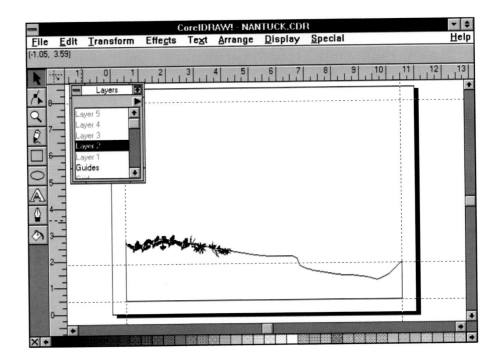

Figure 1.13:
Creating the foreground.

The Lighthouse

The lighthouse is a grouping of 29 objects, most of which are black rectangles and lines. To create the lighthouse, follow these steps:

1. Draw the first (the tower) rectangle, convert it to curves, and make the upper side more narrow than the bottom.

 While creating the lighthouse, use guidelines and position them where needed to ensure that the elements of the lighthouse snap together for proper alignment.

2. Create two more rectangles to form the platform, snapping them into place.

3. Above the platform, draw another rectangle for the light housing (the area of the lighthouse that houses the light), and set the fill to None and the outline to 0.028".

4. Draw another rectangle, and place it over the lower portion of the "open" rectangle to create the solid portion of the light housing.

5. Add a rectangle for the roof, convert it to curves, and manipulate the nodes for the desired slope.

6. Add five vertical lines to simulate the windows of the light housing between the roof and the lower edge of the open area. These lines should not be evenly spaced.

Spacing the lines unevenly gives the illusion of perspective.

7. Add a vertical line to the top of the platform for a railing support, and draw a solid circle at the top of the line. Fill the circle with black.

8. **D**uplicate the line and circle so that you have four supports on the platform, two on each side of the light housing.

9. **S**tretch & Mirror one of the supports by 80 percent to achieve a support for the rear of the platform.

10. Position the smaller support between the two full-size supports and the light housing. Then **D**uplicate the smaller support and place the duplicate on the other side.

11. Add a line for the railing, and convert it to curves so that you can edit the nodes to connect with the top of the supports. This creates a nice slope to the railing between the posts.

12. Add an ellipse to the center of the light housing to depict the actual light, and position it so that it comes up to the horizontal center of the unit.

13. The last three items to create are a circle at the apex of the roof, a vertical line to simulate the lightning rod, and a rectangle on the left side of the tower. Select all of these objects, and **G**roup them (see fig. 1.14).

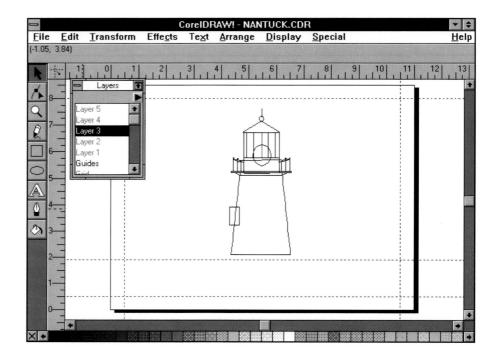

Figure 1.14:
Creating the lighthouse.

The Walkway and the Frame

The walkway to the lighthouse fills the lower right segment of the drawing with some interesting objects to break up the stark foreground. The walkway is composed of simple lines drawn at the appropriate angles to connect the lighthouse with the right margin of the page.

Create the walkway by following these steps:

1. Make sure that Snap To **G**uidelines is on when you position the right ends of the lines at the right of the drawing so that the ends do not go beyond the edge.

2. Select all objects on this layer, and **G**roup them (see fig. 1.15).

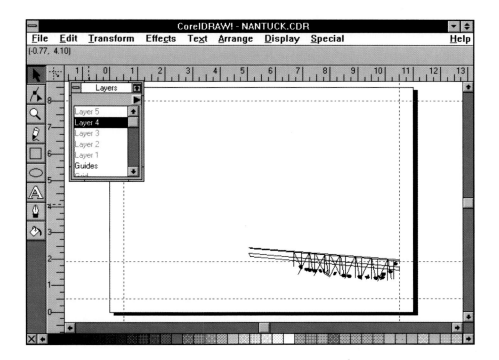

Figure 1.15:
Creating the walkway.

To create a frame, follow these steps:

1. Make sure that Snap To **G**uidelines is on. Then draw a rectangle within the margin guidelines. Set the rectangle's fill to None and the outline to 0.28".

Adding a frame not only gives a finishing touch to the work but also covers objects that did not snap to the margin guidelines.

2. Sign your work. You have just completed a piece of computer art, so why not sign it? Place your signature block in the lower right corner of the drawing.

I usually use Present typeface at 10 or 12 points. Because the foreground is black, I set the text's fill to white.

3. Select all objects on this layer, and **G**roup them. Now the drawing is complete (see fig. 1.16).

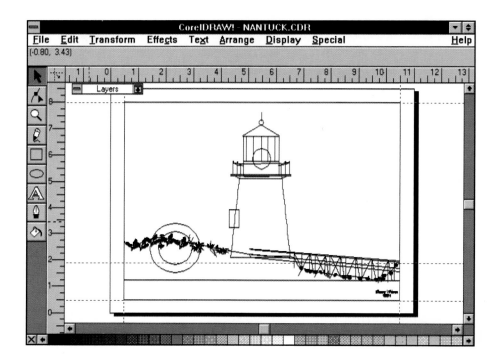

Figure 1.16:
The completed drawing.

Tropical Hallway

by Stephen Arscott

Mississauga, Ontario Canada

Equipment Used

486 IBM PC-compatible

Output Equipment Used

Lasergraphics LFR plus film recorder

Stephen Arscott is a free-lance computer graphics artist who works in metro Toronto, Canada. He has been using CorelDRAW for the past three years to produce presentation graphics/speaker-support slides. This piece of art was created for self-promotion and depicts a hall-way at the Bavaro Beach Hotel, Dominican Republic.

Procedure

This image originally was created on a landscape slide page for future output to 35mm slide.

1. Draw the sky by creating a rectangle the size of the page, and gradating it from a light blue to a darker blue.

2. An irregular shape is created as part of the background foliage. Create a bitmap fill for this shape by first laying out a loose, irregular pattern of shapes (roughly the shapes of leaves). These need only be black and white and fill a square-shaped area (see fig. 1.17).

3. Select **C**reate Pattern from the **S**pecial menu, and create a bitmap pattern using the marquee. The bitmap you create is automatically added to the list of pattern fills. The irregular shape you created earlier to represent the foliage backdrop now can be given this bitmap fill. Assign two dark shades of green to this bitmap fill. **D**uplicate and reduce the size of the background shape and fit one into each section between the posts (see fig. 1.18).

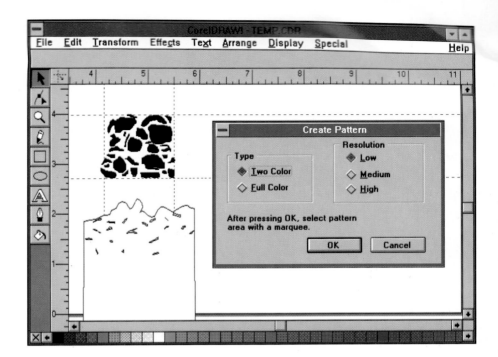

Figure 1.17:

Creating your own bitmap fill.

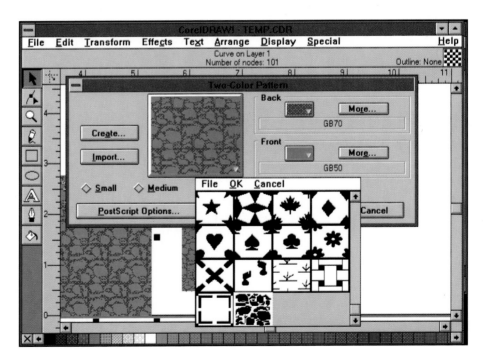

Figure 1.18:

Using your own bitmap fill.

4. The palm leaves are drawn in over the bitmap area. They originally were hand-drawn in black and white and then scanned into the computer with a hand-held scanner. The resulting TIFF files were then brought into CorelTRACE, traced, and then imported as vector art into CorelDRAW. Six palms were scanned into the computer and duplicated, skewed, rotated, mirrored, and layered until a loose collage of leaves was created. Rely on these features to create the dense look of the foliage, reduce the size of the leaves, and heighten the illusion of perspective the further you get from the viewer (see fig. 1.19).

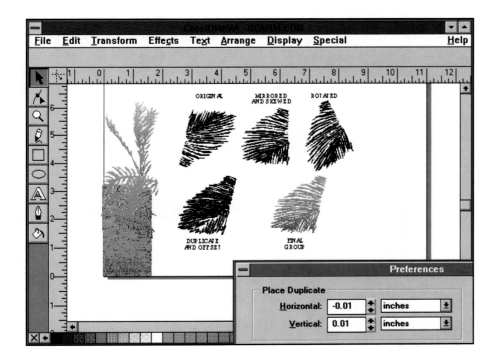

Figure 1.19:
Creating the palm leaves.

5. Fill these palms with a green gradated fill, and then **D**uplicate and offset the entire group. This duplicate group is layered behind the original and given a lighter shade of green to provide a highlight on the leaves.

6. To create the hall, a single vanishing point is established. Guidelines drawn from this central point represent the future placement of the floor, walls, ceiling, floor, and railings (see fig. 1.20).

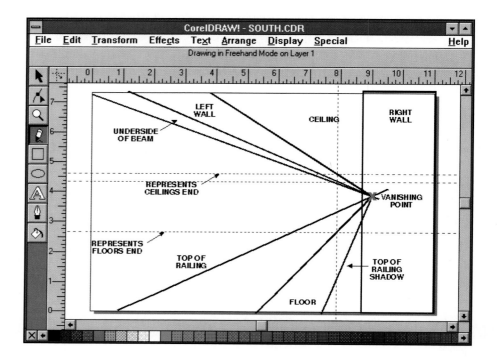

Figure 1.20:
Establishing your perspective.

7. Create the left wall as a rectangle with evenly spaced poles in a plan view. A plan view refers to what the image looks like when viewed head-on in two dimensions (see fig. 1.21).

8. Select Edit Perspective from the Effects menu to shape the plan view to fit the perspective guidelines. Continue to adjust the perspective until the perspective fits the guidelines and the poles remain perfectly vertical (see fig. 1.22).

Give the objects in perspective (the wall) a gradated fill that becomes less saturated with color (lighter) as it approaches the vanishing point to increase the illusion of depth.

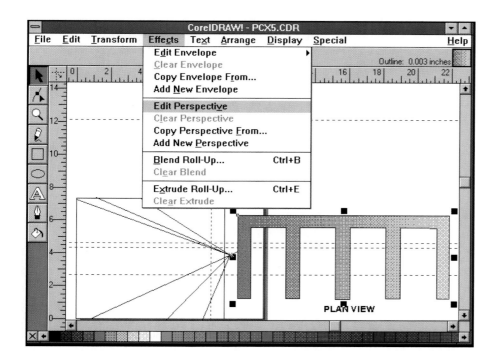

Figure 1.21:
Editing the perspective of a plan view.

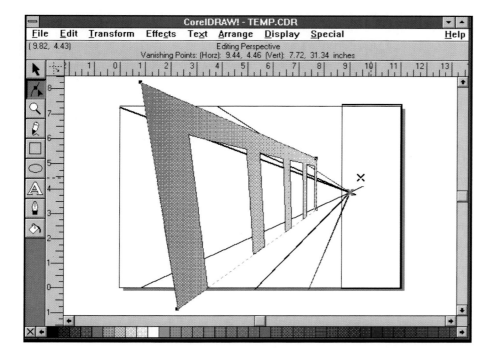

Figure 1.22:
Editing the perspective.

9. Draw the underside of the beam, ceiling, and floor. These objects can be drawn by using the Pencil tool and shaping the areas to the perspective established by the guideline. The underside of the beam is important because it determines the width of the sunlit sides of the poles (see fig. 1.23).

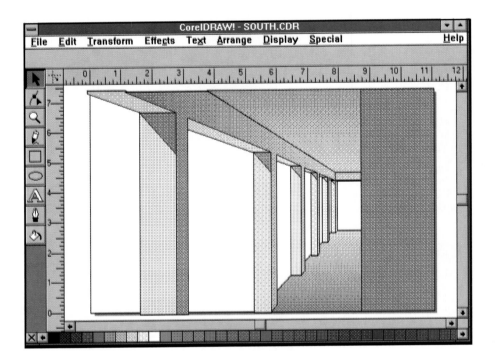

Figure 1.23:

Adding the finishing touches to the wall.

10. Use the Rectangle tool to draw rectangles for the poles. A shadow is drawn at the top, then the two objects are duplicated, reduced in size, and placed farther back in the perspective. Duplicating the shadow with the pole ensures the consistency of the angle of the light source. Reduce the color saturation of each pole and shadow as each gets closer to the vanishing point.

11. The railings are created in much the same way. First create
(in plan view) a group of rectangles (one rectangle that has
been duplicated and evenly spaced). **C**ombine the group
into one object, and select Edit Perspecti**v**e from the Effe**c**ts
menu to shape it to fit the perspective guidelines established earlier. This railing group then is given a top railing,
shadows, and highlights. Then the entire group is duplicated, reduced in size, and fit into each section (see fig. 1.24).

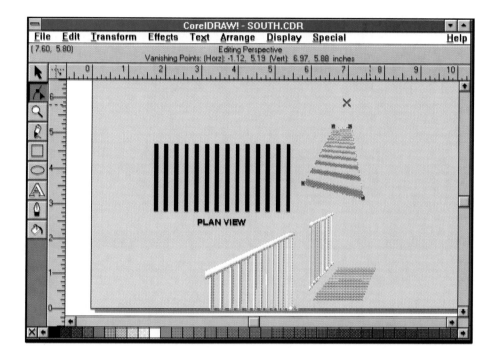

Figure 1.24:
*Creating the railings and
shadows.*

12. The shadows on the floor are created the same way. One
set is created and shaped to fit the perspective guidelines,
and then duplicated, sized, and placed within the same
perspective.

13. The door is a group of rectangles with different shades of the same color to create the illusion of an emboss (see fig. 1.25).

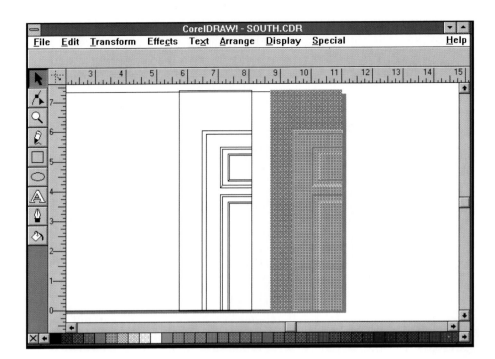

Figure 1.25:

Creating the contoured door.

Rendering Form Effects

"There is nothing worse than a brilliant image of a fuzzy concept."

—*Ansel Adams*

Photo Shoot

by *William Schneider*

Athens, Ohio

Equipment Used

386/33 Northgate
8M of RAM
ATI Ultra video card
NEC 4D 16" monitor
Microtek 300Z flatbed scanner

Output Equipment Used

ICOM, Inc., an Autographix slide
service in Columbus, Ohio

As both a photographer and illustrator, William Schneider frequently uses photographs as starting points for CorelDRAW illustrations. This picture of a joyous photographer, taken while he was studying for his Masters of Fine Arts in photography, began as a black-and-white self-portrait. Sometimes the serious side of art gets tedious, and you have to do something off-the-wall to keep your wits.

With the help of the often-overlooked CorelTRACE module, the black-and-white photograph was converted to a dynamic color image that garnered Schneider a bonus prize in the third annual CorelDRAW World Design Contest.

Procedure

1. Select a photograph that can be traced well. On-camera flash and other frontal lighting methods cast shadows directly behind the subject, and do little to help show the shape of the subject itself. This photo, made with a low 45-degree sidelight, has adequate shadow modeling in the face for tracing. The high-contrast sheen of the folds in the jacket also trace well (see fig. 2.1).

When you take the photo, use side-lighting on the subject—it works better than front-lighting.

2. Scan the image with the grayscale setting at moderate resolution (100-150 dpi). Because the image will be traced, a high-resolution scanner setting is not necessary. High-resolution scans slow image-editing work on the computer. Crop unnecessary detail by using the scanner controls.

3. Open the scanned image in CorelPHOTO-PAINT, and select the important picture areas by using the Scissors Selection tool. In this example, the photographer and his camera are selected, omitting the busy background (see fig. 2.1).

Figure 2.1:
Use the Scissors Selection tool to select the important picture areas.

4. **C**opy the selected area to the clipboard. Find the dimensions of the scanned image in pixels, and make a new file that has the same dimensions (see fig. 2.2).

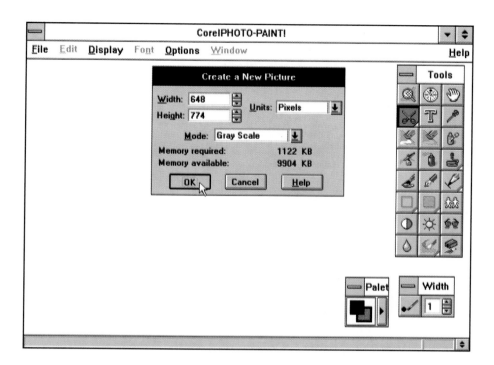

Figure 2.2:

Creating a new file with the same height and width as the original tile.

To find the image information of an open file in CorelPHOTO-PAINT, click on the upper left control button of the image, and select **I**mage Info from the dialog box.

5. Fill the new file with a gradient fill from black to white, top to bottom.

6. The newly created gradient background shows some banding from top to bottom. The resulting trace, if performed now, also would show straight horizontal lines. Add noise by using the **E**dit, **F**ilter, **A**dd Noise command to break up banding in the smooth gradient fill. The **A**dd Noise filter randomly varies the gray pixel tones, blurring the boundary line between adjacent tones in the gradient, reducing visible banding. A modest amount of random noise can be added by using a variance of 10 and a flat distribution (see fig. 2.3).

7. The background needs more smoothing before the photograph can be pasted. Apply **B**lend filter with the **B**lending Amount set to 50 percent and the **W**ide aperture option checked several times to smooth the background. The

background should not have any visible banding at this point in the process, and the minor speckling added by the noise filter should be diminished.

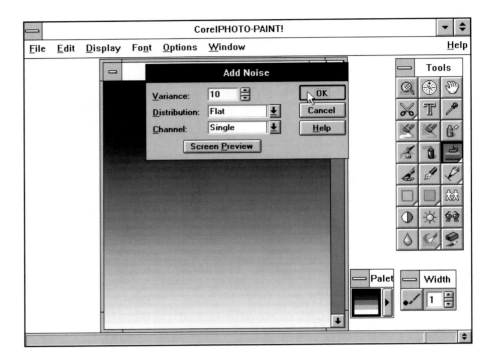

Figure 2.3:

*Use the **A**dd Noise filter to reduce banding in the gradient fill.*

8. **P**aste the image from the clipboard, and position it within the image area (see fig. 2.4).

9. Save the new file as a different name, just in case the tracing doesn't work out as expected. This eliminates having to rescan the image for each trial.

10. Open CorelTRACE, and create a new tracing option called Smooth Outline. The settings selected (in the Tracing Options dialog box shown in figure 2.5) help reduce the number of nodes that result from the trace.

CorelTRACE can generate thousands of nodes when tracing large or detailed bitmaps. An image with an excessive number of nodes creates a large, complex CorelDRAW file that may not print.

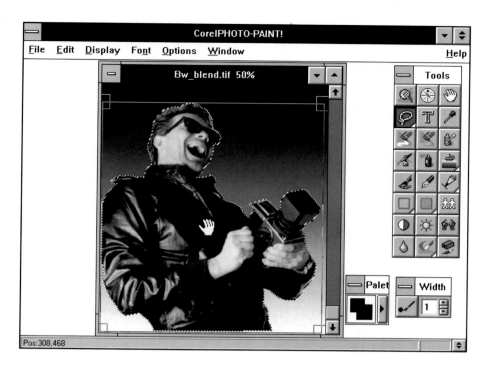

Figure 2.4:
Paste the clipboard image onto the gradient background.

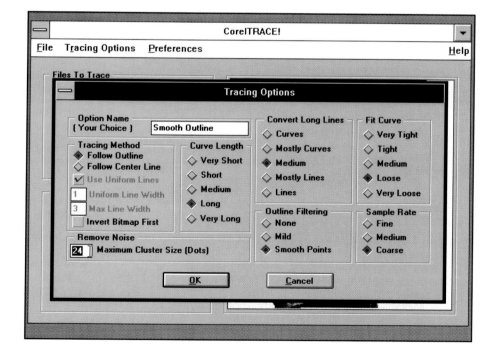

Figure 2.5:
Create a new Smooth Outline tracing option in the Tracing Options dialog box.

11. Under **P**references, **C**olor Reduction, uncheck Convert to Monochrome, and set Reduce grays to 4 Gray levels (see fig. 2.6).

Using a higher number of grays might make the image more photographic, but the image becomes much harder to edit.

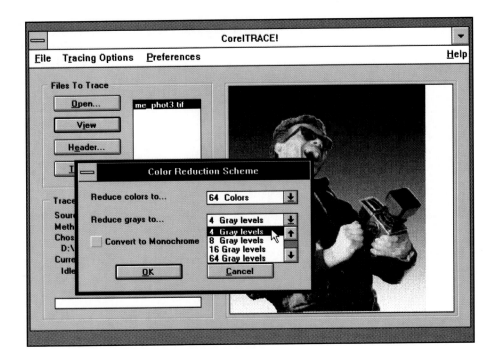

Figure 2.6:

Choose 4 Gray levels to give the image a more graphic appearance and to ease image editing.

Some users have reported that running CorelTRACE from the CD-ROM disk disables their ability to set the number of grays. Although it appears that the desired number of grays is set in the Color Reduction Scheme dialog box, the actual output does not reflect the choice made. If this is the case, copy the program from the CD-ROM, and run it from the hard drive.

12. Although the trace was made with loose settings, my final trace still showed 2,365 nodes and 205 objects (see fig. 2.7). At this point, there still is a lot of work to do. Note that the background gradient was rendered into four bands with rough boundaries between the bands. These bands are a result of the background noise and blending steps during

bitmap editing. Without the noise and blending steps during bitmap editing, the boundaries would be straight horizontal lines.

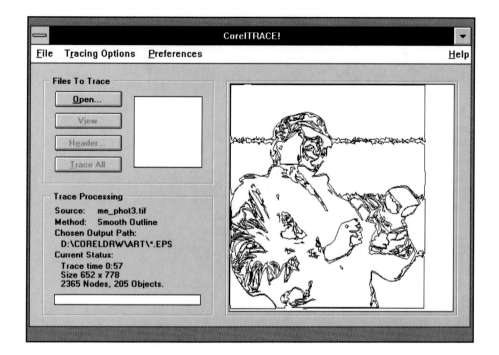

Figure 2.7:
Even with the custom tracing option, this traced image has over 2,000 nodes!

13. The resulting EPS file, when imported into CorelDRAW, appears as a black-and-white image, ready for colorizing and node editing (see fig. 2.8).

14. Add several flesh colors to the palette for easy access and time savings (see fig. 2.9).

15. Serious node editing begins. The goals are to reduce node count, edit the shapes on the face and camera, and select colors for the image. This takes about two full days of work (and lots of patience) to complete. Although reducing the node count was a priority when designing this particular image, a decidedly graphic look was retained. See figures 2.10 and 2.11 for a before-and-after comparison of the face detail.

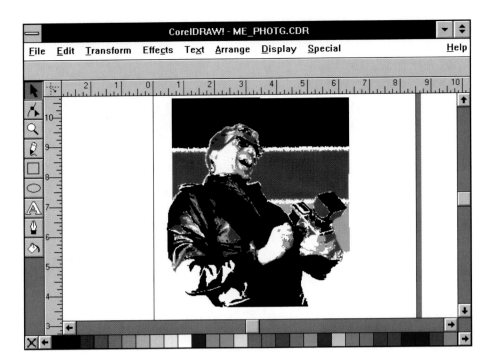

Figure 2.8:

Import the CorelTRACE EPS file into CorelDRAW for coloring.

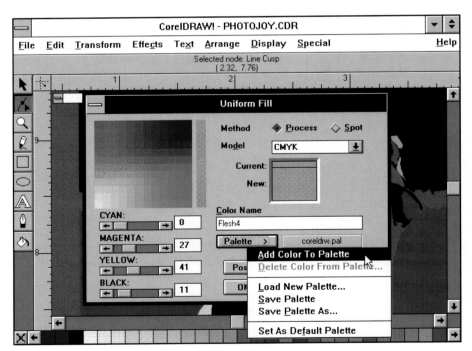

Figure 2.9:

Use the Uniform Fill dialog box to add new colors.

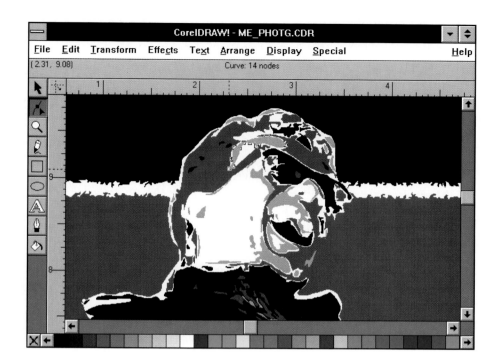

Figure 2.10:
The face before node editing exhibits typical appearance of a raw trace.

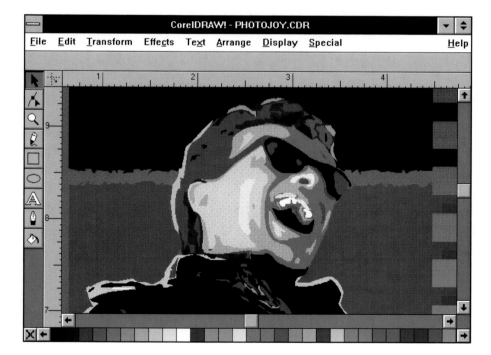

Figure 2.11:
The face has simpler, more graphic areas of color after node editing.

16. Draw two fan-like, closed shapes that suggest the paths of light rays emerging from the camera's lens to imply action. Give both objects gradient fills, and then blend together using 10 steps (see fig. 2.12).

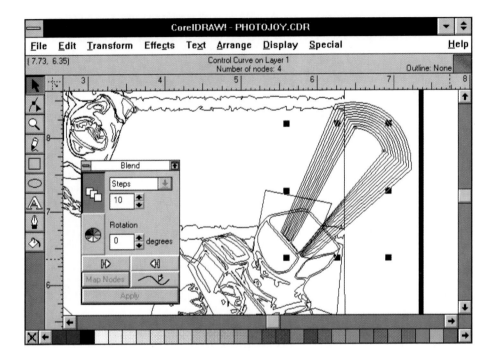

Figure 2.12:

Use 10 blend steps to blend the two fan-like shapes coming from the camera lens.

17. Draw a rectangle slightly above the camera body. Position a copy of the rectangle directly above the first one by holding down the Ctrl key and the left mouse button, dragging upward, and clicking the right mouse button momentarily during the drag. The right mouse button click (while moving) leaves behind a copy of the original rectangle. Use the **R**epeat command several times to make multiple copies of the rectangle, evenly spaced apart. Select all the rectangles, and **C**ombine them into one object. Fill the combined rectangles with a gradient that becomes more chromatic as it approaches the camera (see fig. 2.13).

18. Drag a copy of the rectangles to a new position by clicking on the right mouse button while dragging the originals. Place the rectangles behind the first set, and fill them with a darker color to simulate shadows. The location of the rectangles should imitate the direction of light in the original photo for continuity. Brea**k** Apart and delete the rectangles that do not look like shadows, especially those against a black background.

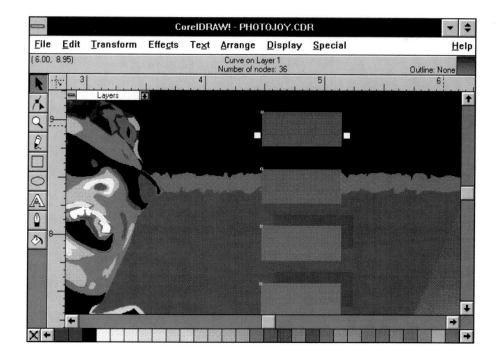

Figure 2.13:
*Use the **C**ombine command to combine objects so that they can be filled with one continuous gradient.*

19. Use the Pencil tool to rough sketch an abdomen for the photographer. Then use the Node Edit tool to shape the newly drawn object (see fig. 2.14).

20. Fill the lower half of the photographer with a gradient fill that blends into the background color at the bottom of the picture. Add text. (I downloaded the Rhyolite Vertical typeface from CompuServe.)

Check out the Desktop Publishing Forum on CompuServe for many freeware and shareware fonts. Both TrueType and PostScript fonts are available.

21. The file is checked by printing to a laser printer, and then sent by modem to the slide service center for the final output in color.

Figure 2.15 illustrates the completed design.

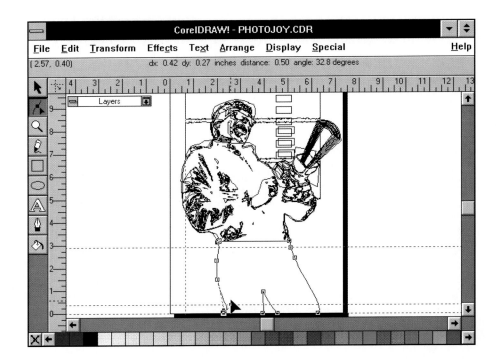

Figure 2.14:
Use the Pencil tool to "rough-in" an object and the Shape tool to fine tune it.

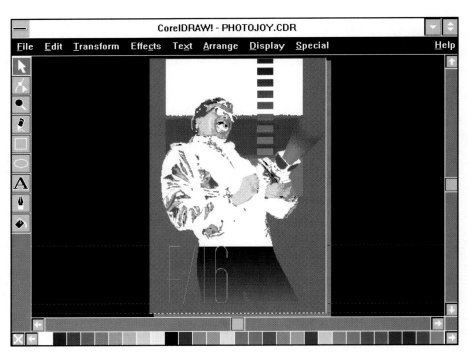

Figure 2.15:
The completed artwork.

Drama and Mood Effects

"Great art picks up where nature ends."

—Georges Braque

Old Folks

by Giuseppe De Bellis

New Design Concepts
Fair Lawn, New Jersey

Equipment Used

486/50 computer system
16M of RAM
ATI video accelerator board

Output Equipment Used

400 dpi CANON CLC500
Fiery image processing unit

Giuseppe De Bellis is an architect for the N.Y.C. Board of Education and a free-lance graphics designer. He has used CorelDRAW, since its first version, on a daily basis for both professions.

The author was inspired by an old friend and teacher he had in high school. This teacher is a fine artist who reproduces scenes of everyday life on canvas.

The author always tried to live up to what his old teacher taught him. The "Old Folks" design is based on the same principle, taking a scene of the life of Mediterranean peasants.

Procedure

1. Create a hand-drawn sketch of the people only (create the floor later). Make sure that you apply pressure on the pencil as you draw so that all the lines are dark and well-defined.

2. Scan in the newly created drawing on a high-resolution scanner. A 600 dpi scanner is sufficient for this operation. Save it as a TIFF or BMP image.

3. Start CorelTRACE, and open the scanned image.

   Change the Tracing Options to the following settings (see fig. 3.1):

Tracing Method	= Follow Outline
Curve Length	= Medium
Convert Long Lines	= Medium
Outline Filtering	= Mild
Fit Curve	= Medium
Sample Rate	= Fine

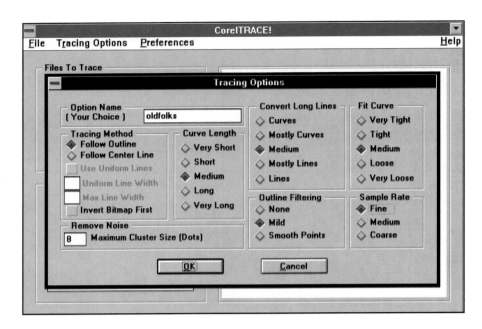

Figure 3.1:
The Tracing Options dialog box.

4. Begin the tracing process (see fig 3.2).

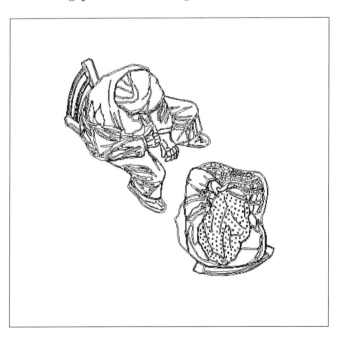

Figure 3.2:
The traced drawing.

5. Start CorelDRAW, and open the newly traced image. Clean up all unwanted lines, dots, and marks.

6. Connect all the nodes of the various objects that belong to the same path.

Using the Node Edit tool, find all the open curve segments, and join the beginning of each open curve segment with the end of each open curve segment. By doing so, you can fill these single continuous curves with colors later.

7. Start the painting process by opening the Fill roll-up window and clicking on Fountain Fill.

8. Choose the start and end colors. Click on the left button to specify the start color; click on the right button to specify the end color.

9. Change the angle of the linear or radial fill by dragging the control in the preview box located in the roll-up window. Make sure that you have chosen an angle that indicates the imaginary light source direction so that all other fills will follow the light source of the drawing accordingly (see fig. 3.3).

10. Repeat the preceding step for all the objects associated with the people.

11. Now you can design the floor. Select **L**ayers Roll-Up from the **A**rrange menu. The Layers roll-up window appears.

Assigning a new layer to the floor helps organize the drawing by assigning groups of elements to specific layers.

12. Click on the arrow in the Layers roll-up window. Then click on New. Make your selection, and click on OK.

13. Double-click on the layer that contains the people, and unselect the **V**isible option (see fig.3.4).

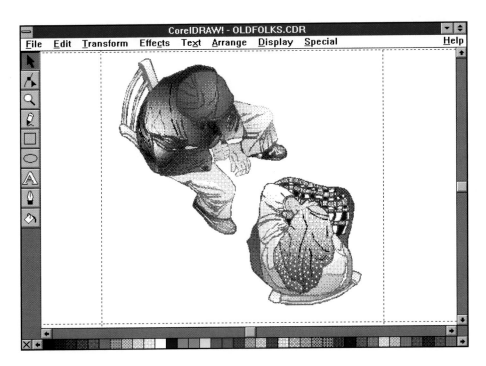

Figure 3.3:
The finished people layout.

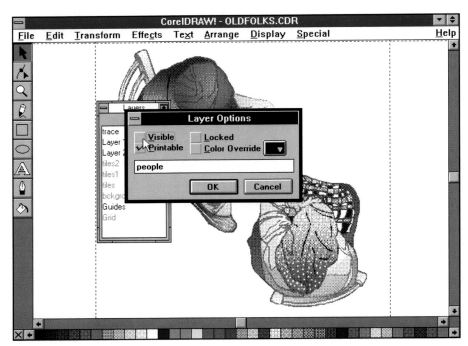

Figure 3.4:
The Layer Options dialog box.

14. Draw a 1" square. Using the Shape tool, round the corners of the square. Then fill the square with a fountain fill on a 45-degree angle.

15. After the tile is defined, draw a random number of small ellipses on the tile to achieve the cement look. Fill the ellipses by using a lighter shade of the tile color.

Group all the objects of the tile (square and ellipses) so that the tile is easier to select later on.

16. Select the tile, and click the right mouse button to duplicate the tile. Then press and hold the Ctrl key, and drag the tile to the right. Be sure to leave 1/16" of space between the two tiles.

17. To complete the row of tiles, press and hold down the Ctrl key and press R (repeat) five times. This process creates a total of seven tiles.

18. Now **G**roup the seven tiles. Then press and hold down the Ctrl key, drag the selected tiles marquee below the original tiles, and click the right mouse button to duplicate them. Make sure that you leave 1/16" of space between the two rows.

19. To complete the entire floor layout, press and hold down the Ctrl key, and press R (repeat) five times. Five additional rows of tiles are created for a total of seven.

20. To obtain a checkerboard look, alternate the tiles with different color shades (see fig. 3.5).

21. Draw a square as large as the floor, and fill it with 50-percent gray. Create the mortar between the tiles by sending the square to the back of the tiles.

22. To make the border around the floor, create two squares—one as big as the floor and the other 1" larger. Draw the first square around the floor. Then, with the Pick tool, press and hold down the Shift key, drag out one side of the square, and click the right mouse button to duplicate it.

23. Select both squares, and choose **C**ombine from the **A**rrange menu. Fill the combined squares with dark brown. This process creates a 1" border, leaving the inner square transparent.

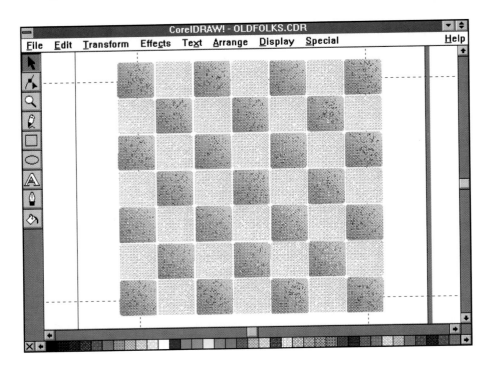

Figure 3.5:

Creating a checkerboard effect.

24. Select all the tiles, and use the Pick tool to rotate them 15 degrees (see fig. 3.6).

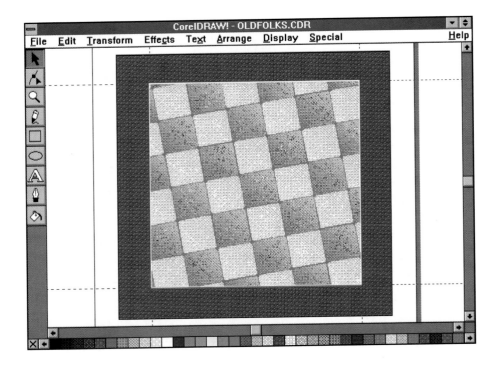

Figure 3.6:

Rotating the tiles 15 degrees.

25. In the People layer, select the **V**isible option from the Layer Options flyout menu. Make sure that this layer is the top layer.

Figure 3.7 shows the completed artwork. This design won a first prize in the 1993 CorelDRAW World Design Contest.

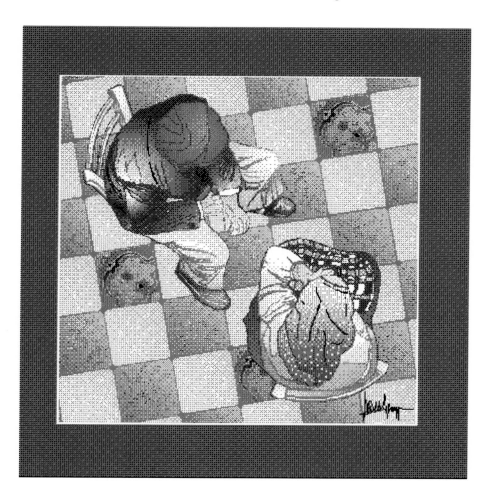

Figure 3.7:
The completed artwork.

Snow Scene

by Stephen Arscott

Mississauga, Ontario, Canada

Equipment Used

486 IBM PC-compatible computer

Output Equipment Used

Lasergraphics LFR Plus film recorder

Stephen Arscott is a free-lance computer graphics artist working in Toronto, Canada. He has used CorelDRAW for the past three years to produce presentation graphics and speaker-support slides. He created this piece of art for self-promotion. The picture depicts a barn amid the drifts of a typical Canadian winter.

Procedure

1. Create seven different shapes. These shapes represent the sunlit areas for the top of each drift. Then draw another shape that represents the shadow area of each drift (see fig. 3.8). There will be a total of 14 shapes—one sunlit area and one shadow area for each drift.

   Draw the shapes by using the Pencil tool. Then shape the objects into their final form by using the Node Edit tool.

2. Give each of the shapes a linear gradient fill at an angle of 45 degrees. The sunlit areas of the drifts, for example, range in color from a light blue to a bright orange.

3. **D**uplicate each drift, and reduce each drift in size by 25 percent.

4. Fill the reduced copies with a gradient fill. Use a fill color that is lighter than the original colors used. Use a lighter shade of the original blue, for example.

5. Then, blend these two objects together in 20 steps to create the watercolor effect (see fig.3.9). You can choose the number of blending steps from the Steps option in the Blend dialog box.

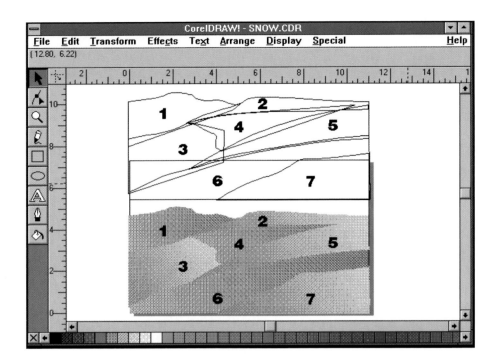

Figure 3.8:
Creating the snow drifts.

Make sure that you map the same node from each object. You want to have the two objects blend together in a smooth and linear fashion. An uncontrolled blend can result in an unwanted mess.

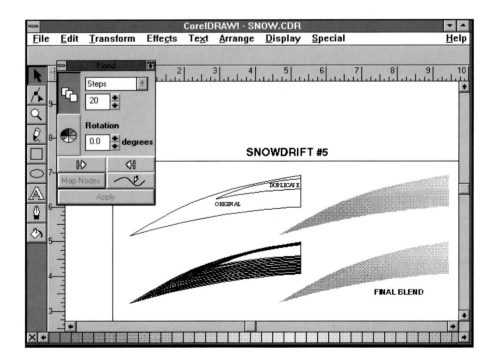

Figure 3.9:
Create the watercolor effect by using the Blend dialog box to blend the two objects.

Both objects must have the same type of fill. CorelDRAW does not blend a solid filled object with a gradient filled object.

6. Create the shadows of the drifts the same way you created the sunlit areas of the drifts. Use darker shades of blue, however, in the gradient fills.

7. Create the irregularly shaped highlights and shadows on the drifts by using the **P**encil tool. Give each shape a gradient fill similar to the background, whether it is in shadow or light. Use blended objects to ease the transition from the light areas to the areas in the shadow (see fig. 3.10).

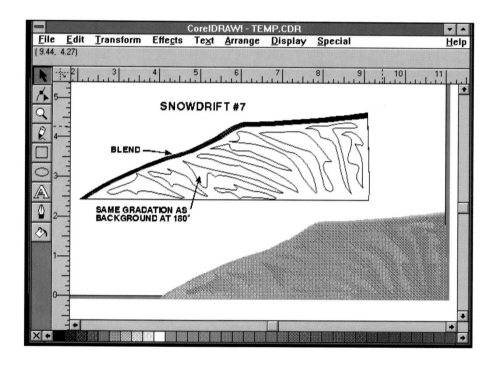

Figure 3.10:
Blending objects eases the transition from light to shadow.

8. Create the fence by first drawing the posts. Create a rectangle, and fill it with a solid dark brown color.

9. **D**uplicate the rectangle on top of itself, and reduce the width of the copy.

10. Fill the duplicate rectangle with a lighter shade of brown, and place it within the original, off-center toward the light. Blend the two objects.

11. Create an ellipse for the top of the post.

12. Using the Pencil tool, draw the fence wire, and give it a black outline. Figure 3.11 illustrates the preceding five steps.

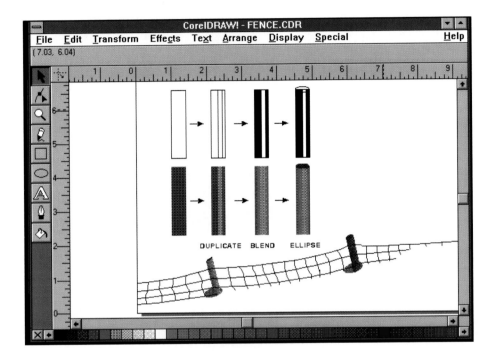

Figure 3.11:
Creating the fence.

13. To create the pine trees, draw an irregular shape similar to the final shape of the tree.

14. Fill the shape with a horizontal gradient fill, from dark green (in the shadow) to a brighter green (in the sunlight).

15. Create the pine branches by using a series of lines, rotated at different angles and assigned different colors. Give each line the same arrowhead, which is found in the Arrows section of the Outline Pen dialog box (see fig. 3.12). Choose an arrowhead that looks like the branch of a pine tree.

Make sure that the pen size is fairly wide so that only the arrowhead is showing and not the lines. Your arrangement of lines should not be recognized simply as a group of lines. These lines are arranged over the basic shape of the tree, and one tree is a smaller duplicate of the other.

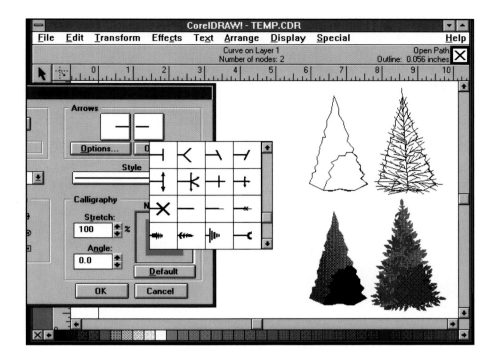

Figure 3.12:
Choose the arrowhead type from the Arrows section of the Outline Pen dialog box.

16. The small clumps of snow are drawn freehand and given the same gradient fills as the snow drifts.

17. The barn is made up of a group of rectangles that are filled with different shades of brown.

18. Place darker lines of brown on the rectangles to separate the barn boards (see fig. 3.13).

19. Create the snow on the roof the same way that you created the snow drift. Create two objects by using the Pencil tool. The second object is smaller and on top of the first. Fill each object with a different gradated fill, and blend them together to create the watercolor effect.

20. Create the sky by using two gradient-filled rectangles. The rectangles meet at the middle of the gradation and are drawn the entire width of the page. Note that the color at the top of the bottom rectangle is the same color as that at the bottom of the top rectangle (see fig. 3.14).

21. The sky is arranged to the back, behind the rest of the drawing.

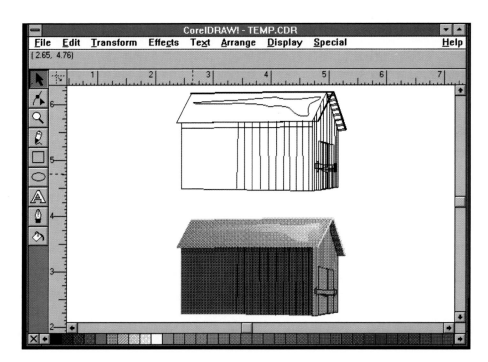

Figure 3.13:
Creating the barn.

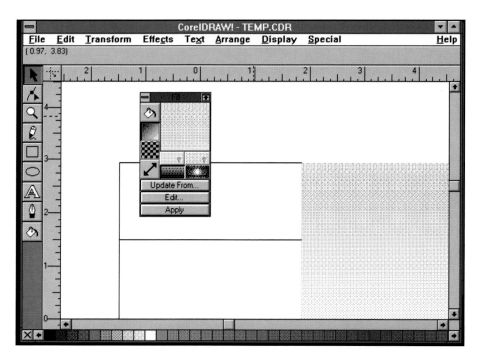

Figure 3.14:
Creating the sky.

The Brooklyn Bridge

Gerry Wilson

The Brooklyn Bridge

by Gerry Wilson

Bay Ridge Graphics
Brooklyn, New York

Equipment Used

Northgate 386/33
16M of RAM

Output Equipment Used

Iris 3024

Gerry Wilson is a self-employed computer graphics artist who specializes in historically accurate illustrations of military equipment. This award winning piece was developed especially for the CorelDRAW contest.

Procedure

The Background

1. Set up your page to letter size in landscape mode, and use guidelines to establish 3/4" margins.

2. Choose Snap To **G**uidelines from the **D**isplay menu. Be sure to leave this option selected throughout the process.

   Use the Snap To **G**uidelines feature when it is important to align elements in a technical drawing precisely.

3. Draw a rectangle to fill the page within the margin guidelines. Set the outline for this rectangle to None and fill with pale yellow.

   You will be using several guidelines in this drawing. If you do not like the default color or it does not give you enough contrast with the drawn objects, change it by clicking on Guides in the **L**ayers roll-up menu.

The Basic Bridge Tower

1. The bridge tower is a basic black rectangle with several gradient objects placed on top to simulate the structure's highlights and shadows. The Brooklyn Bridge shape is distinctive, so I recommend that you study the final drawing and try to follow the basic outline as you add nodes.

2. Draw a 6 3/4" × 3 1/2" black rectangle, 5 1/2" in from the left side.

3. Snap the bottom edge to the lower guideline, and convert the shape to curves so that you can begin to define the shape by adding nodes.

 I suggest that you begin by altering the right side of the rectangle. Add a node and a horizontal and vertical guideline to the points where the shape changes and ensure that it is snapped to the guidelines. Work your way up the right side and across the top. If you study the completed drawing you will notice that there are three distinctive outcroppings along the top. Each outcropping has a straight vertical edge on the left. When the top is completed, move down the left side, which is straight except for the area near the top.

4. Draw a rectangle in the center left of the tower for the first opening, and convert it to curves. It should have a pointed top and a sloped bottom as in the illustration.

5. **D**uplicate the finished shape of the opening, position it to the right of the first opening, and stretch it upward a bit.

6. When satisfied with the positioning, select all three objects, and **C**ombine them. The result gives you the basic tower with the roadways cut out so that the background shows through (see fig. 3.15).

7. Select all objects on this layer, and **G**roup them.

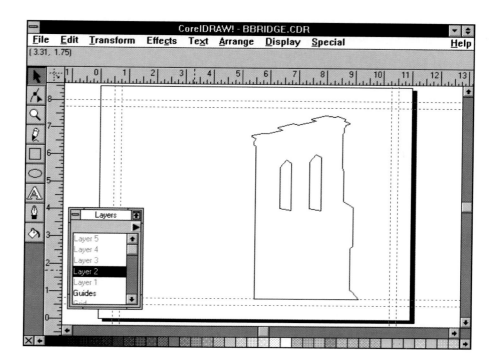

Figure 3.15:

The basic tower with road-ways cut out.

Tower Details and Shadows

1. You can achieve both the highlights and the shadows in a few easy steps by carefully adding eight rectangles with gradient fills of gray and five lines. It may look complicated, but it isn't. Work slowly, and follow the completed drawing.

2. Draw a rectangle at the top center outcropping, convert it to curves, and set the fill to 20-percent black.

3. Snap the left nodes to the previously drawn guidelines. Then marquee-select the two right nodes with the Shape tool, and snap them up to the other guidelines. Repeat the process for the right outcropping.

4. Six highlight objects must be placed on the tower. Draw a rectangle along the upper left side of the basic tower, and convert it to curves. Set a gradient fill of 30-percent black at the top to 70-percent black at the bottom. Edit the upper nodes so that the top of the rectangle follows the shape of the tower but does not cover the left outcropping.

5. Place a second rectangle along the lower left side, and convert it to curves. Set a gradient fill of 30-percent black at the top to 70-percent black at the bottom, and edit the upper right node so that the top slopes downward.

6. Draw a third rectangle in the lower center of the tower. Convert the rectangle to curves, and edit the nodes so that this rectangle looks like the one in the finished drawing and is positioned beneath the left cutout (roadway opening on the left of the tower).

7. Add a smaller rectangle with the same gradient fills to the lower center of the tower. Convert it to curves, and delete one node so that you have a triangle.

8. Moving up the tower, add the highlight rectangles that will surround the roadway openings. Place a rectangle above the left cutout on the basic tower, convert to curves, and set the gradient fill from 10-percent black at the top to 50-percent black at the bottom.

9. Follow the finished drawing, adding nodes as required so that you obtain the desired shape and give some emphasis to the top to highlight the outcroppings.

   The finished object actually should overlap the right side of the cutout to provide the effect of both highlight and shadow. Repeat the process for the right highlight. Note that the right cutout does not come all the way down the left side of the cutout but overlaps the right side of the cutout.

10. Five simple lines complete the tower. Place two at 0.028" line width across the top portion of each highlight object, and align them with the slant of the top of the basic tower. The last line is a vertical line set at 0.013" line width and is used to break the right highlight object.

11. Select all objects on this layer, **G**roup them, and save your work. The tower is complete (see fig. 3.16).

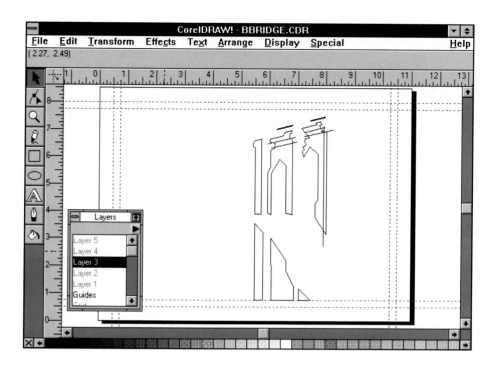

Figure 3.16:
Completing the tower.

The Roadways and Cables

1. The Roadways and Cables layer consists of three groups of objects. The roadways on the bridge have a structural mesh cover that provides an opportunity to add some interesting detail to the drawing. Throughout this step all objects are black.

Black is used to highlight the most distinctive part of the drawing.

2. Begin with the right roadway. Place a rectangle to the right of the tower. Convert the rectangle to curves, and snap the left nodes to the vertical guideline for the right of the tower and the right nodes to the page margin.

   The object should slant down to the right as in the finished drawing.

3. The remainder of this section consists of three lines with a line width of 0.028". The first, or upper line, represents the

near side of the top of the structural mesh over the roadway and follows the same slope as the roadway block. The second line represents one of the inner structural beams on the top of the roadway. The third line comprises all of the vertical and crossways top beams. Use the double-click method to draw the line in a zigzag fashion. This line should have beveled corners. Select the four objects in this section, and **G**roup them.

4. The left, or longer, roadway follows the exact same principle and also consists of a rectangle and three lines drawn in the same fashion. The upper line should be drawn straight across the tower and snapped to a vertical guideline at the left edge of the right highlight object. **G**roup all four objects when satisfied with the positioning and aspect.

5. The cables are lines that have been converted to curves and shaped to simulate the slopping suspension cables on the bridge.

6. Select all the objects on this layer, and **G**roup them (see fig. 3.17).

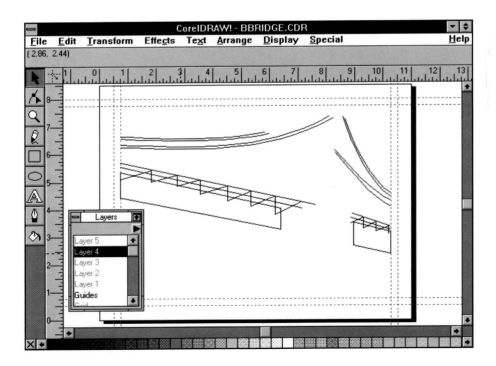

Figure 3.17:
Drawing the cables.

The Title, Frame, and Signature Layer

1. Add the title to the lower left foreground. I like to use Corel's President typeface.

2. Create a special frame for the drawing by adding guidelines 0.50" from the edge of the page and snapping the rectangle to the new guidelines.

3. Draw another rectangle within the preestablished margins (0.75" from the edge of the page).

4. Select both these objects, set the fill to None and the outline to 0.028", and **C**ombine them.

5. Draw a solid black square in each corner, and snap each square to the two sets of margin guidelines.

6. Place your signature in the lower right corner between the lines.

7. Select all objects on this layer, and **G**roup them.

Figure 3.18 illustrates the completed artwork (in Wireframe mode).

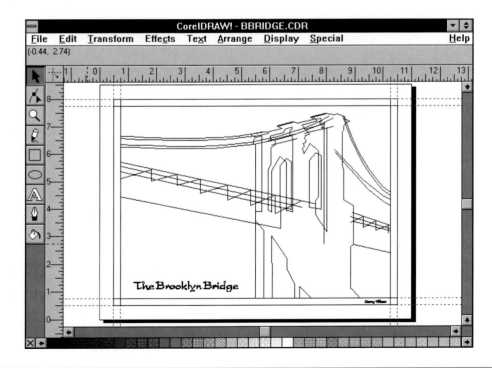

Figure 3.18:
The completed design.

Illusion of Space Effects

"Copy nature and you infringe on the work of our Lord.
Interpret nature and you are an artist."

—*Jacques Lipchitz*

Wm. Mogensen 1991

Viking-3 Concept Spacecraft

by William Mogensen

Mogensen deSIGN
Shadow Hills, California

Equipment Used

386DX hot-rod clone
40Mhz
8M of RAM
An over-stressed, highly stacked 80M
RLE hard drive

Output Equipment Used

HP PaintJet
HP LaserJetIII/PostScript
Signlab 2.01
IOLINE 3700SIGNPRO

Bill Mogensen, owner of Mogensen deSIGN, lives in Shadow Hills, California, with his wife, Leslie, and two daughters, Kristen and Erin. He has used CorelDRAW since 1989 for commercial signmaking and graphics design. He also is an operations engineer at Jet Propulsion Laboratory in Pasadena, where he uses CorelDRAW for presentations and technical illustrations.

This image is the artist's concept for a return Viking Mission to the planet Mars, and his attempt to illustrate, in some small way, the profundity of mankind's remote exploration of alien worlds.

Procedure

1. Determine your source of illumination. In this case, the primary illumination comes from the left, with a small amount of reflected illumination from below. Start with a black-filled rectangle, one slightly smaller than the page size.

2. Next, create a large circle (representing the planet Mars) with the Ellipse tool, and constrain it to a circle with the Ctrl key. Use no outline and a radial fountain fill of black to red with a –42-percent horizontal offset to help simulate the look of an illuminated sphere. Drag the circle (sphere) to the lower part of the rectangle, allowing the lower third of the circle to spill off the page. You will fix that later (see fig. 4.1).

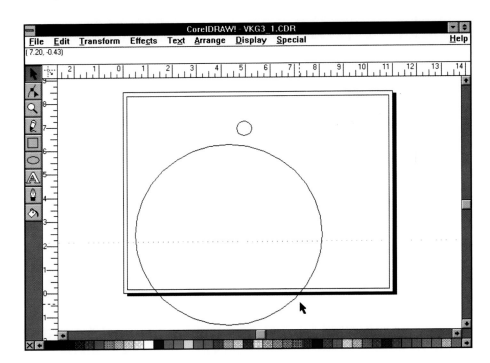

Figure 4.1:

Wireframe image of Mars (large circle) with moon of Mars (small circle).

3. **D**uplicate the large sphere, and reduce its size. This smaller circle (sphere) represents one of the moons of Mars. Place the small circle above the large sphere, and alter the colors. I used black to navy blue with a –50-percent horizontal offset. The darker shades help to show the vast distance separating the two objects.

4. Select the large circle (Mars), and convert it to curves. Using the Node Edit tool, select a point on Mars where the line of arc intersects the border of the black rectangle. Double-click on the line to activate the Node Edit dialog box, and add a node. Double-click on the new node, and select **C**usp. Perform the two previous modifications on the circle, where the other side intersects the bottom of the rectangle.

Next, delete any nodes that lie on any part of the circle in the area outside the rectangle. Then double-click on the curve outside the rectangle, and convert it to a line segment. Use the Node Edit tool to make the necessary adjustments to the new cusp nodes so that the bottom of the circle does not spill off the page.

5. Use the Ellipse tool to create a series of small circles (.04-.08" in diameter) for the stars in the background. Fill them with 100-percent white. You can use the + key, Ctrl-R (repeat), and horizontal and vertical flips to copy large areas of the stars. Then place the stars wherever appropriate. When satisfied with the stars placement, **C**ombine them into one object to reduce the total file size and to speed up screen redraws (see fig. 4.2).

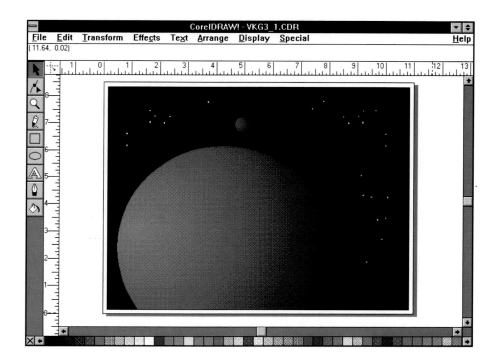

Figure 4.2:
The planet, its moon, and the surrounding star fields.

6. Save this as the background image, and open a new file. Although it is not an actual spacecraft design, the spacecraft in this image is based on component parts of actual unmanned space probes, such as Voyager, Pioneer, Ulysses, and Magellan (see fig. 4.3).

The component parts in this image are just geometric shapes created in CorelDRAW and manipulated by using various tools to simulate filled and shaded geometric solids. Keep in mind that no matter how complicated something might seem, it usually is made up of simple, individual parts (see fig. 4.4).

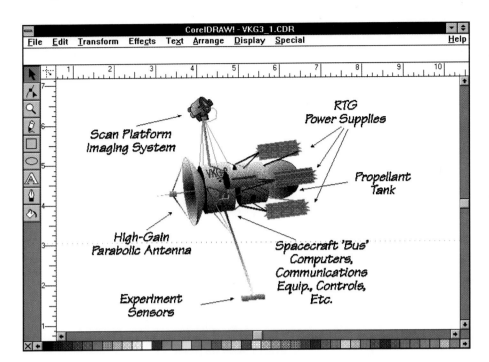

Figure 4.3:

Major component parts of a deep-space planetary probe.

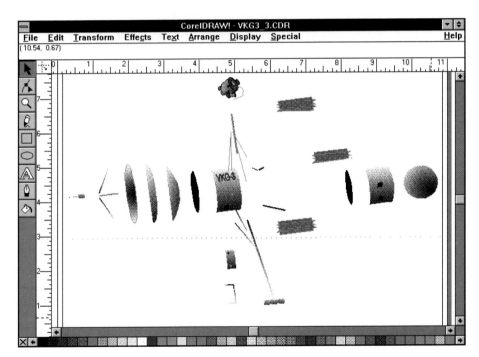

Figure 4.4:

Major components of spacecraft in exploded form.

You can work on the various elements separately, then **C**ombine or **G**roup the elements together to create the final image. The image shown here originally was created in CorelDRAW Version 2; each element was constructed, extruded, and filled or shaded individually, with particular attention paid to the light source for shading.

Most components use radial or linear fountain fills with black and white, and various horizontal and vertical offsets. Remember, almost any effect can be achieved with CorelDRAW, so experiment until you are satisfied. Version 3 makes this type of work easier with its expanded extrusion commands for shape, position, lighting, and color.

7. Start with the major elements (in this case, the parabolic high-gain dish antenna, the spacecraft bus, and the propellant tank). After these components are assembled to your satisfaction, you can add the various other parts to complete the design.

8. The last step is to create cast shadows on any spacecraft parts that are appropriate (see fig. 4.5). Take one step at a time, and make good use of CorelDRAW's **D**uplicate and **C**opy features. Experiment with the fills and outlines (or lack of outlines) until you achieve the look that you want. Continue to **G**roup the various parts to the preceding elements as you create them.

9. Now you can import the file containing the background, and arrange it to the back. Make minor changes to the positions of the major parts of the illustration. Look for balance and proper use of negative space. Add highlights (such as glowing lights) and pieces of miscellaneous hardware to the spacecraft, but do not go overboard (see fig. 4.6).

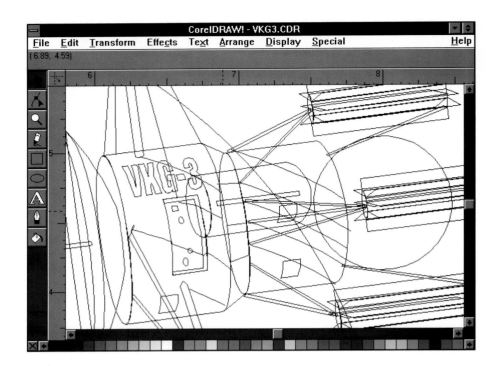

Figure 4.5:

Close-up of spacecraft bus or body to show how "cast shadow" lines are placed.

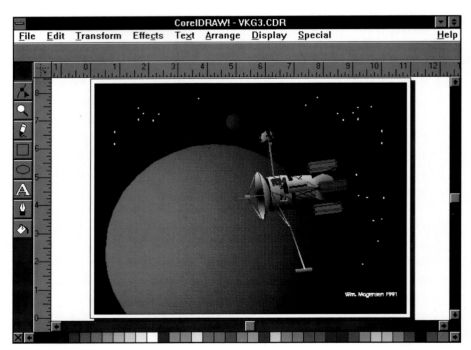

Figure 4.6:

The completed design.

Action Effects

"Treat nature in terms of the cylinder, the sphere, the cone, all in perspective."

—Paul Cézanne

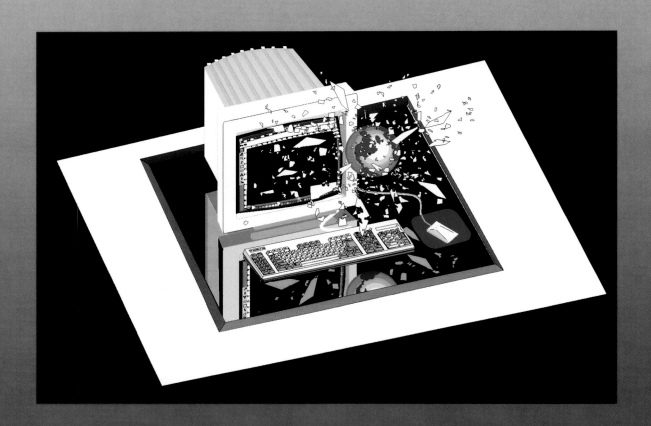

Oops!

by Joe Donnelly

*Capital Communications Inc.
Nepean, Ontario, Canada*

Equipment Used

386/33 IBM compatible
4M of RAM
110M hard drive
ATI VGA Wander graphics card
NEC Multisync 2A monitor
NEC Silentwriter 2 printer

Output Equipment Used

High-resolution 1200 dpi Linotronic

Joe Donnelly is owner and president of Capital Communications Inc. in Nepean, Ontario, Canada. He started the company two years ago in his senior year of university studies. Since then he has worked on projects ranging from simple to full-color design for magazines and newspapers on the local, regional, and national levels. CorelDRAW is the main software used for all his projects.

Oops! originally was designed for the 1991 CorelDRAW World Design Contest. The design's complexity, however, exceeded the limits of CorelDRAW 2.0 and had to be simplified before it could print on a PostScript printer. The design was fixed and subsequently entered in the 1992 CorelDRAW World Design Contest.

Procedure

This piece of art is composed of five major parts: the keyboard, monitor, globe, glass shards, and smoked-glass tabletop.

The Keyboard

1. The starting point for this piece of artwork is the keyboard. Draw a three-dimensional key. Begin by drawing a rectangle, which is the top of the key, and then draw a trapezoid, which is the front of the key. Round the corners of the rectangle using the Node Edit tool.

2. Add two separate text characters to the left side of the rectangle to represent the writing on the keys (see fig. 5.1).

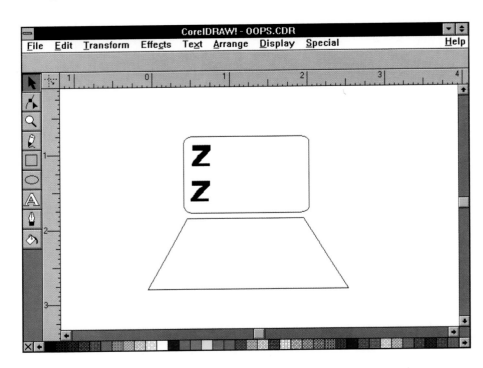

Figure 5.1:

The basic shapes for a key.

3. Select the rectangle and text elements. Enter rotate and skew mode by clicking a second time on the selected elements. Move the cursor over one of the side handles. Click on and drag the handle vertically 11 degrees (indicated on the status line). Then click and drag the top/bottom handle horizontally 33 degrees.

4. Convert the rectangle to a curve by using the Con**v**ert To Curves command from the **A**rrange menu. Using the Node Edit tool, double-click on each side. Choose **t**oCurve, and curve the sides of the key downward to represent the concave shape of the key.

5. Vertically skew the trapezoid 11 degrees, and position it below the rectangle to form the front of the key.

6. Use the Pencil tool to draw the final side of the key. Draw a trapezoid shape with two of the sides meeting the top and front of the key (see fig. 5.2).

 Use the Node Edit tool to achieve precise alignment.

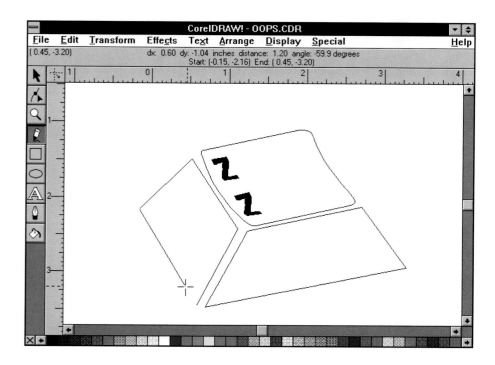

Figure 5.2:

Drawing the third side of a key.

7. After you draw all three sides, use the Node Edit tool to position each side flush with the top of the key.

8. Because the light source for this piece is from the upper right of the picture, the top of the key bears the lightest tone; the front of the key bears the second lightest tone; and the side of the key bears the darkest tone. I chose variations of pale yellow and chalk for the light keyboard keys. Begin by selecting a color from the palette (pale yellow, chalk). Change the color model to CMYK (this enables you to change the various components of your selected color). Alter the color by varying the black, yellow, magenta, and cyan values until the color matches those of your keyboard. A thin black outline of 0.1 point was added to all three sides of the key.

9. Spend some time creating this first key because it will form the basis for all the remaining keys on the keyboard. After you are satisfied with the first key, draw guidelines to show the alignment of all the remaining keys (see fig. 5.3). You will only need four guidelines drawn in relation to your first key to draw your first row and column of keys. After these keys are duplicated and placed, draw your next guide for the second row.

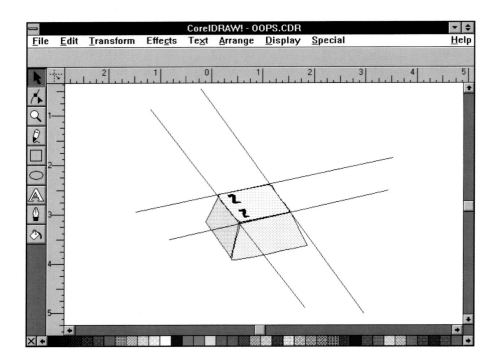

Figure 5.3:

Guidelines for drawing the keys in perspective.

In CorelDRAW 3.0, the guidelines can now be put on the non-printing Guides layer and locked. This enables you to use them as a guide and, at the same time, not have them interfere with your drawing and editing. Any object (lines, arcs, or shapes) can be placed on the Guides layer. This enables you to snap your drawing to these objects for precise alignment.

10. **G**roup the elements of the first key. Then **D**uplicate the grouped object, and offset it above or to the right of the original key. Continue duplicating the key and offsetting it. Remember that the keys closest to the bottom left are in the foreground. All duplicate keys placed after this key should be arranged to the back (see fig. 5.4).

11. Use the preceding steps to construct the dark keys. The fills are variations on drab olive and khaki, with a 0.1-point black outline on all objects.

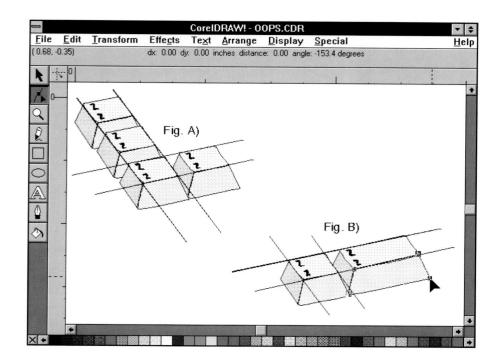

Figure 5.4:
Duplicating and arranging the keys.

12. The long keys, such as the Ctrl, Tab, Shift, Alt, and so on, also are adaptations of the first key created. Use the Node Edit tool to lengthen the top of the key. Select the two rightmost nodes, and extend them to the right until the key is 1 1/2 to 2 times the length of an ordinary key. The length of the key depends on the key that you are drawing. Examine your keyboard to find the correct proportions for the keys.

13. After you lengthen the top of the key, stretch the front of the key in a similar way.

Always remain true to your guidelines as you lengthen a key. This ensures that you create a keyboard in proper perspective (see fig. 5.4).

14. After you finish a row or column of keys, move the guidelines to the next row or column and continue working until the drawing contains all the keys on a keyboard.

15. Place the lettering on each key as you did in step 2. Then, change the default letters on each key to match the letters and numbers on a keyboard.

16. The keyboard case is made up of six rectangles, varying in size. Each rectangle covers groups of the keys. These rectangles also are skewed vertically 11 degrees and horizontally 33 degrees. The rectangles behind groups of keys contain a black fill. The large rectangle behind all the keys is filled with a dark chalk value. Arrange these rectangles to the back of your drawing, behind the keys (see fig. 5.5 and fig. 5.6).

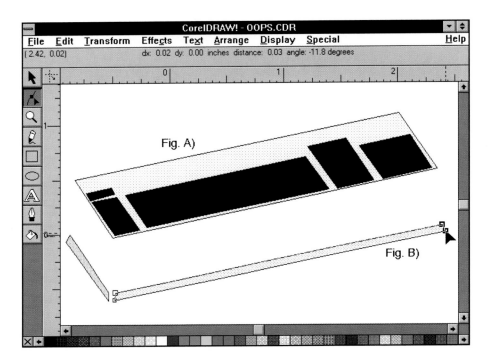

Figure 5.5:

The shapes and arrangement of the keyboard case.

17. The front and side of the keyboard case are then constructed in a similar fashion to the individual key. Create a trapezoid and a rectangle as you did in step 1. Then use the Node Edit tool to convert to curves and skew and stretch the objects to the desired length. Place the object by using the Node Edit tool to ensure proper alignment.

18. **G**roup the keyboard, and place it off to the side of the desktop so that it does not get in the way of the next item.

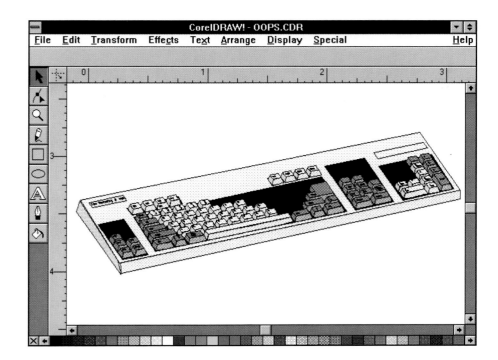

Figure 5.6:
Keyboard case placed behind the keys.

The Monitor

1. The next object to construct is the monitor screen. Maximize the CorelDRAW screen, and print the screen to the Clipboard by pressing Alt-PrintScreen. Paste the captured screen into your document (see fig. 5.7).

2. Trace each element on the screen, exactly as you see it— the tool bars, scroll bars, color bars, rulers, and so on, including the writing on the windows and menu bars. After you complete the tracing, delete the bit map. You will have an exact duplicate of the Corel screen in CDR format.

3. **G**roup all of these elements of the screen. Using the envelope feature, curve the screen elements vertically up and down, as shown in figure 5.8. (You create a single arc for the top and another for the bottom.)

4. Skew the enveloped screen vertically 11 degrees to match the angle of the keyboard.

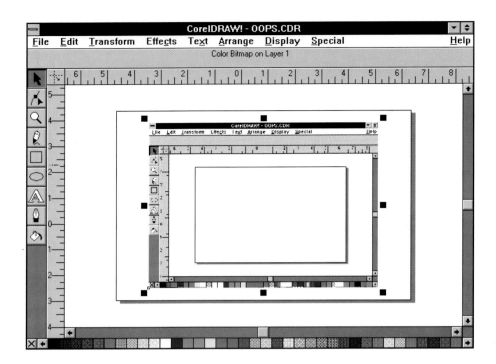

Figure 5.7:
Pasting the captured screen into your document.

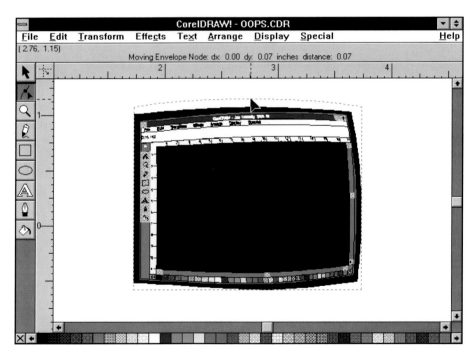

Figure 5.8:
Curving the screen elements.

5. The monitor is made up of a front rectangle panel, skewed again at 11 degrees vertically, and a top panel (also a rectangle), skewed at 11 degrees vertically and 33 degrees horizontally (similar to the keyboard).

6. Use the Pencil tool to draw the third side. Keep the same perspective as established by the first two sides (see fig. 5.9).

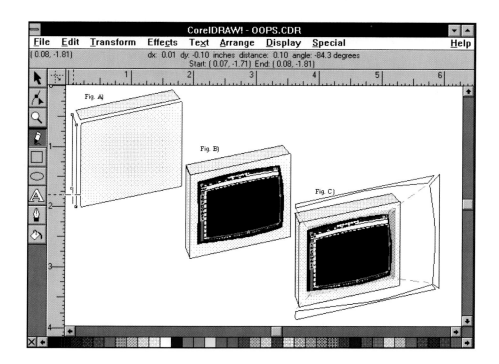

Figure 5.9:

Drawing the third side of the monitor.

7. Fill the monitor face with a gradient radial fill with a dark to light brown color.

8. The vertical side of the monitor is filled with a linear fountain fill of 180 degrees from light to dark. The top of the monitor also contains a 101-degree linear fountain fill.

9. Place the CorelDRAW screen drawn in step 2 in the center of the monitor. Add curved rectangles to the right, top, and bottom of the screen to give the impression of depth.

10. Fill these shapes with darker shades of brown and olive.

11. Draw the shapes for the side and top of the rear of the monitor, and arrange them behind the front elements. They should be filled with the same shades as the top and side of the front elements.

12. The back of the monitor contains gradient fills with the lightest values at the front, gradiating to dark in the back to resemble a front-lit monitor (see fig. 5.10).

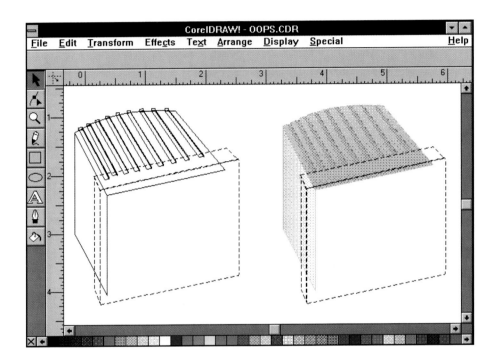

Figure 5.10:

The shapes and fills for the back of the monitor.

The Globe

1. The globe is created by using the blend feature. Construct two circles. Create one large 60-percent black base circle. Then create a small 10-percent black highlight circle. Blend the two shapes with 70 blend steps, to give a smooth gradient (see fig. 5.11).

A similar effect can be achieved by using the radial fill option and offsetting the center point.

2. The map on the globe was taken from the CorelDRAW clip-art collection. Load a map of the world, **U**ngroup all objects, and isolate North and South America, as well as northern Europe, Russia, and Africa. Delete the remainder of the world.

3. Rotate North and South America, and position them at the front of the globe. Rotate Europe, and position it on the far side of the globe.

4. Use the Node Edit tool to add nodes and delete excess nodes on the map so that it conforms to the curvature of the globe.

5. Fill the land mass with green and a 70-percent gray outline to complete the globe.

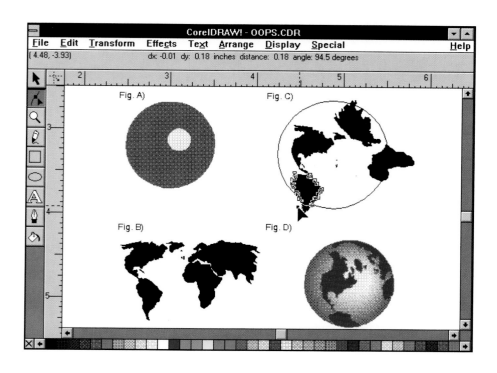

Figure 5.11:
Constructing the globe.

The Glass

1. The shattered glass is created by drawing a number of irregularly shaped polygons using the Pen tool.

To ensure a more realistic drawing of glass, construct the glass shards from line segments only. This gives the impression of sharp, shattered fragments.

2. **D**uplicate the various shapes, and scatter them around the globe. Vary the sizes of the shapes, and rotate some of the pieces to give the glass variety.

3. Isolate a number of shards. Enlarge these pieces to 1/10th the size of the globe.

4. Use the Node Edit tool to drag some of the corner nodes so that they point, in perspective, toward the globe (see fig. 5.12).

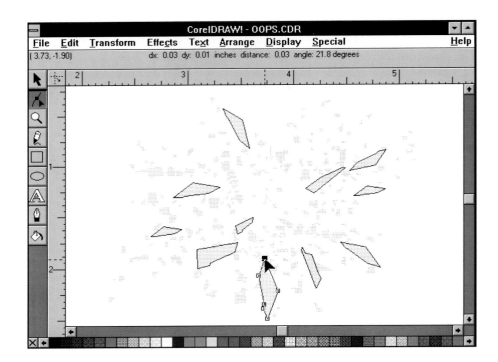

Figure 5.12:

Adding perspective to the glass shards.

5. Select all the glass shards, and **C**ombine them to form one object. Fill the object with 10-percent black and add a 0.2-point black outline.

Assembling the Drawing

1. Position the keyboard. Place the assembled monitor behind the keyboard. Place the globe, with the glass shards, above the keyboard (see fig. 5.13).

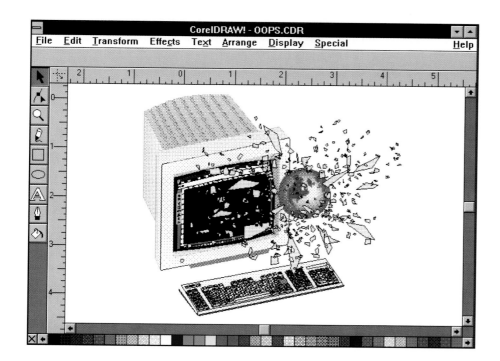

Figure 5.13:

Arranging the first four objects of the design.

2. The reflections in the smoked glass are a vertical mirror of all the objects you just constructed.

   Duplicate each of the groups (the monitor, globe, and glass shards), and mirror them vertically downward.

3. The colors of the objects must be darkened by at least 50 percent, making the glass shards a darker shade of gray, the continents a darker shade of green, and the monitor case a darker shade of brown. This gives the impression of a darkened reflection.

4. Arrange all of the mirrored objects below and behind their counterparts (see fig. 5.14).

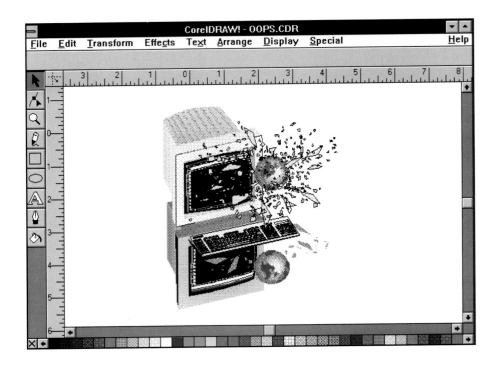

Figure 5.14:

Arranging the mirrored objects.

5. Enlarge a skewed rectangle to encompass most of your drawing. This forms the borders for your piece of smoked glass.

6. Using the Pencil tool, trace the negative space between the objects (monitor and keyboard) and the edge of the rectangle (see fig. 5.15).

When drawing in three dimensions, it is necessary for the viewer's eye to have a point of reference (where the ground is). Drawing this base (the negative space in step 6) provides this point of reference for your eye.

7. Fill these two shapes with black and position them on either side of the monitor. This completes the surface of the piece of smoked glass.

8. Draw rectangles and trapezoids, as you did when creating the keyboard, to create the four sides of the smoked-glass panels surrounding the monitor. Skew and node edit the points in place to give the look of a beveled edge. Fill these edges with 60-percent black (see fig. 5.16).

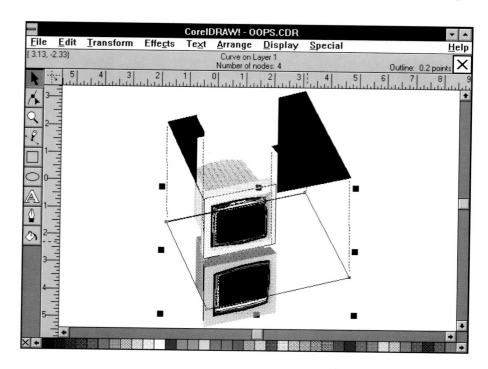

Figure 5.15:

Tracing the negative space between objects.

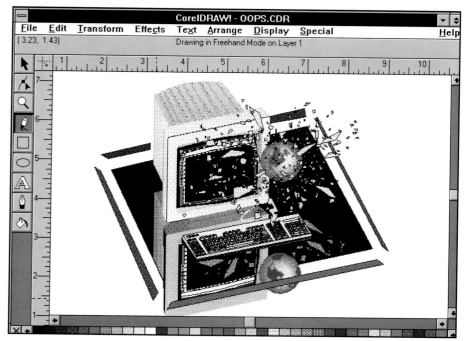

Figure 5.16:

Adding the sides to the smoked-glass plate.

9. After the beveled edges are in place, draw and fill the shapes with white and no outline to mask the parts of the reflected image that may overhang the bottom of the beveled edges (see fig. 5.17).

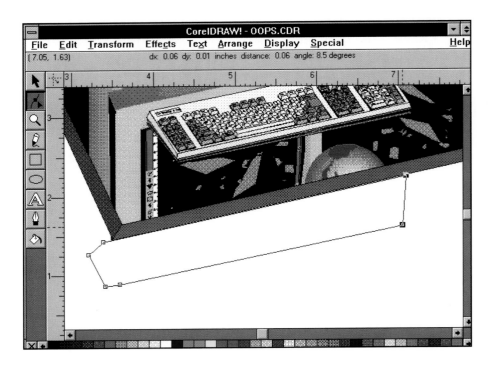

Figure 5.17:
Masking parts of the reflected image.

10. To add the finishing details, draw:

- a mouse pad with a skewed rectangle with rounded corners

- a mouse—constructed from various polygons

- a mouse and keyboard cord from Bézier curves (see fig. 5.18).

11. Finally, draw one last skewed rectangle, fill it with white, and arrange it to the back of all the other elements to frame the final product as illustrated in figure 5.19.

That's it! Fifty-one simple steps to producing your very own Oops! If any of the above steps confuse you, and you have access to the ArtShow3 CD-ROM from CorelDRAW, simply load my drawing, and disassemble it. The best way to discover how an artist did a computer design is to take it apart. Hopefully, you will find that even the most complicated designs are based on the simplest shapes and ideas.

Have fun!

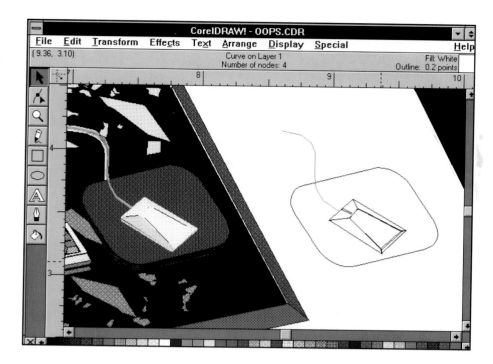

Figure 5.18:
Creating the mouse and keyboard cord from Bézier curves.

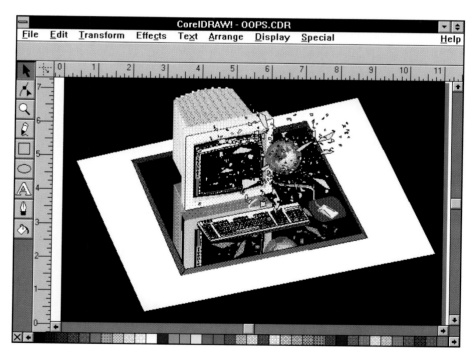

Figure 5.19:
The completed design.

6

Creating Reflections

"Art is a lie that makes us realize the truth."

—*Pablo Picasso*

The First House of Self, the way the world sees The Native and how he views others around him. Libra is the first sign. Everything beautiful appeals to this person. One who loves art for its own sake. Will go into social circles, the theatre and all associated fields are of great attraction. The Native wants and needs harmony around him. Tendency to dream, a bit indecisive. Venus is the ruler in the Tenth House of Career. The Native must be his own boss, yet he is a gentle person. In this House we find Saturn, so the appearance is more reserved. A hard worker, persistant, good reasoning ability, good concentration, sometimes beyond his years. Must practice more self-confidence!

Here is Neptune, the personality is highly sensitive, one who reacts to many vibrations. A great love of music. A "daydreamer" with a highly-developed and provocative imagination. Should put dreams into action. Talkative, nervous, has a great need for self-expression. Aspects of Saturn and Neptune, __ close to Neptune, a very good aspect __ facility as well as spiritual insight __ This is also good for __ watch not to give in to de__ conflicting, showing __ far-flung tendencies __ re is some inconsisten __ d action. Does expe__

Saturn is __ ility to organize and __ discipline and hard w__ talents. There is mu__ come from friends or m__

Neptune sq__ pheaval, as Native is "high__ of a different drummer. High__ ment because of it! Neptune is __ Pluto. This shows a great opportunity for spiritual advancement. Unusual intuitive scientific ability. Can guide others to respond to better ideals, possibly in career, or with co-workers.

The Second House __ ved. There is a Libra and a Scorpio. This shows a double connection in finances, much will be spent on beautiful items, monies could come from partnerships, in home and posessions.

Astrotext

by Gary David Bouton

Exclamat!ons
Liverpool, New York

Equipment Used:

Greentree (IBM-compatible) 486DX 50MHz
16M of RAM
Logitech 256 grayscale hand-scanner

Output Equipment Used:

Genigraphicsô PS4000 Line film recorder

Gary David Bouton is the owner of Exclamat!ons, a company that polishes rough ideas. "Astrotext," the winning entry in the January Miscellaneous category of the CorelDRAW (1992) World Design Contest, was created as an experiment in reflections and lighting. Gary previously had done work with bitmap photo and image-editing software, and this was his first effort with a vector-based drawing program.

A Brief Overview

To do an illustration in a vector-oriented program that contains elements of realism, such as surfaces, lighting, or reflections, requires a measure of preplanning. Because every glint, imperfection, color mottling, or other element of character must exist as a separate object, you cannot go back and "paint over" an area as you can with a bitmap illustration.

I recommend doing a rough sketch of your design before you sit down at the PC. It's the most direct way to visualize your idea. Even if you are not experienced with physical drawing tools, this practice serves to create a visual "catalog" of the items that need to be separately rendered. Also, by sketching a design, you get a better idea of which elements go in front or behind others.

CorelDRAW 3.0 enables users to layer a design and define what each layer is called. I name my layers according to which elements exist on different planes.

("Ball" is the layer on which I am rendering a ball, which goes on top of the "Background" layer, and so on.) Layering is an important feature of CorelDRAW 3.0, because without it you cannot hide a complex image on a particular layer. If you do not use layers, the screen redraw time on smaller systems is tediously long, and you cannot clearly see through a complex section of a piece of work.

Patience, planning, and a worn-out toothbrush were the keys to finishing "Astrotext."

Procedures

1. The starry background in Astrotext frames the main attraction—the reflective ball floating above the parchment. A simple route to render a ponderously large number of stars is to draw a page-sized rectangle and fill it with a tiled pattern of bitmap stars. To create that bitmap fill of stars for a background, you have to "paint" a bitmap fill pattern in CorelDRAW's Two-Color Pattern Editor. The advantage of adding a cosmos full of stars behind Astrotext's globe is that the finished file size is smaller.

    A tiled pattern throughout the page, such as the one shown in figure 6.1, is uncomplicated and requires a small amount of bytes to create. The disadvantage of creating a bitmap of "stars" on an 8 1/2" × 11" page is that the tiled pattern becomes static. In other words, the pattern that the tiling creates is obvious.

    You can see the repeats created from this tiling of a single bitmap pattern in figure 6.2. In an effort to break up the monotonous pattern, I tried to use two or three different bitmap pattern fills in combination scattered throughout the page, but it was getting to be as much work as the second method I finally used! I abandoned the bitmap pattern as an option because what I gained in creating a simpler file, I lost in aesthetics.

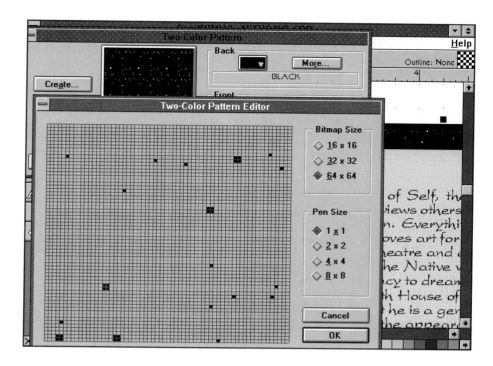

Figure 6.1:
A view of the bitmap Pattern Editor in CorelDRAW 3.0.

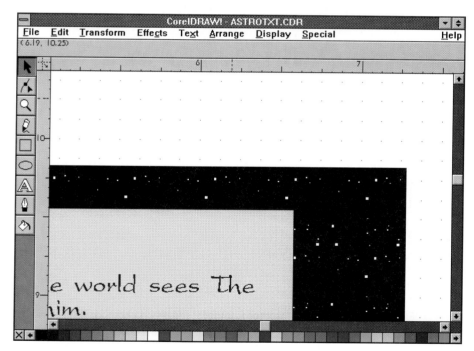

Figure 6.2:
A close-up of a tiled, bitmap pattern.

A more complicated route to creating realistic stars involves using physical media (an actual, live pad of paper and ink), a scanner, and a utility such as CorelTRACE. CorelDRAW and similar software are terrific at creating perfect designs, but it is sometimes frustrating to try to achieve an organic quality about your design work.

A "splatter" painting, created with ordinary paper, ink, and a household hygiene product renders the best random pattern for the starfield.

Take a toothbrush, dip it in some Parker fountain pen ink, and splatter the ink on a white piece of paper. Continue splattering the ink until you achieve a random effect that looks like a "negative image" of a starry night.

Then scan the paper, convert it to vector art, and adopt it into the background with some tinkering and tuning. Vector art typically is smaller in file size than a bitmap rendering—except in this case. The disadvantage to using this technique is that a large file size translates to slow redraw time, even on a 486. The advantage to using the technique, however, is that you can manipulate each and every star as an individual object.

2. Use a scanner to digitize the splattered piece of paper. Set the scanner options to Line Art and 100 dpi. Save the scanned art as a TIFF file.

3. Open CorelTRACE, open the TIFF file of the starfield, and convert the TIFF file to EPS format.

CorelTRACE saves the work in the directory in which it finds the native file. Remember this when you go to import the EPS file later.

4. Open CorelDRAW and select **L**ayers Roll-Up from the **A**rrange menu. Edit Layer One, and call it Background. You will import the vector-converted stars in a few steps, but first you need to create the background on the first layer to place stars on it.

A flat, black background does not evoke the sort of drama I am trying to convey in this illustration. Make the background to Astrotext swoop and fade to a pale color on the bottom. First, create a 3" tall vertical rectangle on the bottom of the page. Fill the rectangle with a radial fountain fill from a 100-percent white in the center to a very pale blue or azure. Set the Edge Pad on the radial fill to 10 to 15 percent to give the fill more contrast.

Write down the CMYK value of this azure or pale blue, because you will need it shortly.

5. Now you are set to create a page frame that blends into the 3" radial-filled rectangle. Place three guidelines on the top, left, and right sides of the page border. Place a fourth horizontal guideline about 2" above the fountain fill rectangle. Select Snap To **G**uidelines from the **D**isplay menu.

   Using the Rectangle tool, create a page frame by starting at the top, left of the page border and dragging the cursor down to the bottom guideline (which is about 5" from the bottom of the page border). Fill this rectangle with the deepest solid fill, but use a minimum of black from the CMYK palette.

   Double-click on the bottom line with the Shape Tool to access the Node Edit dialog box, and select **t**oCurve. Deselect Snap To **G**uidelines because you do not want them affecting the next step in any way. Pull on the control nodes on opposite sides of this bottom line (curve) until you achieve a gentle sweeping effect on the rectangle's bottom (see fig. 6.3).

6. Set the horizontal and vertical values in the Place Duplicate option from the **S**pecial, Pr**e**ferences menu to zero inches. This places duplicate objects exactly on top of the original. **D**uplicate the dark, swoopy, dark-filled curve (rectangle), then assign it a solid fill value identical to the CMYK color you used in step 4.

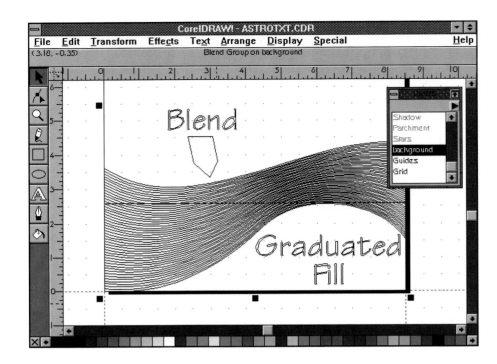

Figure 6.3:

Adding a blend between the swooping-bottom rectangle and a slightly modified duplicate of it.

7. Pull on the bottom two nodes of this lighter duplicate with the Shape tool, then drag down until the bottom slightly overlaps the radial fill rectangle. Select the lighter duplicate, and send it to the back (Shift-PgDn) of the Background Layer. Select both swoopy rectangles. Then select **B**lend Roll-Up from the Effe**c**ts menu, blend the two objects in 40 steps, and click on Apply. The eye should perceive no difference between the smoothness of this blend and that of the fountain-filled rectangle on the bottom.

If a straight 100-percent black value is set for the background, there is no "cycling" in the blend, and the background shows a black-to-white graduation instead of a nice flash of deep blue.

8. Select **L**ayers Roll-Up from the **A**rrange menu, and choose Edit. Set the attributes to this Background layer to Locked, Visible, and set the Color Override color to a value that soothes your eyes.

9. **O**pen a new Layer, and call it Stars. Select **I**mport from the **F**ile menu, and import the EPS file of the stars (see step 3).

They will come into CorelDRAW as a group. While the stars are still grouped, select a white fill and no outline for them.

10. **U**ngroup the stars. Marquee-select a section and use CorelDRAW's drag/click right mouse button feature to sprinkle them all over the page. Do this until the page is randomly peppered with stars. You do not have to stay within the lines of the page border because you will clean up the Stars layer later.

Because you will be adding a parchment design to the center of the Astrotext illustration, many of the stars you randomly distribute will be hidden by the addition of the parchment—which sort of makes several of them unnecessary. Many other stars will be faded into the blend. Stars that do not contribute to the drawing simply create a bigger CorelDRAW file, so you can dispatch them later. Figure 6.4 is an example of how the Wireframe view of Astrotext will look after some unnecessary stars have been cleaned out.

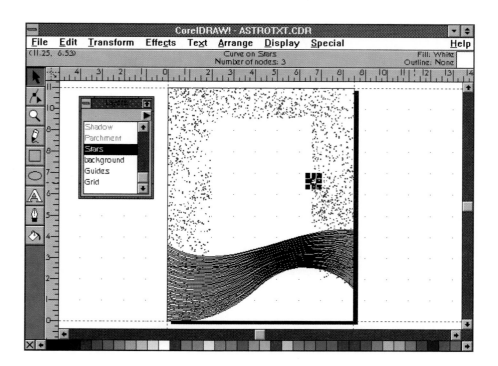

Figure 6.4:

Wireframe view of Astrotext after unnecessary stars are deleted.

11. Lock the Stars layer, and make it invisible. (Otherwise, the screen redraw time is very long and you'll go blind continuing the piece.)

12. **O**pen a new layer, and label it Parchment. Draw a rectangle proportional to a piece of paper. Using the Envelope tool (set to Single Curve), sweep out the bottom portion of the parchment so that it appears to come toward the viewer. To make the bottom sweep symmetrical, hold down the Ctrl key while you tug on one of the bottom corners. Convert the parchment rectangle to curves.

13. Vector art is clean—a little too clean to be believable sometimes. Add tiny imperfections to the parchment, such as bent corners, a tear on an edge, and uneven lighting (use a graduated fill of two slightly different colors) to simulate real-world characteristics (see fig. 6.5).

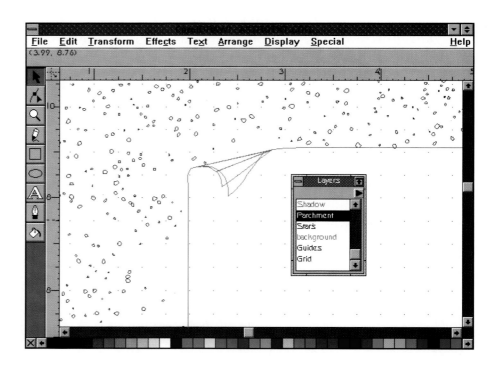

Figure 6.5:

Close-up Wireframe view of one of the parchment's "flaws."

14. Add a shadow to the bottom of the parchment. Use a linear fountain fill, at about a –62 degree angle, with a high value Edge Pad of about 20, graduating from a rich warm gray to a lighter value on bottom. Make certain that the shadow

stands off from the lightly filled bottom of the Background layer by turning on the Background layer's visibility to check (see fig. 6.6).

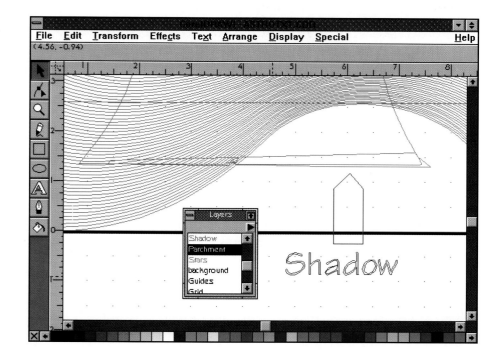

15. Lock the Parchment layer, and set the color override to a dark pastel. Make the Background layer invisible.

16. **O**pen a new layer, and call it Text. You should create the text and save it in a directory as a TXT file prior to creating this piece because it's quicker to compose text in a word processing program than in CorelDRAW. Using the Text tool, marquee-select a text area within the outline of the parchment.

    This text area for the paragraph text should come about 1/4" from the left-hand parchment outline, 1/4" on the right, and 1/4" from the top of the parchment outline. Stop dragging at about the 5" mark on your vertical rule, or where the two vertical nodes on your parchment begin to fan the parchment outline toward the viewer.

If you can't tell where the fanning out begins, use the Shape tool to select the parchment outline, then pull a guideline down to the two vertical nodes. You see nodes a lot better when you use the Shape tool to select an object.

After you have marquee-selected the paragraph text area, type a single character on the keyboard, then press Ctrl-T to bring up the Text dialog box. Delete the character you just typed—it was typed to access the dialog box. Now click on **I**mport, and import the text (see fig. 6.7).

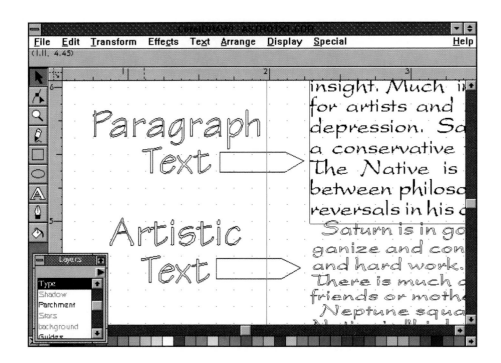

Figure 6.7:

Paragraph text is surrounded by a text border. Artistic text is not.

17. The rest of the text can be imported, or manually entered. This remaining text, however, needs to be artistic text, not paragraph text, because the envelope effect is used on the bottom of the text on the parchment.

Artistic text has a 250-character limit, so you must import several small chunks of text at a time to complete the text on the parchment page.

Carefully align the artistic text strings so that it appears to be one seamless page of text, rather than a huge block of paragraph text, and four or five little strings of artistic text. Figure 6.7 shows an example of how the two different types of text butt together.

Artistic text in CorelDRAW can be enveloped, as well as have other Effects applied to it, whereas paragraph text cannot. There is a limit in Corel, however, as to how many characters can exist in one string of text. Depending on the complexity of the typeface, the limit of characters is an average of 250. With a complex typeface, such as Present Script, the actual character count is around 230 to an individual artistic text string. When you exceed CorelDRAW's limit, a warning appears stating that the excess text will be dropped. In that case, you will have to do some editing.

18. Select E**d**it Envelope from the Effe**c**ts menu. Shape the first block of artistic text so that the left and right margins follow the slope of the parchment outline. You will have to do this with each successive block of artistic text, until the blocks appear to be fanning toward the viewer like the parchment does.

You might want to consider converting all the artistic text blocks to curves, breaking them apart, combining typographic characters that have a "counter" in them (like a *d* or an *o*), then grouping the whole thing.

The reason for this is that unless the PostScript language printer/film recorder you use for final output has a RISC or MIPS processor (which it probably doesn't), the printer instructions for this piece will overwhelm it. Three billion little descriptors that comprise the "broken up" text, however, are much more palatable to the PostScript printer.

19. Lock the Text layer, and make it invisible. You should have only the outline of the Parchment layer on your workspace now.

20. **O**pen a new layer, and call it Ball. Create a symmetrical circle in the middle of the Parchment. Using the Node Edit (or Shape) tool, make the circle a half circle. Watch the status bar to see when you reach 180 degrees. **D**uplicate the semicircle, position the rotation node to the center and bottom of the semicircle, and rotate it 180 degrees. You now have two hemispheres aligned to create a symmetrical circle.

21. The secret to creating reflections and chrome is to understand that a reflective surface has no character of its own—it simply mimics and distorts its surroundings. To create the ball, use a sky blue (reflecting the sky) color on the top of a "chrome" object, then add a horizon (a very dense, concentrated color, such as brown), and a ground color (usually a dark brown on top that graduates to a lighter brown).

    Fill the top half of the ball with a graduated fill depicting the sky—a blend from an azure to powder blue is good. Litter the top half with artifacts (extraneous shapes of items that the ball is reflecting) by using a few circular highlights and a few abstract shapes (see fig. 6.8).

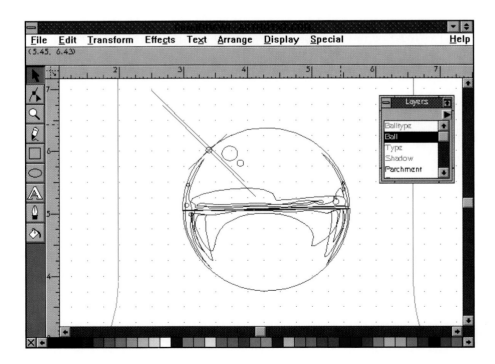

Figure 6.8:

Wireframe view of completed ball, with sky, horizon, ground, and a few highlights and shadows.

22. Put highlights and shadows in the ball's ground and sky areas for realism. Chrome objects reflect unpredictably; sometimes a photograph of chrome on a car picks up the photographer or other unwanted things. You might consider a little silhouette of telephone poles, a tree, or other shapes to encourage believability on the viewer's part. Don't get too carried away; you still need to add text as an element of the ball's reflecting properties.

23. The last piece that goes into the ball is the horizon. Make it dark, and blend it into the ground piece(s). A striking contrast should exist between the sky element and the horizon, and a very mottled transition between the horizon element and the ground element. White, circular highlights add realism to the chrome ball. Imitate what a camera lens might pick up by placing a white circle on the rim of the ball, and a "white cross star" effect on top of the white highlight with two 0.003" wide white lines.

Cross stars are an effect created by irregularities in the coating of a camera lens.

Spherical objects create highlights toward the outer rim and draw light in toward the center.

24. Lock the Ball layer, and give it a color override that is distinct enough to see. Unlock the Parchment layer, and make it visible.

25. Create a shadow (an ellipse) on the Parchment that is cast from the Ball. The Type layer should go over both the Parchment and the Shadow elements. Select a CMYK color slightly darker than the area on the Parchment where the ellipse lands. This is tricky because the Parchment has a slight graduated fill in it. The best way to tackle this is to set your display to 16 dithered colors, and try to match the area. Then switch to 256 pure colors, and see if the matching holds up (see fig. 6.9).

26. Select the two ellipses, and set the Blend command for 15 steps. Apply the Blend.

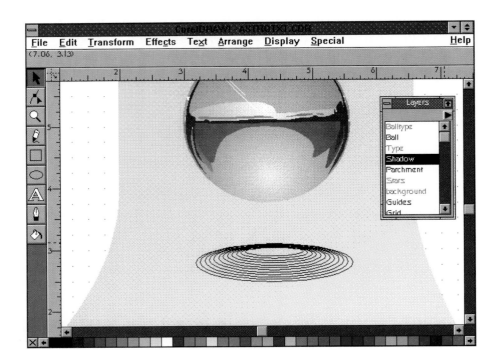

Figure 6.9:

A blend between two ellipses that will become the ball's shadow.

You have no control of the "pattern" of the fill in a single, graduated fill. A graduated fill is always linear or radial. You want what photographers call the "curve" of the graduation to be uneven to achieve a realistic shadow.

27. Clean out the extraneous stars on the Stars layer. Delete the stars that fall inside the border of the Parchment.

28. Now it's time to place some text in the lower half of the ball. This is the most critical step in creating the illusion of the ball hovering on top of the parchment. **O**pen a new layer, and name it Balltype.

29. Pick an area of artistic text on the Text layer that might be reflected inside the ball if this image were real. **C**opy the text, and move it to the Balltype layer.

30. Lock every layer, and make them invisible, except the Ball and the Balltype layers. You need to see the outline of the ball, but the emphasis is on shaping the Balltype at this point, so use a light blue color override on the Ball Layer now.

31. If earlier you converted the artistic text blocks to curves, broke them apart, combined certain ones, then grouped them, it's possible that you now have a large block of text or two on the Balltype layer. Don't worry if the large block of text exceeds the size of the area you're going to drop the copy into.

32. **U**ngroup the groups of text you have on the Balltype layer. Marquee-select a rectangle slightly larger than the bottom-half of the ball. **G**roup those items, then delete the unnecessary text fragments.

33. Select the text grouping, and mirror it both horizontally and vertically. (With a convex surface, objects mirror backward.) Make certain that this copy block has plenty of "bleed" with respect to the bottom half of the ball. **A**lign the upside down text grouping to the horizon of the ball.

34. Using the Shape tool in the envelope mode (unconstrained), start shaping the text grouping to fit inside and to conform to the general geometry of the bottom half of the ball (see fig. 6.10).

35. Lock the Balltype layer. Select Wireframe view (Shift-F9). By adjusting the Layers controls in Wireframe mode, you save redraw time as you make the layers visible one by one.

    Keep the layers Locked, though, as a matter of good practice. You now have about 19 billion objects in this piece, and you don't want them to move by accident.

36. Invite friends over to look at the finished piece. Then get a CorelDRAW World Design Contest form, and enter the piece. (Your own piece, of course. The contest judges might get suspicious of repeated Astrotext look-alikes.) Remember to put extra postage on the envelope because it's going to Canada.

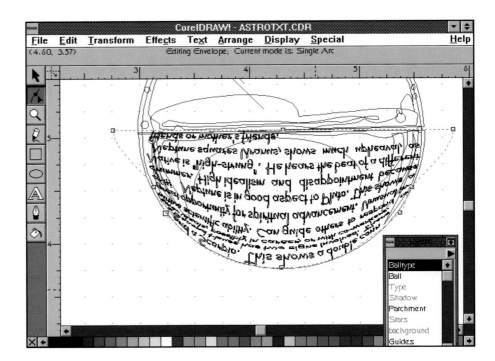

Figure 6.10:

Use the Shape tool to fit the envelope on the text to the ball shape.

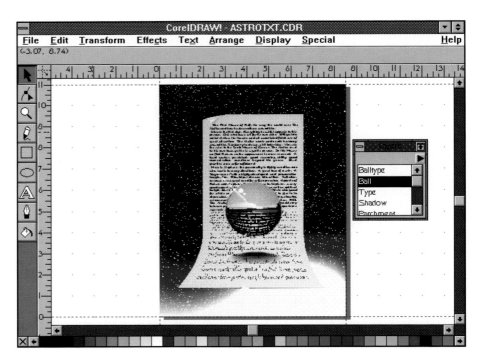

Figure 6.11:

The completed design.

7

Creating Metallic Looks

"Intellectual passion drives our sensuality."

—Leonardo da Vinci

Plymouth Laser

by David B. Libby

Doublegraph Inc.
Vincennes, Indiana

Equipment Used

Packard Bell 286
2M of RAM

Output Equipment Used

Film recorder

David is the president and principal artist of Doublegraph Incorporated, a graphic design and illustration firm. This automotive illustration was conceived as a portfolio piece.

Procedure

1. This illustration originally was drawn in Corel 2.0, and the procedure used was not particularly ingenious. A black-and-white TIFF scan of the original photo was imported into CorelDRAW and used as a template for roughly outlining key shapes.

   Because the bitmap looked pretty much the same in Wireframe mode as it did in Preview mode, the only loss on-screen was in differentiation between similarly-colored areas, all of which looked gray. The advent of CorelDRAW 3.0's editable preview would at least allow tracing over a full-color bitmap. Even a line trace on tracing paper scanned in probably would be more efficient than the method I chose.

2. Start by drawing the main outline of the car with the Pencil tool, and fill it with a deep blue color. The front bumper is drawn separately and filled with the same deep blue color. The outline of the tires, the wheel wells, and the shadow on the pavement are drawn as a single shape and filled with black (see fig. 7.1).

3. After drawing the shapes, use the Node Edit (Shape) tool to adjust the shape of the curves while eyeballing the original photo.

4. Draw shapes for the front bumper vent openings, fill them with black, and accent them with thin, light gray lines to suggest reflective edges.

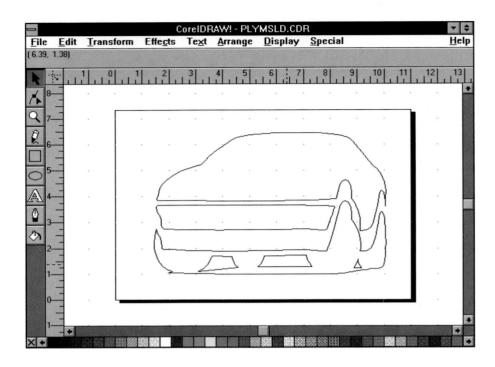

Figure 7.1:

Creating the main outline, front bumper, tires, wheel wells, and shadows.

5. Draw the hood and side body panel next and fill with linear fountain fills that match the photo in direction and general color (see fig. 7.2).

Figure 7.2:

Creating the body with linear fountain fills.

I deliberately picked a subject that I felt would lend itself to rendering with CorelDRAW's tools and features. A couple of strategically placed fountain fills proved to be very effective in this instance.

6. Several other blue body panel sections are added by using linear fountain fills and blends to give the front and side of the car more curvature.

7. Draw the windshield, and give it a medium gray fill. Then add the lighter areas of the windshield to give the illusion of glass and the outline of seats and dash. Draw the side window, and give it a dark gray to light gray linear fountain fill to suggest reflection.

8. Draw the side mirrors in outline first, and fill them with black. Then draw a smaller version of the mirror on top of the mirror outline to approximate the smaller light area, and fill it with a lighter shade. The two shapes then are blended (see fig. 7.3).

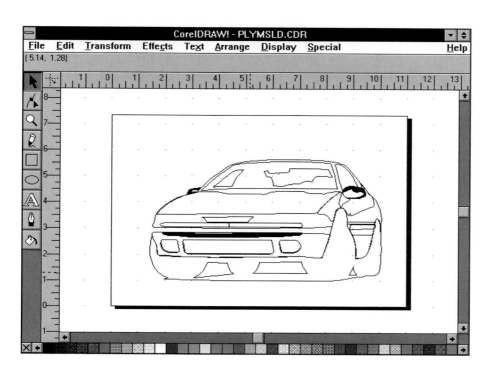

Figure 7.3:

Wireframe view with blends on the mirrors.

9. Details are added by drawing lines; for example, for the hood and door outlines and body panel separations. Draw the windshield wipers and fill with black.

10. Match the color of the headlights and turn signals to those in the photo. Then overlay the headlight and turn signals with a grid of light gray lines to simulate glass lenses (see fig. 7.4).

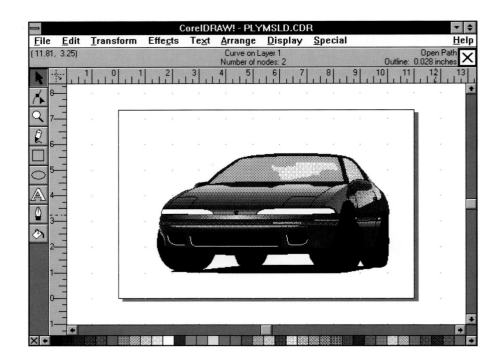

Figure 7.4:

Creating the headlights and turn signals.

11. The wheels and hubcaps are created last (see fig. 7.5), as these are difficult to create. The accuracy and detail needed for these elements is in contrast to the rest of the car, where only a sense of the accurate shapes is necessary to convey the feeling of the original. I worked on the wheels until they looked correct, adjusting shapes and placement, and printing proofs to get a feel for the result. (Did I mention that this was originally drawn several years ago on a 12" monitor in 16 colors at 640 × 480?)

12. Draw a shape for the pavement, send it To **B**ack, and give it a linear fountain fill at a 90-degree angle to suggest the proper perspective.

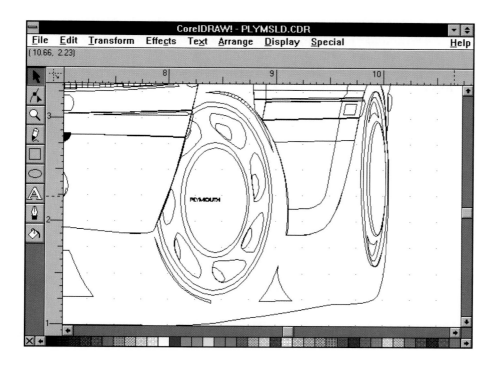

Figure 7.5:
Creating the wheels and hubcaps.

13. I added a rainbow-colored background to this piece. To do this, draw four slightly overlapping rectangles (see fig. 7.6), and give each a horizontal fountain fill to coincide with the next rectangle; for example (from left to right) from red to yellow, from yellow to green, from green to blue, and from blue to purple.

14. Originally, I drew the characteristic engine clearance hump on the hood. I never found a way to satisfactorily blend that object into the fountain fill of the hood, however, so I omitted the hump in the end!

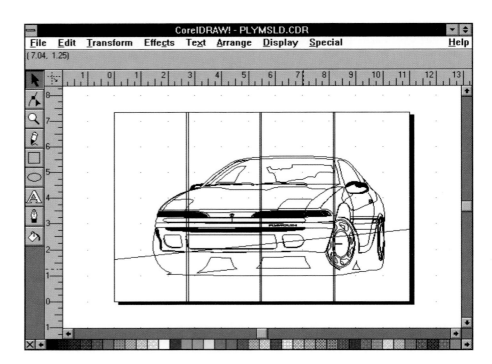

Figure 7.6:

Overlapping rectangles to create the rainbow-colored background.

Creating Glass Looks

"Son pittore ancor io!" (I, too, am a painter!)

—*Correggio*

Reflections

by Wil Dawson

Tulsa, Oklahoma

Equipment Used

386/40MHz IBM clone

This drawing is not a complicated one; it consists primarily of a series of rectangles which have radial and linear fills. All perspectives were created with the perspective feature, and all objects consistently have a 1-point line around them.

Procedure

1. Draw a series of elongated rectangles. Colors used in the original drawing were desert blue, purple, spring green, navy blue, light green, electric blue, pastel blue, forest green, sea green, and deep navy blue. Any colors, however, may be used. Note that rectangles do not need to be a uniform height, as illustrated in figure 8.1.

2. **G**roup the series of rectangles, then **D**uplicate them three additional times up the page, offsetting them to the left and right (see fig. 8.2).

3. Draw a large rectangle behind the colored boxes. This box has a baby-blue fill, as shown in figure 8.3.

4. Group all objects. Use the Edit Perspecti**v**e function to shape the group to approximately the shape shown in figure 8.4.

5. Draw the following building facades over the group of colored boxes. Facades facing left have a radial fill from 100-percent black to 70-percent black. Facades facing right have a radial fill from 80-percent black to 10-percent black. Experiment with the horizontal and vertical offset for the center of the radial fill. Note that the boxes have been omitted for clarity.

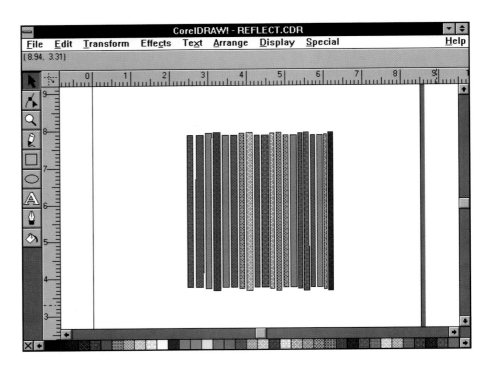

Figure 8.1:

Series of elongated rectangles.

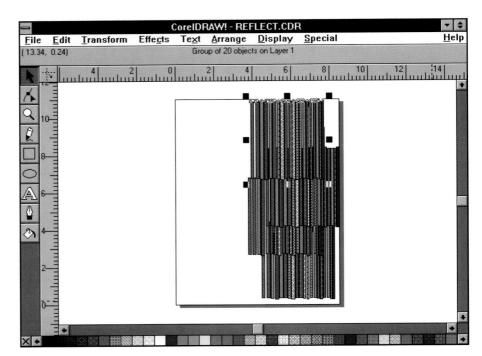

Figure 8.2:

Duplicated group of rectangles.

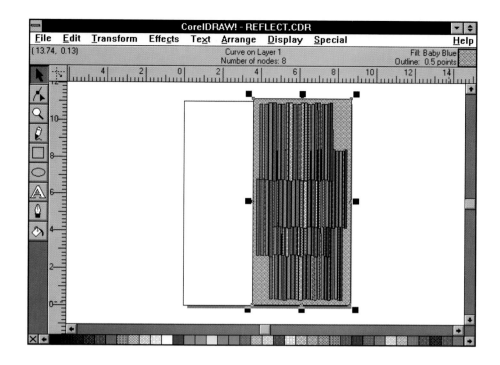

Figure 8.3:

Blue rectangle for background.

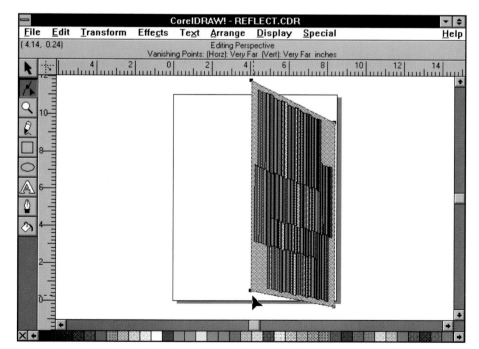

Figure 8.4:

Perspective applied to grouped objects.

Use layers to separate the boxes from the building facades. By using color override on the layer for boxes, you can easily draw the facades on their own layer but still accurately position them (see fig. 8.5).

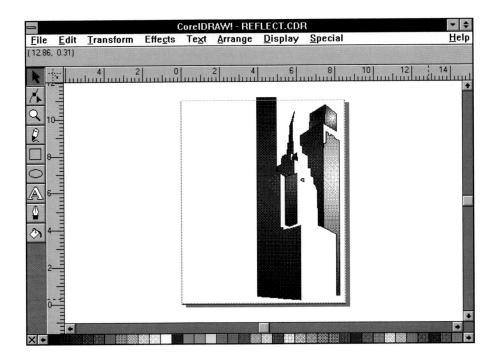

Figure 8.5:

Building faces with radial fills.

6. On the desktop, create the shaded windows that form the lower part of the right facade. Draw an elongated rectangle with three squares under it. These elements contain a radial fill from 80-percent black to 20-percent black. **C**opy these figures seven additional times, and **G**roup them. Then select Edit Perspecti**v**e from the Effe**c**ts menu to shape the group (see fig. 8.6).

7. Drag the group you just created into place. At this point the drawing should like figure 8.7.

8. Draw the following objects to mask the areas behind and in front of the buildings:

 Rectangle on left. Use a radial fill from navy blue to desert blue. Specify a center offset of horizontal 0, vertical 28.

Rectangle on right. Use a radial fill from navy blue to desert blue. Specify a center offset of horizontal 18, vertical 26.

 Top rectangle and triangle. Use a linear fill from C47, M0, Y9, B35 to C53, M38, Y0, B40.

 Bottom rectangle. Make this black.

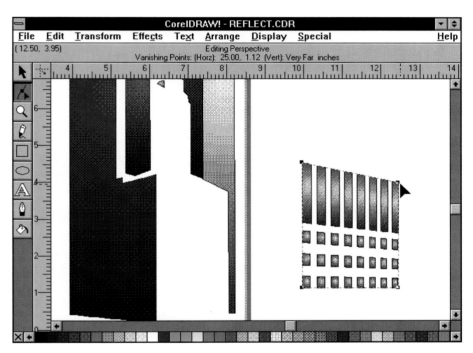

Figure 8.6:

Perspective applied to group windows.

The left rectangle and the triangle remain on top. The other three rectangles should be moved behind the buildings (see fig. 8.8).

9. On the desktop, draw a series of about 15 or 16 rectangles and surround them with one large rectangle, as shown in figure 8.9.

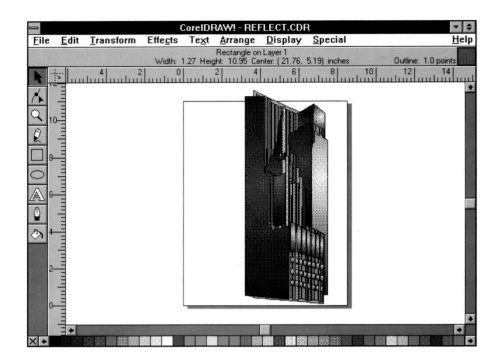

Figure 8.7:
Completed group of buildings.

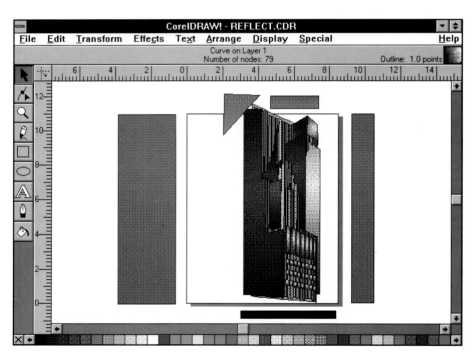

Figure 8.8:
Objects for masking and background.

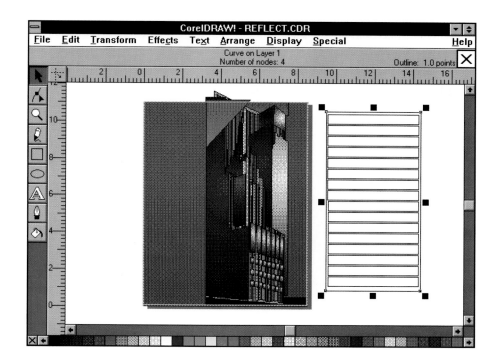

Figure 8.9:
Series of rectangles for windows.

10. **C**ombine these elements to produce cutouts, and give the object a radial fill from 80-percent black to white, with a horizontal offset of 10 and a vertical offset of 26. Choose Edit Perspecti**v**e from the Effe**c**ts menu to give this object the desired shape (see fig. 8.10), and then drag it onto the drawing.

11. Repeat steps 9 and 10 for the left and middle groups of windows. Fill them as follows:

    Left windows. Use a linear fill from black to white with an angle of 18.7.

    Middle windows. Use a radial fill from 30-percent black to 80-percent black. Use a horizontal offset of 25 and a vertical offset of 21 (see fig. 8.11).

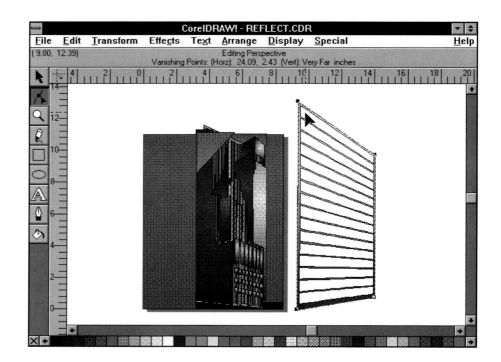

Figure 8.10:
Perspective applied to combined rectangles.

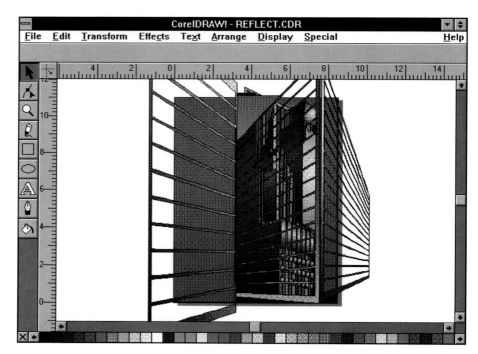

Figure 8.11:
Three overlay groups of windows.

12. As the drawing extends outside the boundaries of the page, you now have two choices:

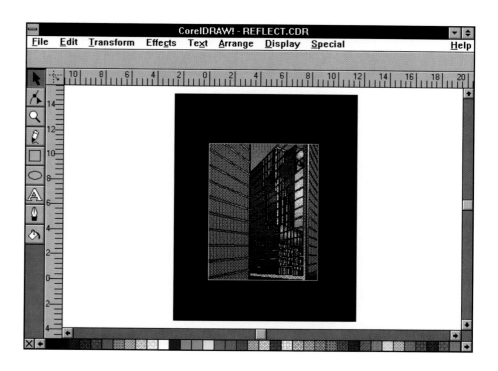

You can mask the unwanted area.

You can use the Node Edit tool to make object boundaries conform to page boundaries.

To mask the unwanted area, draw a large rectangle to cover all objects and a smaller one the size of the paper. **C**ombine these objects to produce the mask. Use a black fill with a 4-point, 30-percent gray outline (see fig. 8.12).

Figure 8.12:

Combined rectangles form mask.

If you plan to use the Node Edit tool to reshape the objects, the drawing should be created on different levels. Different levels enable you to break apart (**U**ngroup) objects, manipulate the nodes, and then recombine or regroup the objects. If all objects are created on one level, this task becomes considerably more difficult.

Figure 8.13 illustrates the completed design.

Figure 8.13:
The completed design.

Creating Wet Looks

"I paint objects as I think them, not as I see them."

—Pablo Picasso

MIKE GILES 1992

Water Reflection

by Mike Giles

Giles Graphics
Jasper, Alabama

Equipment Used

386 DX/40
4M of RAM
Genius mouse
Super VGA monitor

Output Equipment Used

Hewlett-Packard DeskJet 500C

Mike Giles is owner of Giles Graphics in Jasper, Alabama. He has been a CorelDRAW user for three years. He specializes in landscapes and inspirational art. This piece was designed for sale in local art and specialty shops surrounding the Smith Lake area.

Procedure

1. Set guidelines for the perimeter of the picture.

2. Select **E**dit Wireframe from the **D**isplay menu so that the image will not take as long to redraw after each step. Instead of redrawing a filled object, Corel will redraw the outline of each image.

3. Place a horizontal guideline where you want the shore to be.

4. Choose Snap To **G**uidelines from the **D**isplay menu so that the rectangles for the sky and the water do not overlap.

5. Draw a rectangle for the sky background. (Note that all drawing is without outlines until the final stages of the illustration.) Fill the sky rectangle (using CMYK colors) with a radial fill from C100-M60-Y0-K6 to C13-M18-Y0-0.

6. Draw a rectangle for the water background, and fill it with navy blue.

7. Draw a circle with a height of 0.65", and place it over the center of the radial fill. Fill the circle with pink (C1-M9-YO-KO). This is the moon.

8. Turn off Snap To **G**uidelines.

9. Using the Pencil tool, draw the highlight for the water (see fig. 9.1). Use the options found in the Node Edit menu to eliminate any unwanted corners or curves, and fill with pink (C2, M14).

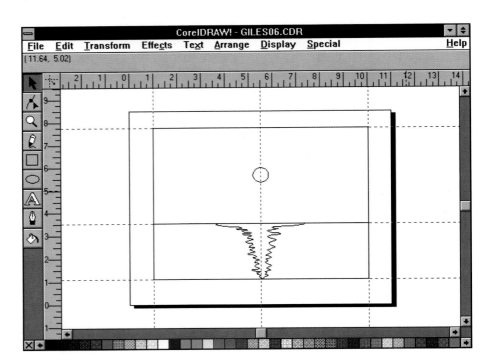

Figure 9.1:
The water's highlight.

Reflections in clear water are darker, whereas, reflections in muddy water are lighter. This picture shows clear water; therefore, the highlight is slightly darker than the moon.

10. While holding down the Shift key, stretch the highlight 850 percent, and click the right mouse button to leave the original.

11. Fill the duplicate with navy blue.

12. Place the highlight in front of the duplicate by selecting Forward **O**ne from the **A**rrange menu (see fig. 9.1 and fig. 9.2).

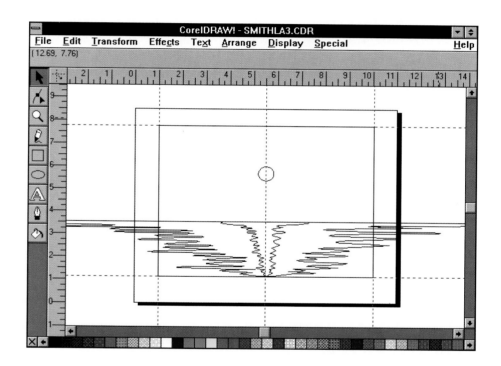

Figure 9.2:
The final highlight.

13. Select the highlight and the duplicate highlight, and blend in 20 steps.

14. Turn on Snap To **G**uidelines.

15. Press F3 to enlarge the view area, and draw large rectangles to cover unwanted sides of the blend. Fill these rectangles with white.

16. Using **L**ayers Roll-Up from the **A**rrange menu, make level 1 invisible, and select New to make level 2 the active layer.

17. Turn off Snap To **G**uidelines.

18. Using the Pencil tool, draw an evergreen tree, making sure that the tree is a closed object.

You can scan in a tree to create a more realistic look, but scanning results in an extremely complex object that can cause memory and printing problems.

19. Using the Node Edit tool, eliminate as many nodes as possible. The goal is to have a tree with less than 100 nodes.

Keep the trees simple. The more complicated the trees, the longer it takes to redraw them.

20. Using the Pick tool, drag and click the right mouse button to make several (four or five) duplicates of the tree. Make some of the trees taller, larger, smaller, shorter, mirrored, and so on. These trees keep the forest from having a "cookie-cutter" look (see fig. 9.3).

21. Fill the trees with a linear 90-percent fill, using pastel blue at the bottom and navy blue at the top.

22. Draw a rectangle the width of the picture and 1/2" high (see fig. 9.4). Place this rectangle on top of the shoreline. Fill with pastel blue.

23. Using the Pick tool, select a tree and duplicate it several times. Place the duplicated trees along the shoreline. Be sure, however, not to place any below the shoreline.

24. Continue using the different tree shapes until the middle of the shoreline is complete (see fig. 9.5).

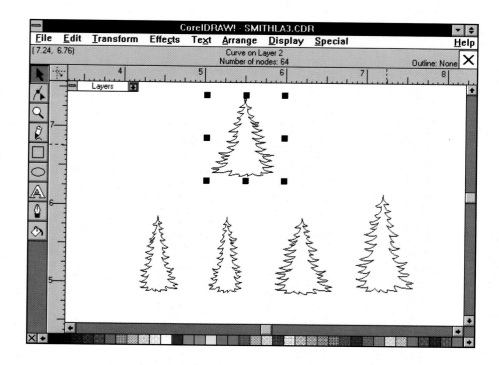

Figure 9.3:
Creating several different trees from a single tree.

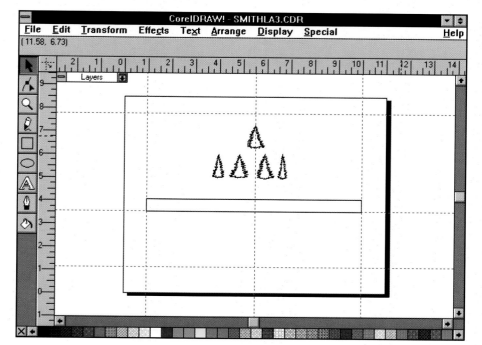

Figure 9.4:
The rectangle fills in behind the trees.

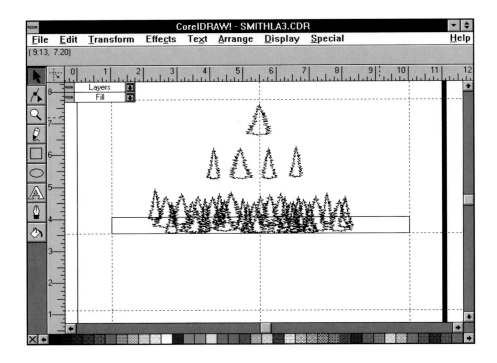

Figure 9.5:

The shoreline.

25. Using the Pick tool, select the shoreline rectangle and all the shoreline trees. Then **G**roup the objects.

26. Using the Pencil tool, draw the left bank. Use the Shape tool to clean up the image. Then fill the bank with twilight blue.

27. Using the Pick tool, select a tree and place duplicates along the left bank. Because these trees are closer, they must be larger. Use the Pick tool to enlarge them.

28. Fill the left bank trees with a 90-percent linear fill, with twilight blue at the bottom and deep navy blue at the top.

29. Follow the same procedure for the right bank (see fig. 9.6).

30. Make Layer 1 visible.

31. Add 0.056 twilight blue border outline and signature (see fig. 9.7).

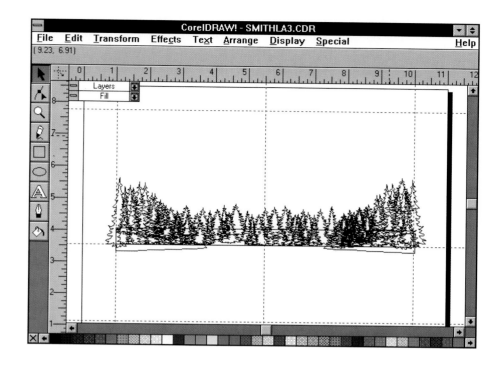

Figure 9.6:
The completed shoreline.

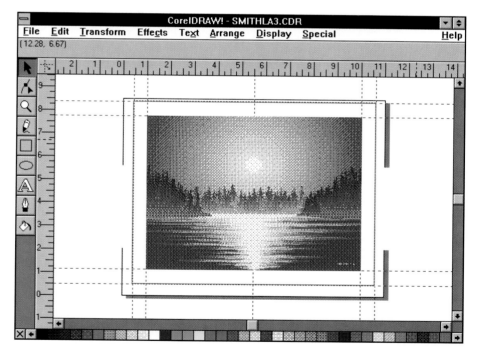

Figure 9.7:
The completed artwork.

Creating the Modeled Look

"There are painters who transform the sun into a yellow spot, but there are others who, thanks to their art and intelligence, transform a yellow spot into a sun."

—*Pablo Picasso*

© Lisa A. Windham 1992

The Bathing Bear

by Lisa Agnes Windham

Virginia Beach, Virginia

Equipment Used

486 CPU IBM-compatible computer
4M RAM
33 MHz
128K cache memory
210M hard drive
5 1/4" and 3 1/2" drives
VGA monitor
Mouse
This file is 182,874 bytes.

Output Equipment Used

QMS-PS 410 Laser Printer for initial proofs
Tektronix Phaser II SD Color Printer for final output

Lisa Agnes Windham is a free-lance graphics designer, with a special interest in animal illustration. Born in Alexandria, Virginia, she received her degree in art from Virginia Polytechnic Institute and State University. Having explored various media throughout her career, she began using the computer for illustration three years ago. The computer provided a uniquely flexible avenue through which she has been able to expand upon her artistic abilities. Lisa always has found animals to be a source of enjoyment, pleasure, and beauty, as reflected in her artwork. She continues to use her love of animals and the encouragement from her family as an inspiration.

This drawing of "The Bathing Bear" was her first attempt at computer illustration.

Procedure

The Head

1. Open a new Corel file. Begin by using the Pencil tool to freehand draw the head of the bear. Continue drawing until the head is a closed object. This part of the head is going to serve as a background template—other objects will be added to the front.

If the drawing appears rough with jagged edges or unnecessary curves, any part of the design can be altered by using the Shape tool's pop-up Node Edit dialog box. You can use this feature to alter an existing form rather than redraw it. To alter the head, double-click on the node you want to edit. Use the options in the dialog box to alter the design as desired (see fig. 10.1).

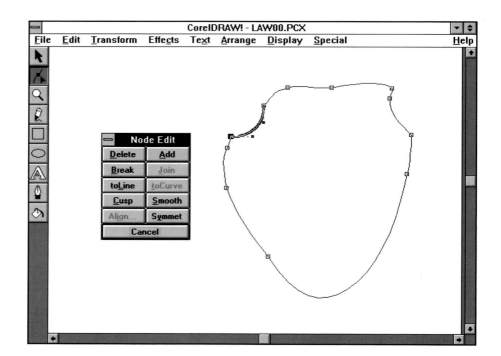

Figure 10.1:
Creating the bear's head.

2. Next, fill the head by clicking on the Fill tool. Two rows of fills appear on the flyout menu. Select fountain fill, and the Fountain Fill dialog box appears.

   Fill the head with a 60-degree linear fountain fill ranging in color from black to sand (see fig. 10.2).

To access the Fountain Fill dialog box immediately, use the shortcut key, F11.

3. Use the Pick tool to select the head. Because the head is serving as a template, it is best to have no outline. To make the head have no outline, select the Outline tool. Two rows of objects appear: the top row illustrates various line widths

and the bottom row illustrates various outline colors. In the top row, select the "X" for no outline (see fig. 10.3).

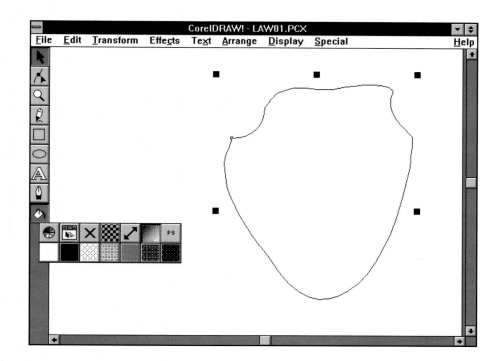

Figure 10.2:
Filling the bear's head.

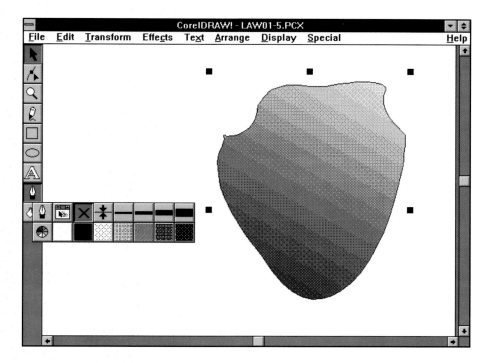

Figure 10.3:
Using the Outline tool.

4. Draw the bear's muzzle next. Follow the steps used to draw the head, and fountain fill the muzzle with a 45-degree linear angle from walnut to sand.

5. Place the muzzle in front of the bear's head, and position it in the lower center of the head, as shown in figure 10.4. This position makes the bear appear as if it is looking down.

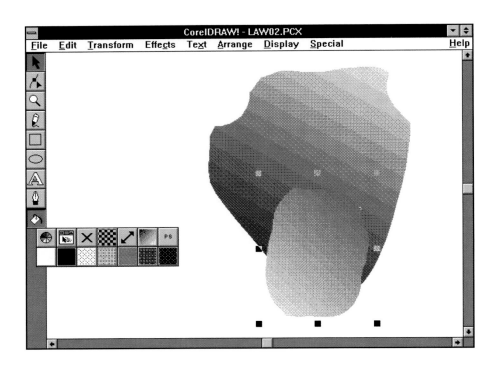

Figure 10.4:
Placing the bear's muzzle.

6. Draw the nose tip, and recall the Fountain Fill dialog box (F11). Use a radial fountain fill from black to 90-percent black. In the same menu under Center Offset, use these settings: horizontal −45 percent, vertical 50 percent, and an Edge Pad of 15 percent. By using the Edge Pad feature, the nose tip appears to have a light source coming from the right.

After this is completed, place the nose tip in front of the muzzle.

When applying highlights and shadows, consider the three-dimensional light source. The light in this drawing is located above, to the right, and in front of the bear. The left side of the bear is darker from shadows cast by the bear's head and body.

7. Draw the tongue with a 0.014-inch black outline (as shown in step 1). Click on the Outline Pen tool, and then click on the Pen icon in the flyout menu to access the Outline Pen dialog box.

   Under the width option in the dialog box, change the outline setting to 0.014-inch. The color should remain black.

You can access the Outline Pen dialog box immediately by using the F12 shortcut key.

8. Next, recall the Fountain Fill dialog box (F11). Use a radial fountain fill from black to ruby red, and change the vertical offset, found under Center Offset, to –26 percent.

9. Draw the bottom lip with a 0.003-inch black outline, and use a linear fountain fill of black to walnut at an angle of 90 degrees.

10. Place the bottom lip behind the tongue, and select both objects. After selecting the objects, place both the tongue and bottom lip behind the muzzle (see fig. 10.5).

11. Create the left ear, and recall the Fountain Fill dialog box (F11). Use a linear fountain fill that ranges from black to sand with a 145-degree angle. There is no outline for the ear because it serves as a template (as discussed previously with the head in step 3).

12. Next **D**uplicate the ear (see fig. 10.6).

13. Flip the duplicate ear by selecting the **S**tretch & Mirror (Ctrl+Q) option from the **T**ransform menu (see fig. 10.7). After the ear is flipped, place the new image in the desired location on the right side of the head.

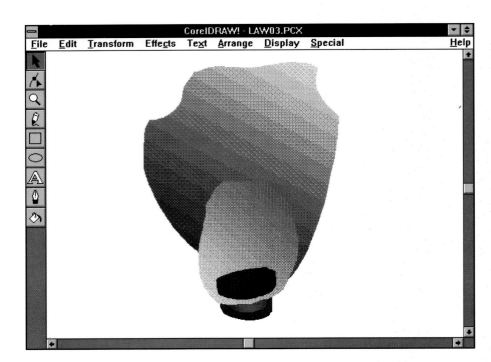

Figure 10.5:
Creating the tongue and lip.

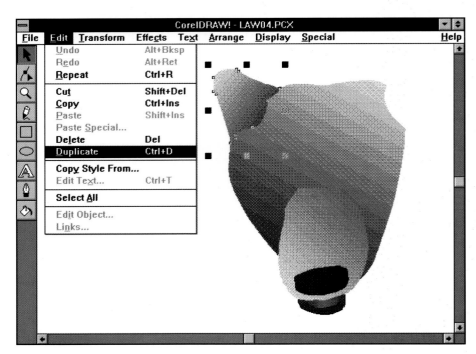

Figure 10.6:
Duplicating the ear.

You can alter and shrink the new ear to make it appear different from the other by using the **S**tretch & Mirror option (Ctrl-Q). Remember, the head is going to be tilted, so the right ear should be smaller.

After the right ear is adjusted, recall the Fountain Fill dialog box (F11), and use a linear fill from brown to walnut with a 75-degree angle.

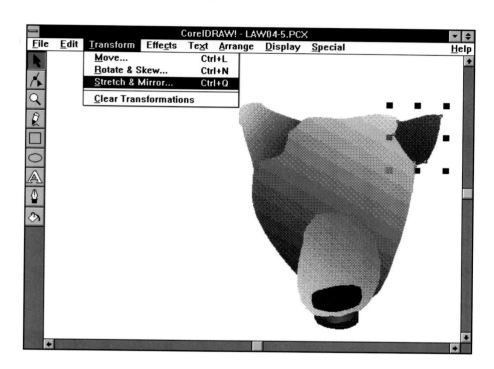

Figure 10.7:
Stretching and flipping the ear.

14. Draw the eyes using the Pencil tool, and fill with black. (I did not duplicate these to achieve a more realistic effect. Remember that the right eye should be smaller, just like the ear.) Add an oval white reflector highlight by using the Ellipse tool, and place the highlight in front of the eye (see fig. 10.8). Position the highlight near the top of the eye to achieve the desired effect and added depth.

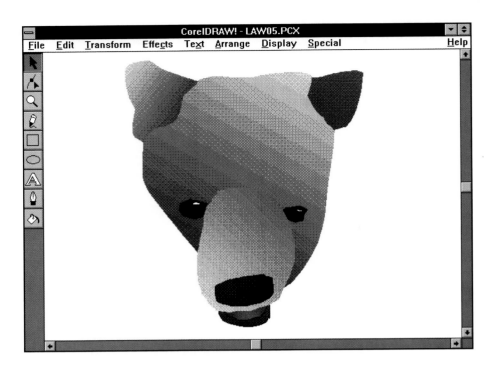

Figure 10.8:

Using the Ellipse tool to create a highlight.

15. Next, create the illusion of shadows and fur. Determine where shadows should fall, remembering the light source determined in step 6. Make those areas darker. Use the Pencil tool to draw a closed zigzag pattern in various sizes and color shades to create fur. Begin by placing fur on top of the ear, as shown in figure 10.9.

16. Continue adding fur, following the contour of the head.

It might be best to begin adding fur in the upper left side and continuing diagonally, increasing various levels of fountain fill as you go. Remember the light source, and make those fur areas appropriately lighter. Some fur patterns can be selected and blended together using the **B**lend command from the Effe**c**ts menu.

17. Group the entire head by using the **G**roup command from the **A**rrange menu (see fig. 10.10).

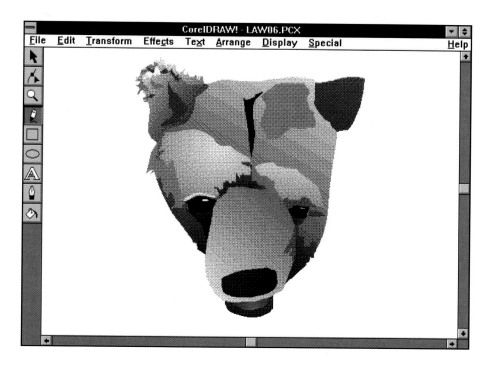

Figure 10.9:
Creating fur.

Grouping objects facilitates moving them and eliminates the possibility of accidentally altering or selecting an individual piece. If an object needs to be moved, **U**ngroup the head, make the necessary adjustments, and regroup.

The Body

18. With the head in place, create the body in two sections by using the Pencil tool. Recall the Fountain Fill dialog box (F11), and use a linear fill from walnut to sand with a 165-degree angle and an Edge Pad of 35 percent for the left side of the body.

By altering the Edge Pad, the two colors become more dominant and eliminate the gradual blend. This is ideal when creating a shadow effect.

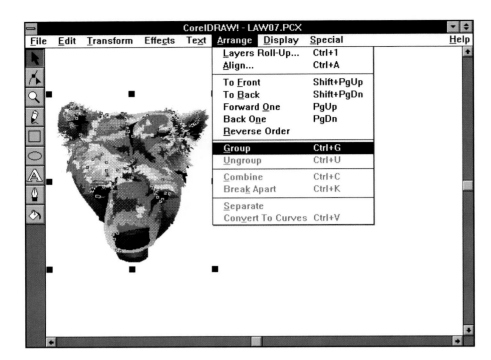

Figure 10.10:
Grouping the elements.

19. On the right side of the body, use a radial fountain fill with lighter versions of the two colors used in the preceding step. Use a horizontal offset of –7 percent, a vertical offset of 14 percent, and an Edge Pad setting of 10 percent (see fig. 10.11).

20. Draw a black shadow in the center, and overlap the two sections of the body (see fig. 10.12). Keep in mind that the foot and leg will be placed in front of the right half of the bear. Also remember the direction of the light source determined in step 6. The two objects cast a slightly larger shadow to the left side. Select the three objects, and send to back using the To **B**ack (Shift-PgDn) command from the **A**rrange menu.

Remove the grouped head from the body, and place it off the working space before you continue the drawing. This makes it easier to group the entire body after the rest of the drawing is completed.

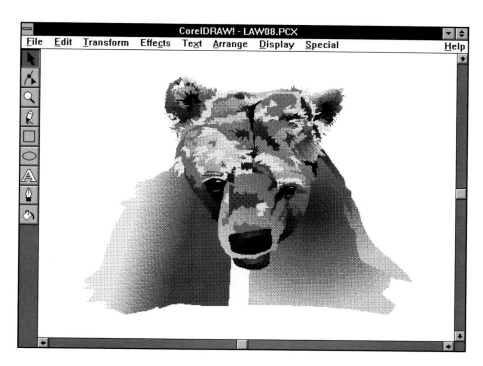

Figure 10.11:
Creating the body.

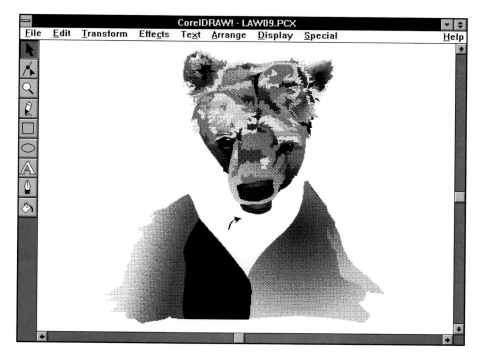

Figure 10.12:
Placing a black shadow.

21. Continue adding fur (as explained in step 15) to the left side of the body, and proceed in a diagonal fashion from left to right, stopping at the shadow. Add fur to the right side, until the desired effect is achieved.

22. **G**roup the entire body.

23. Place the bear's head in the proper position, and move it to the front, as shown in figure 10.13.

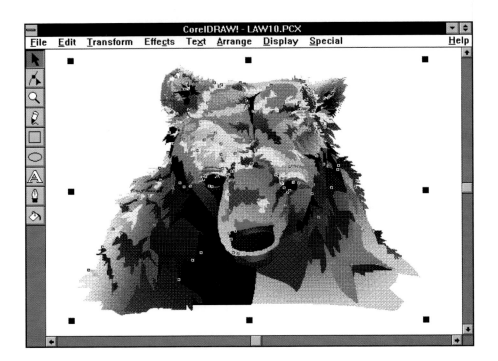

Figure 10.13:
Placing the bear's head.

The Foot and Leg

24. Using the Pencil tool, create the broad base of the foot away from the rest of the drawing. Recall the Fountain Fill dialog box (F11), and use a linear fill from pale yellow to light brown with a 6-degree angle.

25. Using the Pencil tool, draw the foot pad. Recall the Fountain Fill dialog box (F11), and use a radial fill of 50-percent black to black. Next, draw the toes, using a radial fill of black to 50-percent black for each toe. Keep in mind the way the shadow should fall on the toes.

26. **G**roup this portion of the foot (see fig. 10.14).

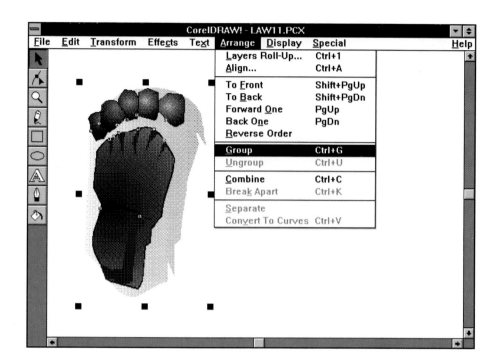

Figure 10.14:
Grouping the foot.

27. Draw the leg to the right of the foot. Recall the Fountain Fill dialog box (F11), and establish a linear fill of yellow-brown to black that resembles fur next to the foot. Create a similarly filled shape near the top of the leg, and blend the two objects (see fig. 10.15).

28. Add fur to both sides of the foot and shadows to the foot pad. Remember to take into account where a shadow might fall due to the light source.

29. Use the Pencil tool to create the toenails, and fill with light yellow. Place the toenails to the back of the foot pad.

30. **G**roup the entire foot and leg as shown in figure 10.16. The bear is now in three grouped pieces.

31. Position the leg in front of the body and head of the bear, and cover the tongue slightly to make it look as if the bear is bathing.

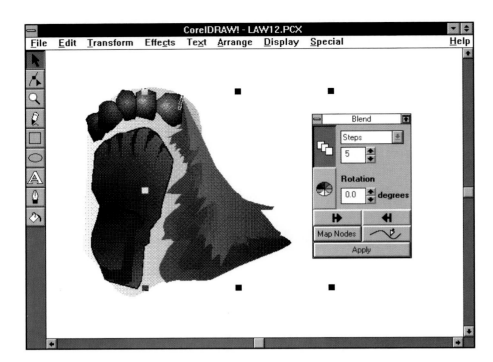

Figure 10.15:
Creating the leg.

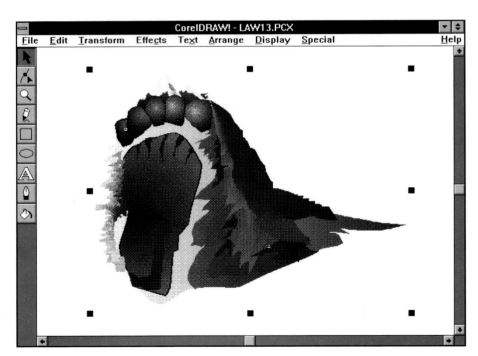

Figure 10.16:
Grouping the foot and leg.

32. After you have everything in position, **G**roup the entire bear (see fig. 10.17).

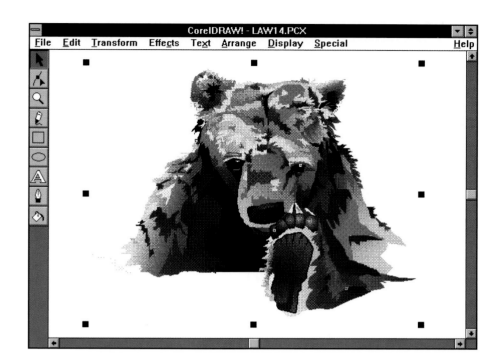

Figure 10.17:
Grouping the entire bear.

Final Effects

33. To create the illusion of water, use the Pencil tool to draw a background with a linear fountain fill of light blue-green to light ocean green. Place the water behind the bear (Shift-PgDn). Using the Pencil tool, draw various highlights and reflections on the water to create the illusion of ripples and shadows. These ripples can be any lighter variation of the water color. I choose to use highlights ranging from white to dark blue. Keep in mind that the areas of water around the bear are darker because of the shadows cast by the body.

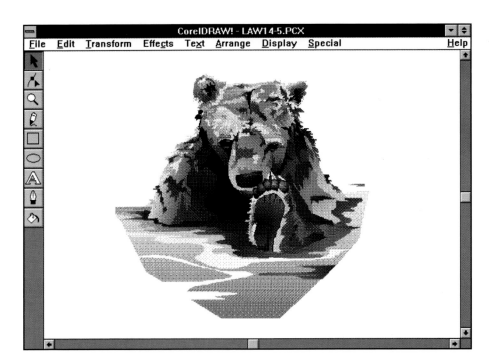

Figure 10.18:
Creating the water.

34. Next, use the Pencil tool to draw the rocks. Recall the Fountain Fill dialog box (F11), and use a radial fill from black to 20-percent black for the left rock. The horizontal offset is 15 percent and the vertical offset is 40 percent. The right rock has the same radial fill as the left, but the horizontal offset is 10 percent, the vertical offset is 48 percent, and the Edge Pad is 10 percent. This makes the highlights appear to come from above. Add darker percentages of black shadows to the rock for depth. When the rocks are completed, send them to the back (Shift-PgDn), and place them adjacent to the edge of the water to serve as a border.

35. The last background element to be created is the sky. Use the Pencil tool to draw the sky in a zigzag pattern allowing the background color of the paper to show through and fill with a light shade of ice blue. A smaller accent of ice blue can be created in the sky. This accent allows for some variation in sky color and makes for a more realistic picture.

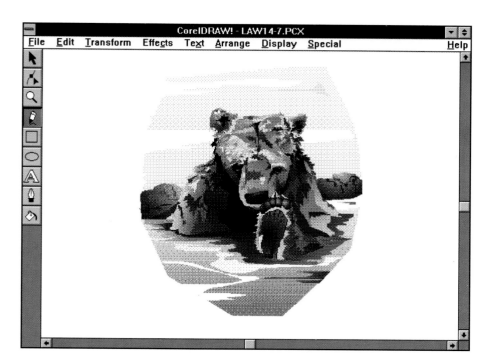

CorelDRAW! - LAW14-7.PCX

File   Edit   Transform   Effects   Text   Arrange   Display   Special   Help

Figure 10.19:

Creating final background effects.

36. A mask is added in these final steps to complete the drawing and eliminate rough edges. Use the Ellipse tool to draw a large white oval with no outline to cover the entire picture.

It is best to pull guidelines from the top and left sides to show the dimensions of the drawing. This can be done by selecting the Show **R**ulers command from the **D**isplay menu. After the rulers are activated, pull the guidelines down from the top and left. The guidelines appear as nonprinting dotted blue lines and can be placed anywhere in the working area.

37. Next, draw a larger white rectangle with no outline, and center it on top of the oval. Select both the oval and the rectangle.

Because both overlapping objects are the same color, choose **E**dit Wireframe from the **D**isplay menu. **E**dit Wireframe changes the color image to outlines of all the objects. This makes it easier and faster to view and select several objects of the same color.

After the oval and rectangle have been selected, combine them by using the **C**ombine command from the **A**rrange menu. This creates the effect of a mask because the white oval now is clear.

38. To complete the effect, place the combined object on top of the picture. The drawing appears as if the viewer can see through the oval. "The Bathing Bear" now is complete (see fig. 10.20).

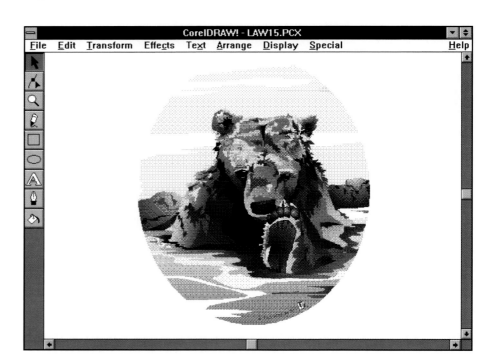

Figure 10.20:
The completed drawing.

Giuseppe De Bellis

Naples

by Giuseppe De Bellis

New Design Concepts
Fair Lawn, New Jersey

Equipment Used

486/50 computer system
16M of RAM
ATI video accelerator board

Output Equipment Used

400 dpi CANON CLC500
Fiery image processing unit

Giuseppe De Bellis is an architect for the N.Y.C. Board of Education and a free-lance graphics designer. He has used CorelDRAW, since its first version, on a daily basis for both professions.

The "Naples" design was inspired by a photograph he took in his hometown in Italy.

He tried to create a watercolor effect so that the final product would not look like a computer-generated drawing.

Procedure

1. Enlarge the original photograph so that it is clear enough to be traced.

   A copy machine can be used for this purpose. A larger photo reproduction of the original is suggested, however, because it is much clearer than a photocopy.

2. Using a sharp pencil, trace the enlarged photo on a piece of vellum or some other type of transparent media.

   The darker and more defined the pencil marks, the better and sharper the scanned image is. Also, draw consecutive lines with few breaks so that you do not have to edit the nodes later.

3. Scan in the traced image on a high-resolution scanner. A 600 dpi, black-and-white scanner will work. Save the image as a TIFF or BMP image (see fig.10.21).

You can use a low-resolution scanner to scan the image, but you will get much better definition of picture with a high-resolution scanner.

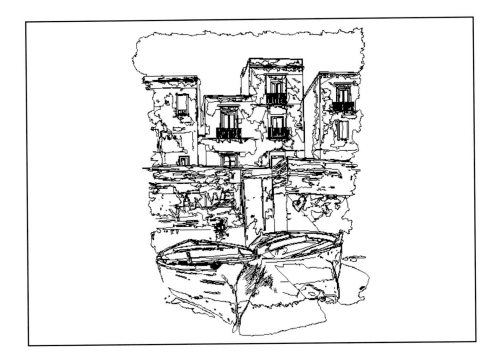

Figure 10.21:

The scanned drawing.

4. Open CorelTRACE, then open the scanned image.

   Change the tracing options to the following, and begin the tracing process (see fig. 10.22).

Tracing Method	=	Follow Outline
Curve Length	=	Medium
Convert Long Lines	=	Medium
Outline Filtering	=	Mild
Fit Curve	=	Medium
Sample Rate	=	Fine

5. Start CorelDRAW, and open the newly traced image. Clean up all unwanted lines, dots, and marks.

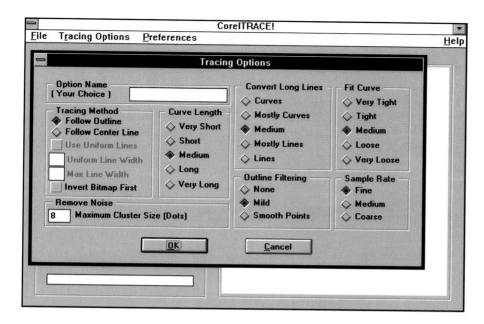

Figure 10.22:
Change the tracing options in the Tracing Options dialog box.

6. Close all the open paths of the objects that form the drawing so that you can fill the objects later.

Using the Node Edit tool, find all the open lines and join them (see fig. 10.23). (This may be the most time-consuming and tedious step.)

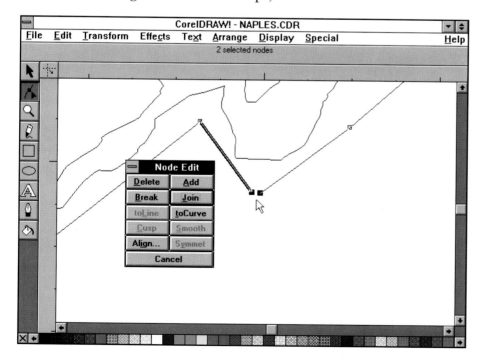

Figure 10.23:
Use the Node Edit dialog box to join broken lines.

7. Prior to starting the painting process, select all the objects that form the drawing by choosing Select **A**ll from the **E**dit menu. Then click on the Outline tool, and select the "X" in the flyout menu. None of the objects will have an outline.

8. Begin the painting process. Select the object to be colored, and choose the colors you want to use from the Uniform Fill dialog box, or select the colors from the palette bar located at the bottom of the CorelDRAW window.

You can use any color that you like. I chose colors to match the original photo as closely as possible.

9. You may need to create some of the colors. To do so, open the Fill roll-up window, and click on Edit. Mix the desired color, save it for future reference, and click on OK. Now apply the new color to the object (see fig. 10.24).

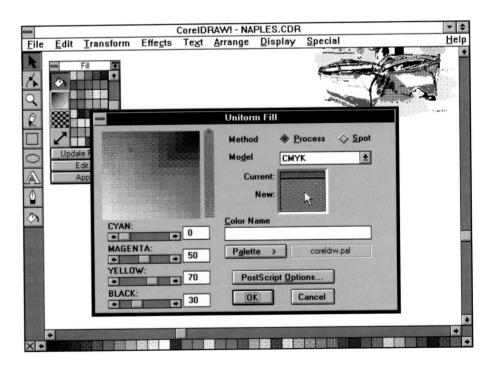

Figure 10.24:

Use the Uniform Fill dialog box to create new colors.

10. Figure 10.25 illustrates the completed artwork. This design won a second-place award in the 1992 CorelDRAW World Design Contest.

Figure 10.25:
The completed design.

Extrusion Effects

"Pop art is the inedible raised to the unspeakable."

—*Leonard Baskin*

Business Card

by Shane Hunt

Slimy Dog Grafix
San Dimas, California

Equipment Used

386 DX20 dinosaur

Output Equipment Used

High-resolution linotronic (to produce negatives for offset printing purposes)

Shane Hunt, owner of Slimy Dog Grafix in San Dimas, California, has been tinkering with CorelDRAW since its inception in 1989. He created this artwork to promote his design business and to illustrate a technique he developed to render transparent images in Corel.

Procedure

One of the shortcomings of CorelDRAW is that it doesn't enable you to fill an object with a transparent pattern. Filling an object with a transparent fill is a nice effect if you are trying to render semiopaque objects or light reflections. To overcome this obstacle, you can create bitmaps for special effects.

Corel's import and export features enable you to create bitmaps that you can incorporate into your design to give the illusion of transparency.

1. First create the transparent object. In this case, I wanted to create letters that looked as if they were molded from green jello! As you will not be able to change the look of the text by adding a heavier outline, choose a hefty font, such as USA Black.

2. Select Edit Perspective from the Effects menu. Use the Shape tool to drag the points in the direction you want.

3. Use the E**x**trude Roll-Up dialog box to give the text a 3D look (see fig. 11.1).

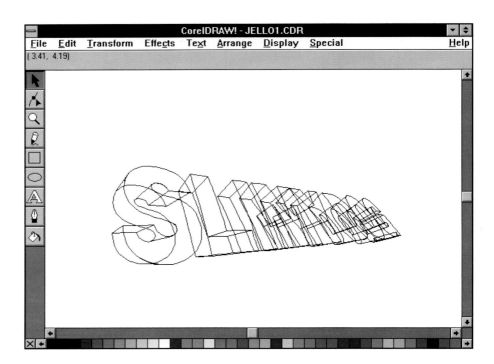

Figure 11.1:

The extrude feature creates a 3D wireframe.

Although CorelDRAW has added excellent shading capabilities to the E**x**trude Roll-Up option, it is the simplified wireframe that we are after. Now that you have the basic shape, you will create the first "effects object" that will be used to create our bitmap. It is important to understand that you will create images that will not be used directly in your design. These images are used to create the bitmaps that are incorporated into the final piece later!

4. Concentrate on the shading of the letters in the foreground. **D**uplicate your wireframe, and set the copy off to the side.

During the import/export process, you will delete many of the "effects objects" that are not used in the finished design! Save another copy of your image to disk just in case of disaster!

5. Convert your text to curves, and break apart the letters into individual objects. This is done so that each object can be shaded individually, rather than as one unit.

6. Choose a fountain fill that becomes darker toward your light source. You'll understand why in a moment. Remember that your goal is to create something that looks transparent, so assign the fountain fill 50-percent to 10-percent black. Also, assign your object no outline attributes (see fig. 11.2).

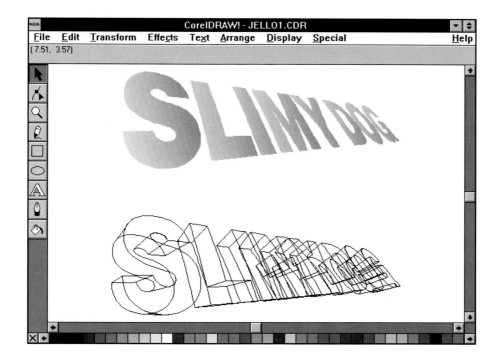

Figure 11.2:
Wireframe text and shading of "effects object."

7. Select only the shaded object, and then choose **E**xport from the **F**ile menu.

8. Export your file in TIFF format by selecting TIFF 5.0 Bitmap, *.TIF from the drop-down list box. The next step depends upon the nature of your project.

If you are outputting the image to a printer, create a 300 dpi, 1:1 (size), black-and-white TIFF file. If you plan to view the image on-screen, experiment with different resolutions. The reason for this is that a bitmap created with shading is made-up of very small dots that produce a moiré pattern when viewed on-screen. This happens when the dot pattern of the bitmap conflicts with the dot pattern of your video screen. This can be seen when you enlarge a bitmap. The checkerboard-like pattern that appears when you view or print the image is an example of a moiré pattern.

9. Now import the bitmap that you created, and assign the outline pen color of your choice. Because you have the option of No Fill with a black-and-white bitmap, your object appears to be transparent (see fig. 11.3)!

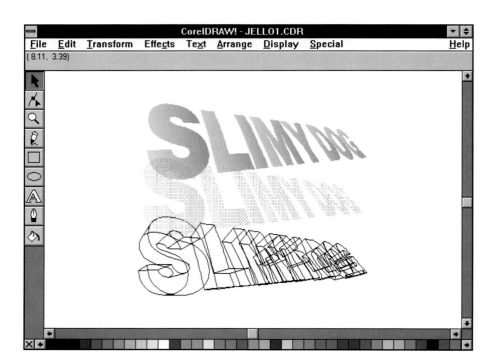

Figure 11.3:

Transparent bitmap reimported on top of the wireframe and "effects object."

10. Align this bitmap over your original wireframe. You can see the wireframe behind the fill, adding to the transparent illusion.

11. Assign fills to the extruded effects, and export them as a 300 dpi, black-and-white, 1:1 TIFF file (see fig. 11.4).

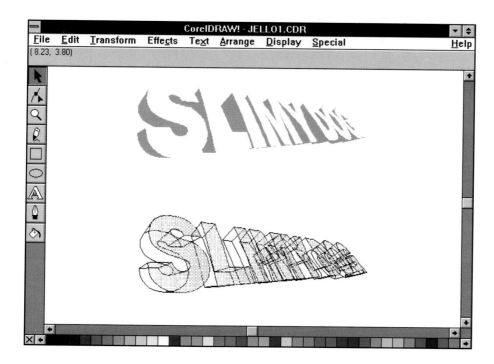

Figure 11.4:

Fill values assigned to "effects objects" to simulate shading for export.

12. Reimport this bitmap, align it with your original wireframe, and assign the desired color values to your objects. You now have a transparent block of text as shown in figure 11.5.

13. To heighten the illusion of transparency, I created blocks of text behind, through, and in front of the "clear" letters (see fig. 11.6).

I wanted the blocks to look like metallic objects slicing through my jello. The blocks actually are constructed of two opposing triangles, each with a 50-percent black-to-white linear fountain fill. By creating an offset white duplicate behind the black letter in the foreground, you get a "glint" (see fig. 11.7).

The end result looks a bit like a razor blade, as shown in figure 11.8.

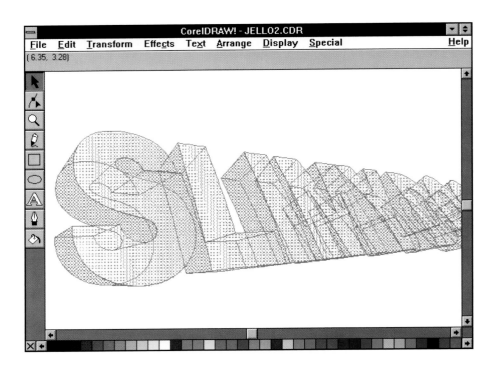

Figure 11.5:

Bitmaps aligned over original wireframe.

Figure 11.6:

Text elements placed to heighten illusion of transparency and add depth.

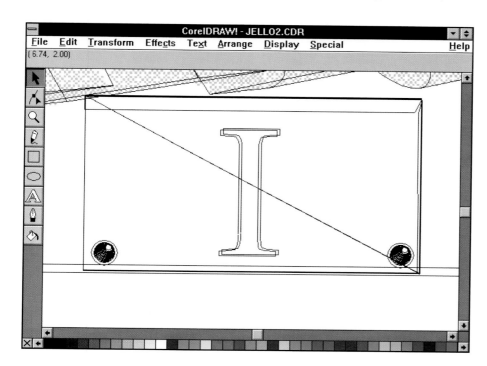

Figure 11.7:
Wireframe view of the "razor blade" letter.

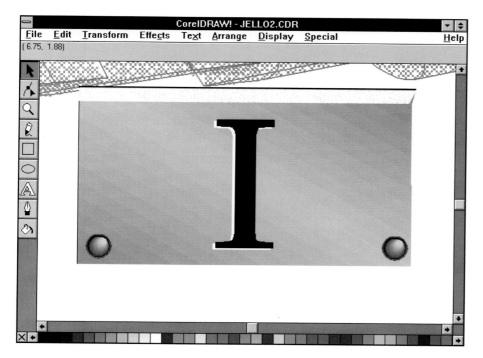

Figure 11.8:
Preview view of "razor blade" letter.

14. To finish my card, I added a photo of myself, but thought it was a bit too pretentious (see fig. 11.9)!

Figure 11.9:

Images added behind transparent text to add depth.

15. I wanted a more interesting look, and after trying a few different backgrounds, I added an outer-space scene. Then I "cut" a hole in the universe and peeked through it! I stuck the falling piece of the hole in the foreground and used the Blend feature to give it the desired shading. Then I added the standard business card text and was finished (see fig. 11.10).

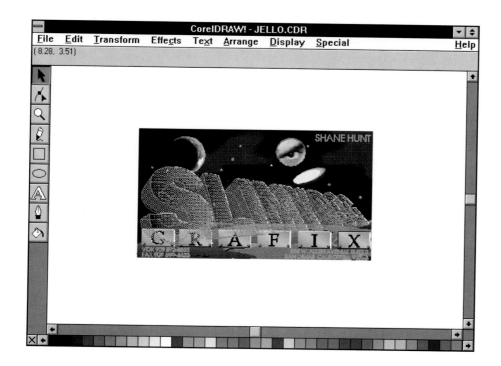

Figure 11.10:
The completed design.

Distortion and Mutation Effects

"To ask the meaning of art is like asking the meaning of life: Experience comes before a measurement against a value system."

—Fairfield Porter

Filmstrip

by Richard Feldman

Slides Plus Inc.
New York, New York

Equipment Used

Austin 486/33DX computer
8M of RAM

Output Equipment Used

High-resolution film recorder

Richard Feldman is president and owner of Slides Plus Inc., a full-service audio-visual production company specializing in slide, multi-image, video, and multi-media production. He has been a CorelDRAW user for three years.

He designed this artwork to be used as part of a direct-mail self-promotion piece for Slides Plus, in which various samples are shown on an actual strip of film.

Procedure

1. Type the copy on two lines by using the Text tool. Use the Motor font (see fig. 12.1).

2. Using the Node Edit tool, select the bottom node of each letter in the word PLUS, and, holding down the Ctrl key, adjust the letters horizontally so that PLUS is justified left and right with the word SLIDES. Make sure that the type is evenly spaced, as shown in figure 12.2.

3. Select the text, and modify it by selecting Edit Perspective from the Effects menu (see fig. 12.3).

4. Use the Pick tool to rotate text (see fig. 12.4). No specific degree of rotation was used. You can rotate the text until it is visually appealing to you.

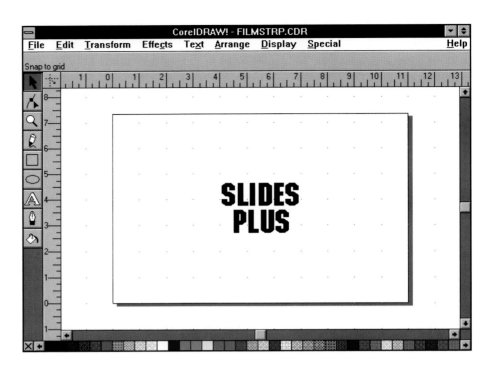

Figure 12.1:
The Motor font used for the text.

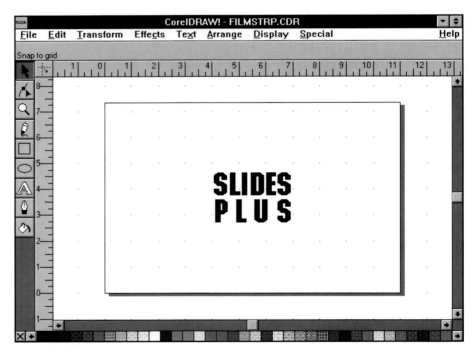

Figure 12.2:
Evenly spaced type.

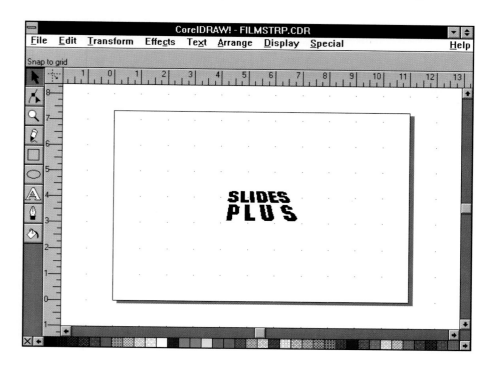

Figure 12.3:
Editing the perspective.

Figure 12.4:
Rotating the text.

5. Fill the text with yellow (see fig. 12.5).

Text is outlined with a hairline black rule. The rule makes the art easier to see as you work with it. Final art will not be outlined.

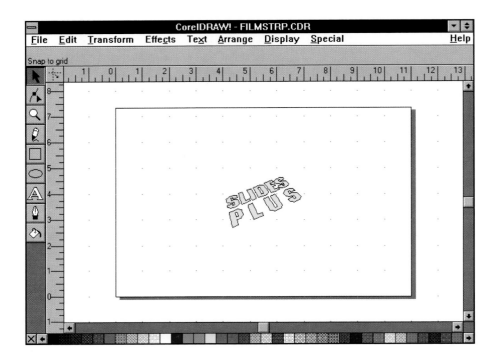

Figure 12.5:
Filling the text.

6. From the E**x**trude Roll-Up, uncheck the Perspective box, and extrude text straight down (see fig. 12.6).

7. Separate the extrude group, and fill it using a linear fountain fill to simulate light coming from the lower right corner, as shown in figure 12.7.

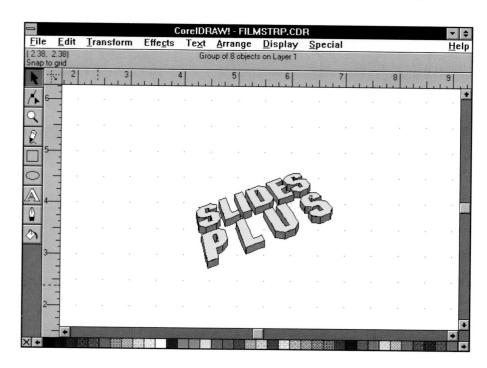

Figure 12.6:
Extrude text.

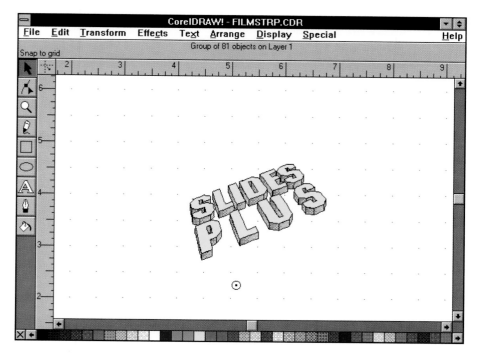

Figure 12.7:
Simulating a light source.

8. **U**ngroup the extruded objects. Use a darker solid fill on those extrude objects that face left and would be in the shadow (see fig. 12.8).

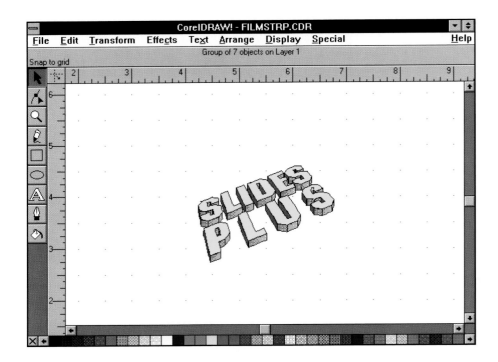

Figure 12.8:

Ungrouping the extruded objects.

9. Select the text object. From the E**x**trude Roll-Up menu, uncheck the Perspective box. Extrude toward the upper left corner. Separate the extrude group, and fill with black (see fig. 12.9).

10. Select the black extrude group, and send it **T**o Back. Then move the black group down and to the right until it lines up with the bottom edge of the first extrude group (created in fig. 12.6) to simulate a realistic shadow (see fig. 12.10).

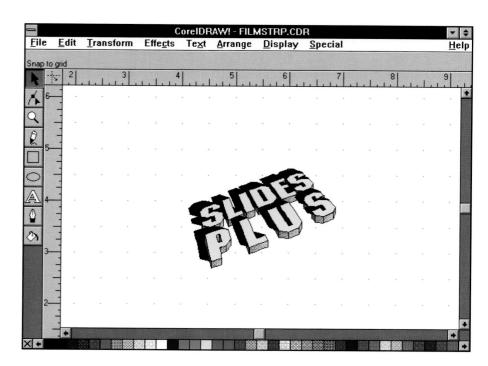

Figure 12.9:
Separating extrude group.

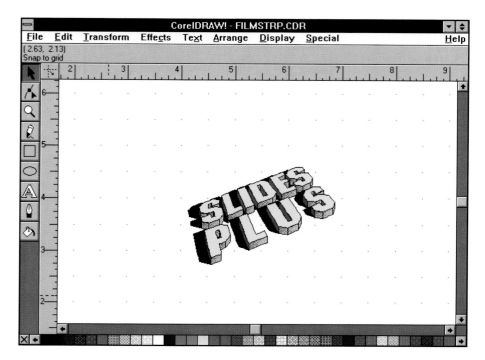

Figure 12.10:
Creating a realistic shadow.

11. Add additional text. Use the Swiss Bold Italic font (see fig. 12.11).

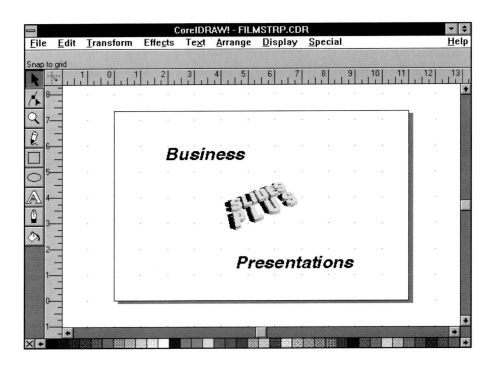

Figure 12.11:
Adding additional text.

12. Fill text with yellow. Click on the Business text object to select it. Then, click on it again to get into skew mode. Select the upper center skew control point, and skew the text 45 degrees left as you press the right mouse button. Fill the new text with black, and send it to the back. Repeat this procedure with the Presentations text object (see fig. 12.12).

Pressing and holding the right mouse button while skewing the text creates a duplicate (which is slanted 45 degrees) and leaves the original in its current position.

13. **G**roup the Business text object with its shadow, and group the Presentations text object with its shadow. Then, rotate each group of text so that it aligns with the SLIDES PLUS text block (see fig. 12.13).

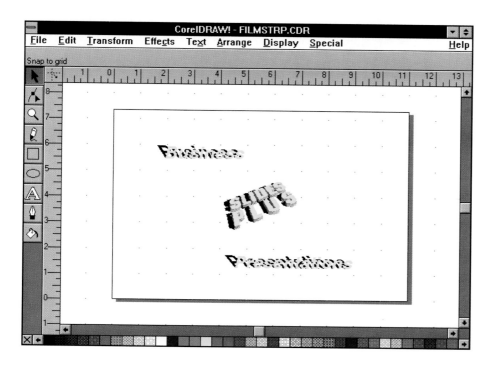

Figure 12.12:
Sending text objects to the back.

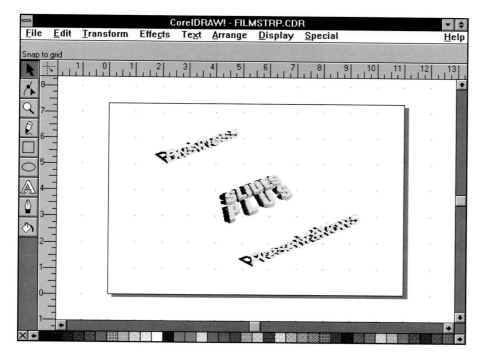

Figure 12.13:
Aligning the text.

14. Move each text block to positions above and below the SLIDES PLUS text block (see fig. 12.14). Adjust the size of the text if it is too large.

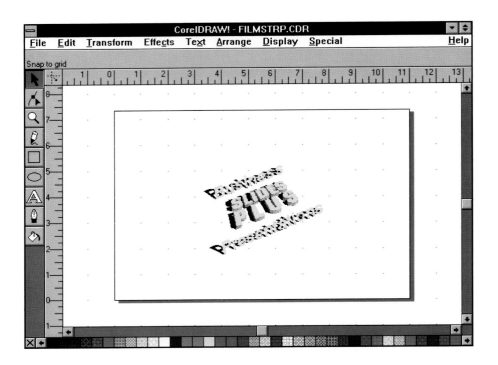

Figure 12.14:

Moving text above and below Slide Plus text block.

15. Draw a rectangle (2 × 3 proportion) around all the objects, and send it to the back (see fig. 12.15).

16. Fill the rectangle with a linear fountain fill, ranging from light on the bottom right to dark at the upper left, as shown in figure 12.16.

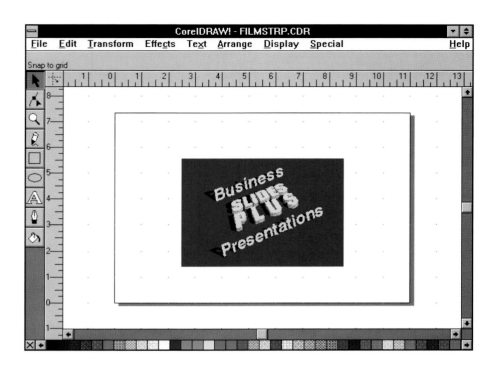

Figure 12.15:
Drawing a rectangle.

Figure 12.16:
Filling the rectangle with linear fountain fill.

17. **G**roup all the objects. Reduce the objects in size and **D**uplicate five times in a line from left to right (see fig. 12.17).

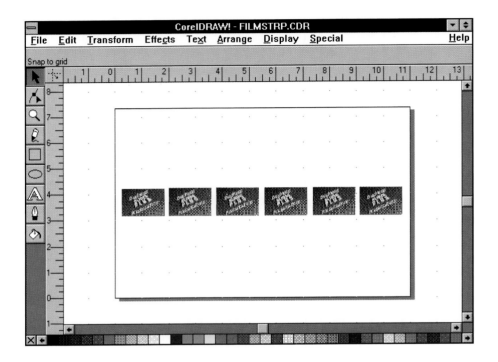

Figure 12.17:
Duplicating objects.

18. **G**roup all the objects. Draw a rectangle around all the objects, and fill the rectangle with black. Then send the rectangle to the back to form the film border (see fig. 12.18).

19. Draw a vertical rectangle (in the upper left corner) to form a sprocket hole, and fill it with white. Use the Node Edit tool to round the corners slightly (see fig. 12.19).

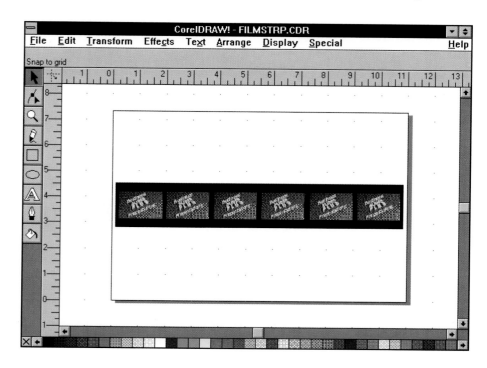

Figure 12.18:
Creating film border.

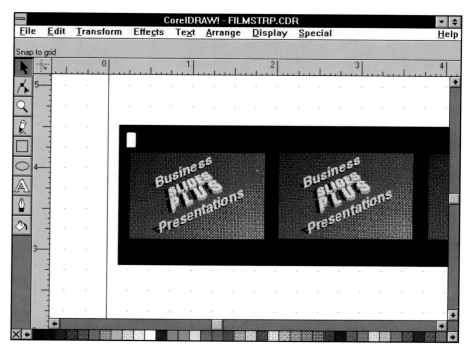

Figure 12.19:
Drawing a sprocket hole.

20. Copy the white rectangle, and position it as shown in figure 12.20.

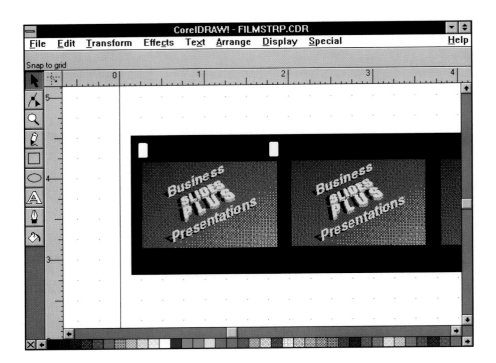

Figure 12.20:

Copying the white rectangle.

21. Select the two white rectangles, and use the Blend feature to create six additional rectangles between them. Then **S**eparate and **U**ngroup them (see fig. 12.21).

22. Select the eight white rectangles, **D**uplicate them, and place them over each frame. Then, duplicate the eight white rectangles, and place them below each frame (see fig. 12.22).

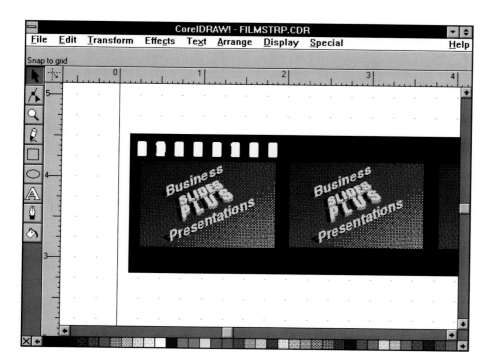

Figure 12.21:
Creating six additional rectangles.

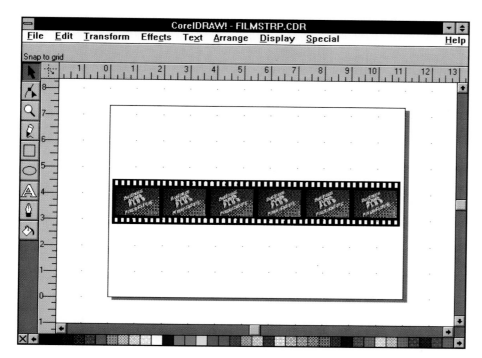

Figure 12.22:
Duplicating rectangles.

23. Select the white rectangles and the black rectangle. **C**ombine them so that the sprocket holes are windows. **D**uplicate them, and send them to the back. Then fill the rectangles with gray, and offset them down and to the right (see fig. 12.23).

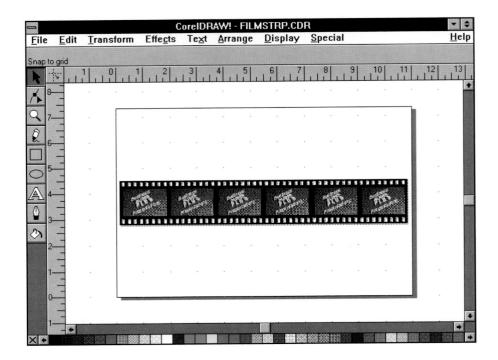

Figure 12.23:
Editing the perspective.

24. Select all the objects, and group them. Edit perspective on the left side by holding control and shift keys (see fig. 12.24).

25. Select E**d**it Envelope from the Effe**c**ts menu. Then choose Unconstrained. Select the top center control node, and move it up approximately 1" and to the right approximately 3 1/2" (see fig. 12.25).

    Repeat this step with the lower center node. (These adjustments are not an exact science; you may need to make a number of adjustments to achieve just the right curve.)

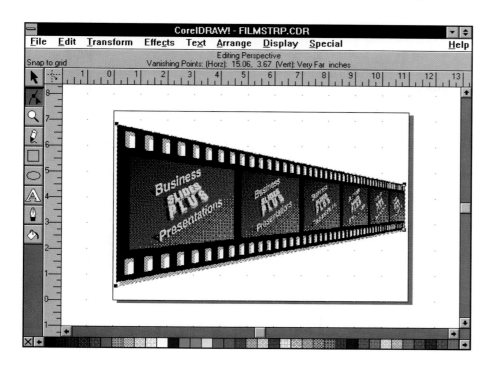

Figure 12.24:
Editing perspective.

Figure 12.25:
Adjusting envelope node.

26. Select the left corner envelope nodes, and pull handles away from the object group (see fig. 12.26).

Figure 12.26:

Selecting the left corner envelope nodes.

27. Select the right corner envelope nodes, and pull handles away from object group (see fig. 12.27).

Figure 12.28 shows the completed artwork.

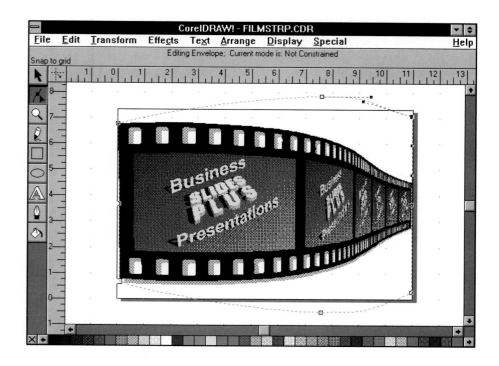

Figure 12.27:
Selecting the right corner envelope nodes.

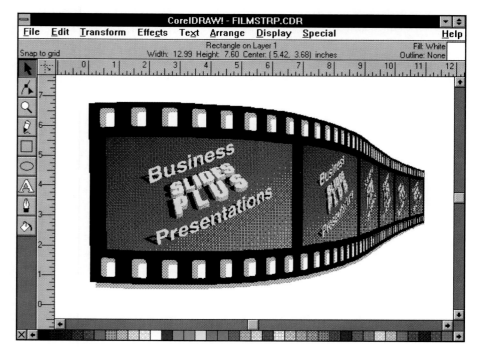

Figure 12.28:
The completed artwork.

FOUNDATIONS
FOR THE
F·U·T·U·R·E

Systems Logo

by Chris Purcell

Compaq Computer Corporation

Houston, Texas

Equipment Used

Compaq Deskpro 486/25 personal computer
28M of RAM

Output Equipment Used

High-resolution linotronic
Seiko Colorpoint color printer

Chris Purcell is a graphic designer working at Compaq Computer Corporation in Houston, Texas. He has been using CorelDRAW for three and a half years.

This logo was developed for a Systems Engineering Conference, which occurs twice a year in Houston. The logo design had to be versatile enough to be printed on many different mediums and produce a new look for the conference.

Procedure

1. Use the Pencil tool to draw a stylized hand. Draw a circle, and add it to the palm of the hand (see fig. 12.29).

2. Marquee-select the elements, and **G**roup them together.

3. Select **R**otate & Skew from the **T**ransform menu, and rotate and skew the group 180 degrees (remember to highlight the Leave Original button). Drag the duplicated group to the right until the two thumbs interlock (see fig. 12.30).

   You may need to adjust the two hands so that they fit as shown in the figure. To do this, **U**ngroup both groups, and use the Node Edit tool to adjust shapes. Remember to regroup the shapes when you are finished.

4. Select both hands, and rotate them 90 degrees, making sure to leave the original. This gives you a second hand group on top of the original.

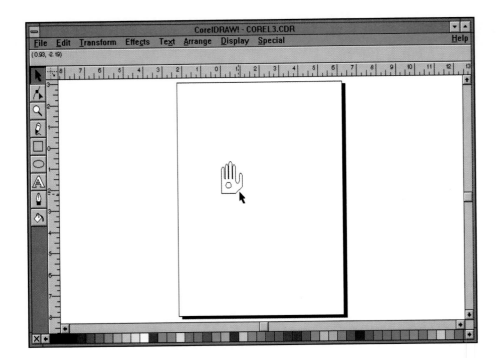

Figure 12.29:
Adding a circle to the palm of the hand.

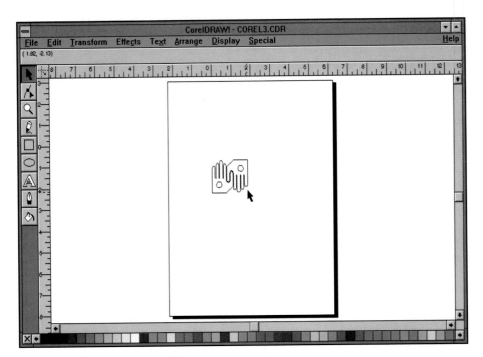

Figure 12.30:
Positioning the duplicated hand.

5. Select Preferences from the **S**pecial menu, set the Nudge measurement to 2", and nudge the duplicated group to the right. Set a baseline guide, select Snap To **G**uidelines from the **D**isplay menu, and align the group to the baseline guide (see fig. 12.31).

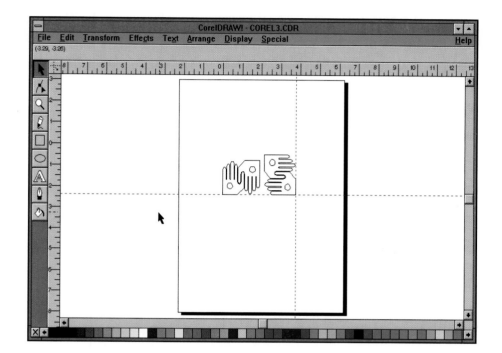

Figure 12.31:

Create the second group of hands, and use the baseline guide to position it.

6. Repeat steps 4 and 5 twice, nudging the shape vertically and then horizontally to make up the block of four shapes (see fig. 12.32). You might want to set additional vertical and horizontal guidelines.

7. Marquee-select all four hand groups, and rotate 45 degrees.

8. **U**ngroup everything. Select the circles, **G**roup them, and temporarily move them out of the way.

9. Marquee-select all the hands, and **C**ombine them (see fig. 12.33). Choose E**x**trude Roll-Up from the **E**ffects menu and set the horizontal measurement to 1.88" and the vertical measurement to –1.06". Deselect Perspective and To Front in the Extrude roll-up window.

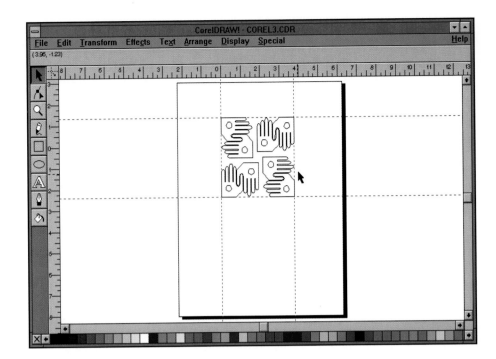

Figure 12.32:
Create the third and fourth group of hands, and position them.

You can adjust the unit while the Extrude roll-up window is still open to achieve the exact position if necessary.

10. To apply color to the extrusion, **S**eparate shapes. Select the newly created extruded shapes, and nudge them to the left. Select line elements of the extrusion, and make the outline 4-point purple. Fill the extrusion with a fountain fill of yellow to red at 90 degrees.

11. To add color to the hands, first break them apart. Then **G**roup them to give each hand a fountain fill of purple to blue at 90 degrees. Make the outline 4-point purple.

When objects are combined, they take on the attributes of one item. When objects are grouped, each item retains its own attributes.

12. Nudge the extrusion back to the hand group by using the Nudge feature.

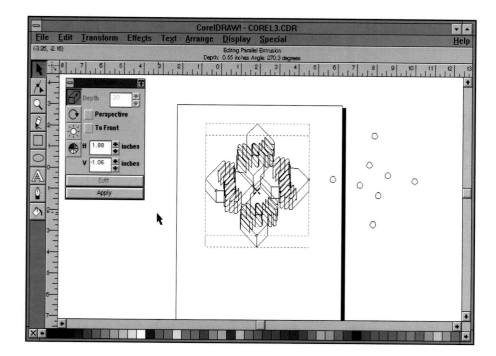

Figure 12.33:

Use the Extrude roll-up window to extrude the hands.

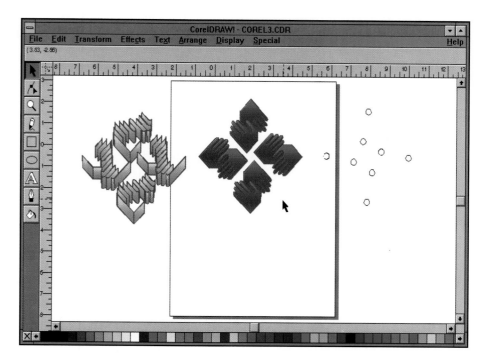

Figure 12.34:

Adding fountain fills to different elements.

13. Select the circle group, and use the Uniform Fill feature to fill it with red. Make the outline 4-point purple, then nudge the circles back to the hand group.

14. Marquee-select all the elements, and rotate them 45 degrees.

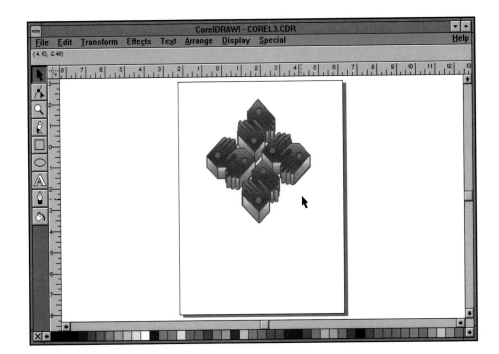

Figure 12.35:
Rotate everything 45 degrees.

15. Draw a square around all the elements, and send it to the back (Shift-PgDn). Fill the square and outline with purple. Select the square, and press the Shift key and click on the left mouse button while dragging a corner handle to decrease the size proportionately. Click on the right mouse button at the same time and leave the original square. Uniform fill and outline the smaller duplicate with black (see fig. 12.36).

16. Select the larger purple square, and rotate it 45 degrees—leaving the original. Slightly increase the size proportionally, holding down the Shift key and dragging a corner. Then send it to the back (Shift-PgDn), as shown in figure 12.37.

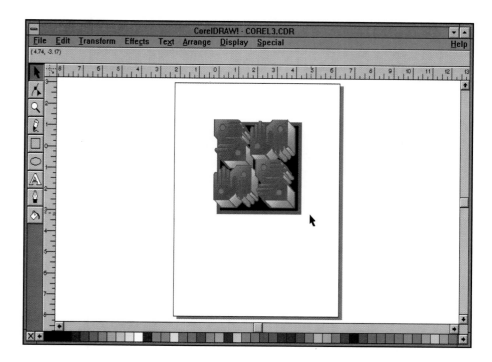

Figure 12.36:
Draw and duplicate squares around the hands.

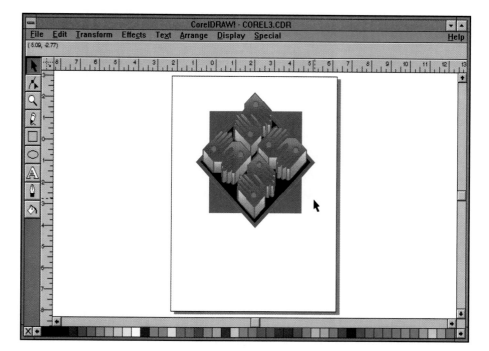

Figure 12.37:
Rotate and duplicate a square, and send it to the back.

17. Use the Pencil tool to draw a circuit board pattern in the bottom right corner of the square (see fig. 12.38). **C**ombine the circuit board shapes, and fill them with light blue and add a 3-point white outline.

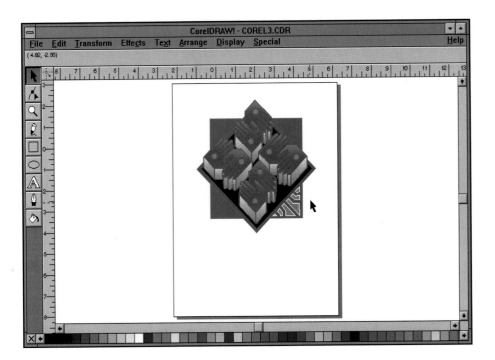

Figure 12.38:

Use the Pencil tool to draw the circuit board pattern.

18. Highlight the circuit board shape, and use the **S**tretch & Mirror command to duplicate the shape horizontally (check the Leave Original box). Select the duplicated shape, press the Ctrl key, and drag the shape horizontally to the left. Position the shape in the left side of the square, as shown in figure 12.39.

19. Select the two circuit board shapes, and use the **S**tretch & Mirror to vertically mirror the shape (check the Leave Original box). Select the new duplicated shapes, press the Ctrl key, and drag the shapes vertically. Position them in the top right and left sides of the square (see fig. 12.40).

20. To create a 3D look for the logo, select the purple diamond shape (rotated square) and the purple square, **D**uplicate them, and send them to the back (Shift-PgDn).

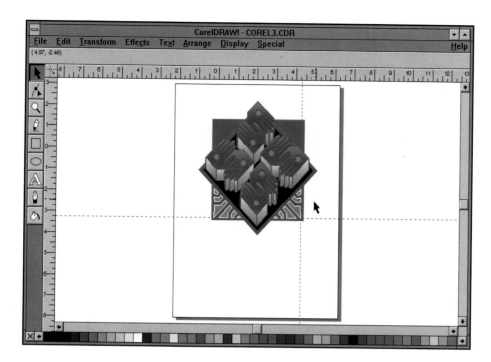

Figure 12.39:
Duplicate and position the circuit board shape.

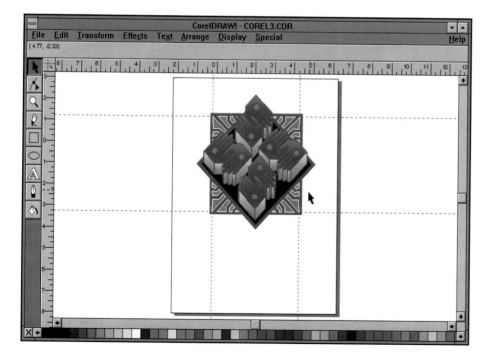

Figure 12.40:
Duplicate and position the third and fourth circuit board shapes.

21. Fill the two duplicated shapes and outlines with a 30-percent black fill. Increase the outline on these two shapes to 16 points to make the newly created drop shadow appear larger (see fig. 12.41).

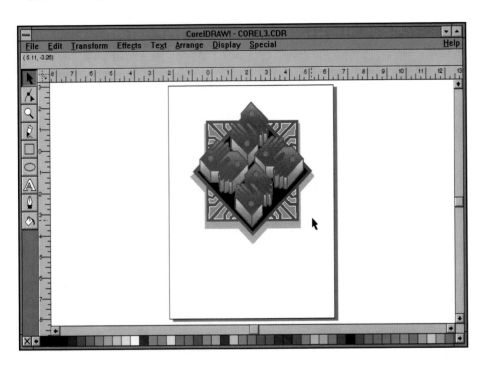

Figure 12.41:

Creating a drop shadow

22. Using the Text tool, type the word **FOUNDATIONS** (all caps). Select the text with the Pick tool, and change the type style to ITC Cheltenham Book by using the Edit Te**x**t feature from the **E**dit menu. Fill the text with black. Position left and right vertical guidelines on either side of the drop shadow square. Move the type flush left with the vertical guideline, then drag the bottom handle so that it aligns flush with the right guideline. Draw a 2-point purple rule under the type from the left to right guideline.

23. Using the Node Edit tool, add three nodes to the rule. Make sure that the middle node is positioned in the middle of the rule and other two nodes are equally spaced on either side of the rule.

24. Select the middle node. Press the Ctrl key, and drag the node down vertically to create a V shape (see fig. 12.43).

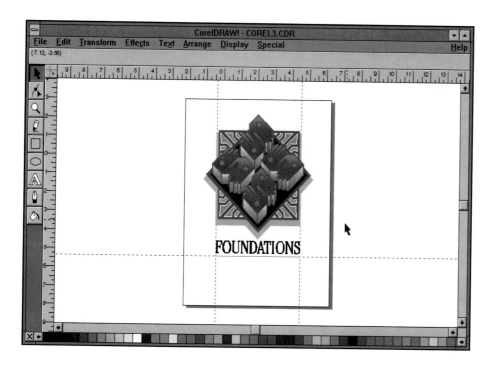

Figure 12.42:
Add text and a rule.

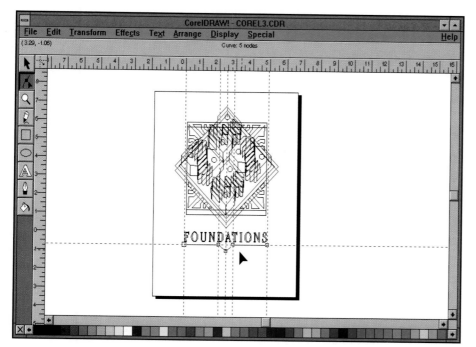

Figure 12.43:
Use the Node Edit tool to create a V shape in the rule.

25. Select and **D**uplicate the type and rule. Then nudge them down .81".

26. Repeat step 25 to achieve the second and third line of text with rules.

27. Using the Pick tool, select the second line of text and edit it. Type **FOR THE** in all caps. Repeat this procedure for the third line of text and type **FUTURE**.

28. Using the Node Edit tool, justify the two bottom lines of type by dragging the bottom right edge of the text to the vertical right guideline.

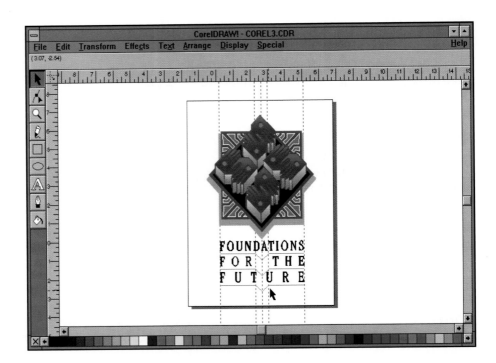

Figure 12.44:
Justify text with the Node Edit tool.

29. To create the diamond shapes between the bottom letters of text, draw a small square, fill it with purple, and rotate it 45 degrees. Place a horizontal guideline in the middle of the text, and place the diamond between the F and U in the word FUTURE.

30. Press the Ctrl key, drag to the left, and click the right mouse button to duplicate the shape between each letter of the word FUTURE (see fig. 12.45).

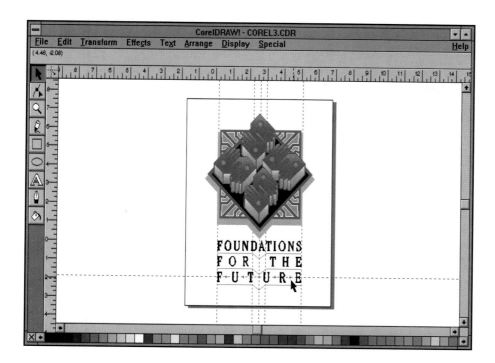

Figure 12.45:
Add diamond shapes to the last line of text.

Figure 12.46 illustrates the completed logo design.

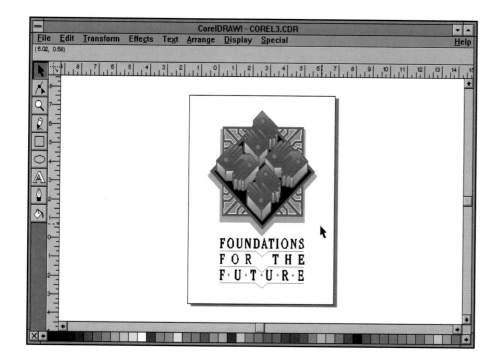

Figure 12.46:
The completed design.

Mixed Media Effects

"The people no longer seek consolation in art. But the refined people, the rich, the idlers seek the new, the extraordinary, the extravagant, the scandalous."

—Pablo Picasso

Ville-Marie (Montréal)
1642-1992

Canada 42

Stamp

by David Gronbeck-Jones

Victoria, British Columbia, Canada

Equipment Used

ASI 386DX/25
4M of RAM
Panasonic CD-ROM drive
Logitech Scanman hand scanner

Output Equipment Used

Hewlett-Packard Deskjet 500C
for color

Hewlett-Packard LaserJet IIP with
Pacific Page Personal Edition
PostScript emulation cartridge for
black and white

David Gronbeck-Jones has used CorelDRAW as a desktop-publishing tool in his main work as a planner and consultant for four years. He also operates Groundhog Graphics as a sideline venture, where CorelDRAW gets a real workout.

David developed this prize-winning piece of art specifically for the CorelDRAW World Design Contest (1992). He would like to make it clear that this is not the design of a real Canadian postage stamp and never was intended to be one. Coincidentally, the Canadian Post Office later issued a stamp for the depicted anniversary event based on the same historic painting.

Procedure

1. Create the stamp mask with a hand scanner as a "line" or black-and-white bitmap, capturing the image of a white, upside-down stamp against a black background. Crop the resulting TIFF file (in the scanner's software) to roughly 1/4" larger than the stamp on all four sides.

   This effect requires a black-and-white bitmap. You cannot apply color options to color or grayscale bitmaps.

2. Import the TIFF image into CorelDRAW as a bitmap, without tracing it. Use the Shape tool to crop the bitmap's outside dimensions to a perfect rectangle. To protect your work thus far, save the file with an interim or temporary name. You may want to use it for another design later (see fig. 13.1).

You should import the TIFF image as a bitmap because the perforations are too complicated to trace accurately and will create an object with a large number of nodes, making it difficult to print to a PostScript printer. Besides, the design to come is the important element of the "stamp."

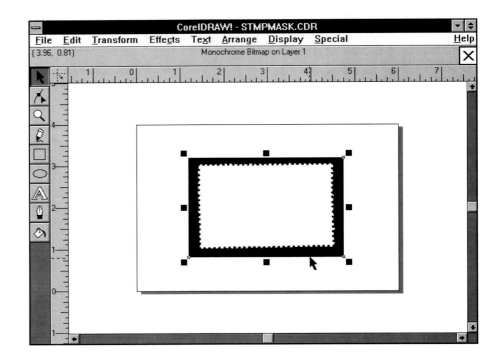

Figure 13.1:
The cropped bitmap.

3. Select the bitmap, then use the Outline tool to change the stamp's mask color to 30-percent gray. A bitmap is colored using the Outline tool. Use the Fill tool for the part you want to leave blank (uncolored). Resave the file (see fig. 13.2).

4. Change the page size to a proportional "fit" for the stamp mask. (I used 6" × 4" landscape.) This keeps the image at a workable size on-screen so that you do not have to magnify it when the file is opened or run in a slide show.

Center the bitmap image on the new page. Then resave the file (see fig. 13.3).

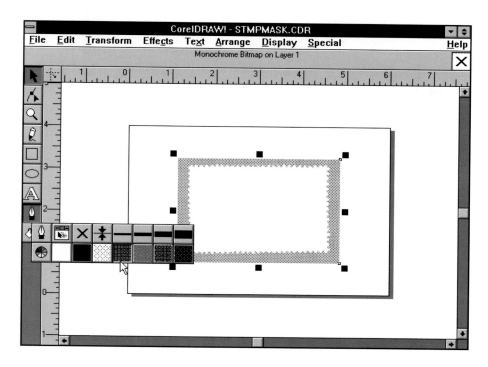

Figure 13.2:
Changing the stamp mask color.

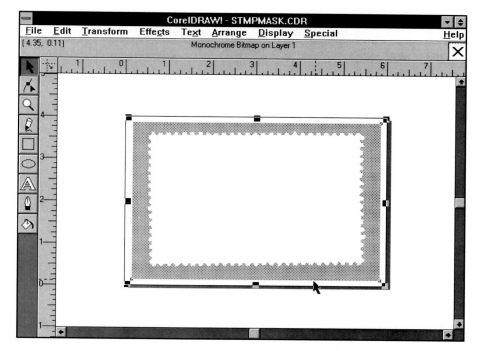

Figure 13.3:
Centering the bitmap image.

5. Then I made a black-and-white line scan of a small halftone-printed version of an old (1740s) public-domain

watercolor drawing of Ville-Marie (now Montreal, Quebec). Import the scan into the working file as a bitmap (not traced) and then crop it to include the desired part of the image in the same proportions as the stamp mask on-screen (see fig. 13.4). Save the file with a new name; you may want to keep the mask for another design.

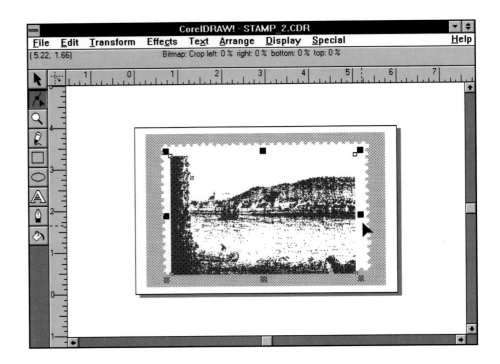

Figure 13.4:
Importing the scanned halftone.

6. Using the Rectangle tool, make a frame (unfilled) for the correctly sized bitmap design. **G**roup the frame object with the bitmap object, and use the Outline tool to select a dark green spot color. (I chose Pantone 350CU.) Then reselect the color as a process color, which will be an "unnamed color."

The Spot Color menu provides a vast range of predefined hues from which to easily select; the Process Color menu does not. Because most files that print in color use process color, this is a handy workaround (see fig. 13.5).

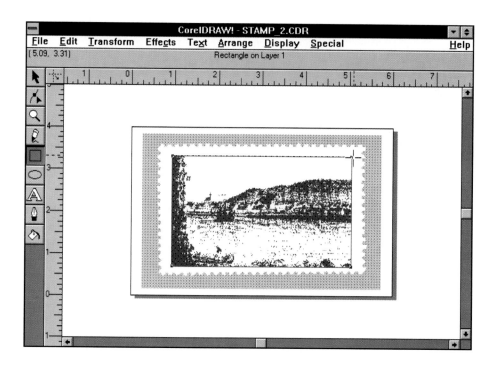

Figure 13.5:
Adding a frame to the design.

7. It is easier to add more color if you magnify the image. Use the Zoom flyout menu All Objects tool or Zoom In tool (see fig. 13.6).

Figure 13.6:
The Zoom flyout menu.

8. To make the image look like a watercolor painting, you must add the appropriate color to it. Because you cannot fill parts of a bitmap with color, you must create new objects. These objects are simple shapes without outlines (rectangles and ellipses) and with colored fills. The shapes need only approximate the part of the design you are coloring to achieve the desired effect.

Then arrange these objects behind the bitmap object. In a black-and-white bitmap with no fill, these objects will show through. In this design, color was added to the sky, the water, and a few of the buildings by using rectangles and one ellipse.

Figure 13.7 shows two buildings' "paint jobs," each of which is made up of two rectangles with typical watercolor brick-like colors (spot colors Pantone 162 CV and 1555 CV are good). These objects must be arranged behind the bitmap (To **B**ack). Resave the file when you are done.

9. If you cannot keep inside the building lines, convert the rectangles to curves, and edit the nodes as required. I did not have to do this (see fig. 13.7).

Figure 13.7:

*Colored objects drawn in front of the bitmap before arranging them **T**o Back.*

Figure 13.8, with the bitmap design cut away from the colored objects, illustrates this coloring process more clearly.

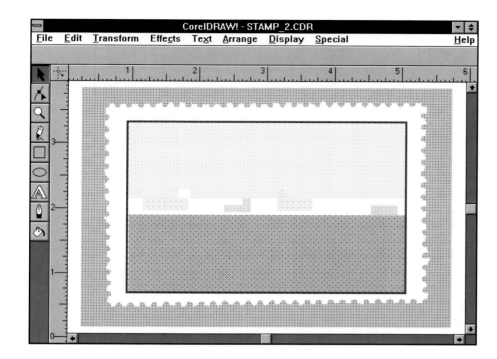

Figure 13.8:

Colored objects with bitmap design removed.

10. Finally, add the text. I used the shareware MIDDLETON.WFN font from CorelDRAW 2.x, and then converted all the text to curves. The upper text is filled with the green color used for the frame and bitmap outline. The lower text is filled with white. No outlines are used for the text objects.

If you create a file with text objects and you are not absolutely certain that a recipient (such as a service bureau) has the same font in its version of CorelDRAW, convert the text objects to curves when you are finished sizing and coloring them. Because most CorelDRAW 3.x users do not use WFN fonts, and because I do not have Middleton typeface in any other format, converting to curves is the only option I had for showing you this design.

Beware, however. Text converted to curves creates a larger file than plain text and can confuse PostScript printers and typesetters if their node limits are exceeded. Another option is to leave the text objects unconverted, and then export the file in EPS format. This, however, also creates a large file, but will avoid a problem with the printer.

Figure 13.9 shows the completed design.

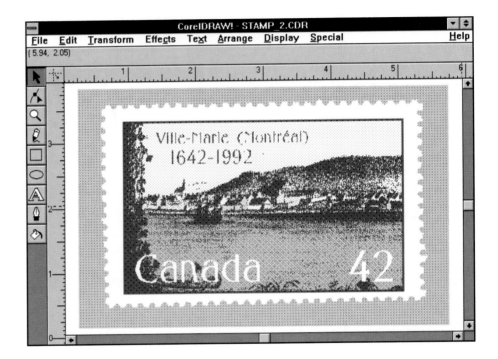

Figure 13.9:
The completed drawing.

HAPPY HOLIDAYS!

Happy Holidays

by William Schneider

Athens, Ohio

Equipment Used

386/33 Northgate
8M of RAM
ATI Ultra video card
NEC 4D 16" monitor
Microtek 300Z flatbed scanner

Output Equipment Used

HP LaserJet III
HP DeskJet Plus with refilled ink cartridge (burgundy ink)

William Schneider has a complete darkroom at his disposal, but he didn't need to use it to design this simple, yet elegant Christmas card. He saved both time and money by placing a cut evergreen branch directly on the glass of his Microtek scanner, and then scanning it. He saved more time and expense by printing the cards at home (in spot colors) with a colored-ink cartridge DeskJet and a LaserJet. The design, which was created by Schneider for personal use, was a first-place winner in the 3rd Annual CorelDRAW World Design Contest in the Holidays and Special Events Category for December 1991.

Procedure

1. Cut several small evergreen branches. Select the best looking one, and place it directly onto the Microtek scanner glass. Scan it as a grayscale image, and save the image to a file.

2. **O**pen the grayscale image in CorelPHOTO-PAINT. Use the **E**dit, Fi**l**ter, Bri**g**htness and Contrast settings to posterize the scan into black and white. Set contrast to 100 percent, and adjust the brightness setting to obtain the right balance of light and dark shading.

You can preview the image before clicking on OK (see fig. 13.10). When finished, the image appears in black and white, although it still is a grayscale image.

When you scan a continuous-tone original for eventual conversion to a 1-bit file (black and white only—no gray tones), scan the original as a grayscale image, then convert it to black and white in your image-editing program. Do not scan it as a black-and-white (line art) image. This extra step enables you to preview and adjust the light and dark balance before you save the file as a 1-bit image.

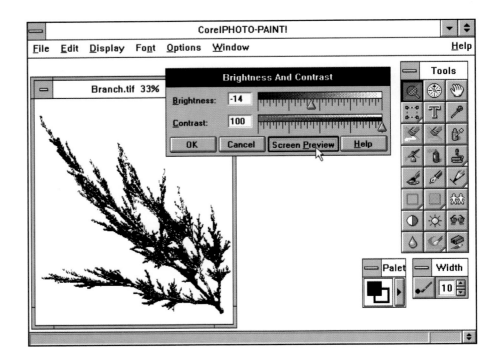

Figure 13.10:

When adjusting brightness and contrast, click on the Screen Preview button to monitor changes.

3. Convert the image using the **E**dit, Con**v**ert To, **B**lack and White command with the **L**ine Art setting, and save the file. The resulting 1-bit black-and-white image should be 1/8th the file size of the original grayscale image. This conversion process saves disk space and speeds printing.

4. Use the Box Selection tool, and select the portion of the 1-bit image that you want to turn into a negative image (see fig. 13.11).

5. Reverse the tones of the selected area with the **E**dit, T**r**ansform, **I**nvert command. Black becomes white, and white becomes black (see fig. 13.12).

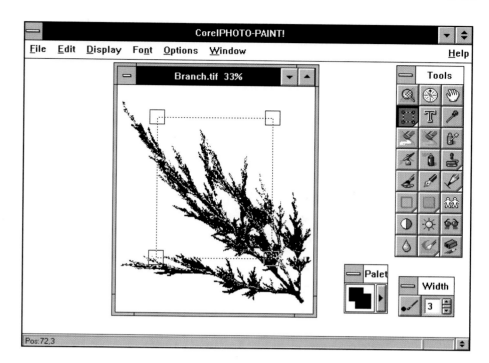

Figure 13.11:
Make changes to a selected area using the Box Selection tool.

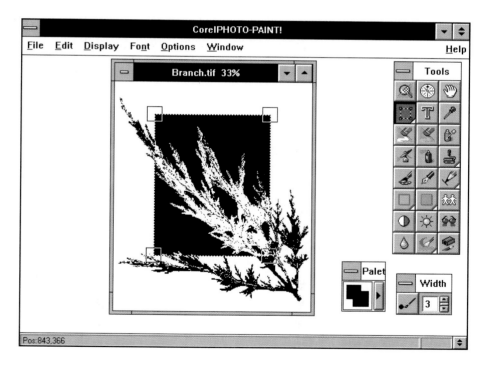

Figure 13.12:
Invert the tones in the selected area.

6. Save the file. The file should be a 1-bit image (black and white) so that the white areas become transparent in CorelDRAW. Grayscale or color images are not transparent when used in CorelDRAW. Those white areas allow an underlying, colored fill to show through the bitmap for the desired effect. Only 1-bit images permit underlying areas to show through, and they show through the nonblack part of the image.

To understand 1-bit bitmaps, think of a string of paper dolls cut out of black paper; anything that is placed underneath the paper dolls shows through the cut out areas. That's how a 1-bit bitmap works.

Now think of a photograph of real dolls placed on top of the same background; nothing shows through the dolls because the paper from the photo is still there. That's how grayscale or color bitmaps behave in CorelDRAW. Nothing shows through the rectangular bounding box of the picture.

7. Set up the page in CorelDRAW with guidelines for folding the card. To design a folded card, position a vertical guideline at 4.25" and a horizontal guideline at 5.5". These guidelines represent the halfway marks on the page where the page is folded. Add additional guidelines to allow for margins near the folds and for trimming the edge of the folded page.

8. Draw a rectangular border around the front panel of the card. Position it within the margin guidelines so that it does not fall onto a fold or a trim area. Use no fill, and a 4-point black outline (see fig. 13.13).

9. Import the black-and-white TIFF file. Position the bitmap on the front-panel portion of the page (see fig. 13.14). Resize and crop as necessary to fit. Be sure to give the bitmap a black outline with no fill.

10. Choose Layers Roll-Up from the Arrange menu, and make a new layer called Color. All objects printed in the second color are placed on this layer.

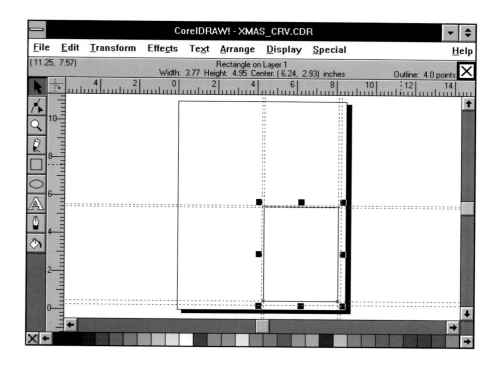

Figure 13.13:
Use guidelines for position-ing fold lines and placing graphic elements.

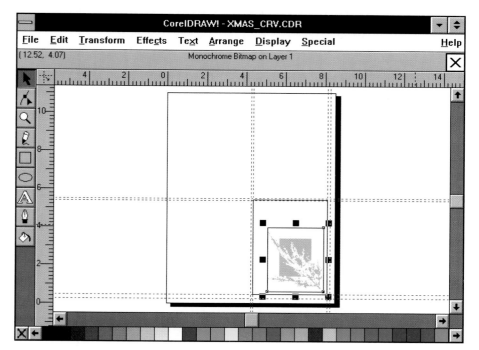

Figure 13.14:
Import the bitmap created earlier into CorelDRAW.

Some background information about the printing process is necessary at this point. The final artwork is printed in black and dark red on ivory-colored paper. The black color is printed with a LaserJet, and the dark-red color is printed with a DeskJet Plus equipped with a refilled ink cartridge. Although a DeskJet could be used for the black color also, the LaserJet has a speed advantage—and it has nonsmearing toner. If a laser printer is not available, a DeskJet alone can easily do the job, with some drying time allowed between the two applications of ink.

The dark-red ink was formulated by purchasing a red-ink refill kit for the DeskJet cartridge, and adding it to a nearly-spent cartridge. The refill kit includes an accordion-like reservoir of ink, which is equipped with a needle for injection into the breather hole of a DeskJet cartridge. The combination of red ink and the remaining small amount of black ink makes a deep burgundy color.

Colored ink refills for various ink jet printers can be obtained from the following company:

Lyben Computer Systems
5545 Bridgewood
P.O. Box 130
Sterling Heights, MI 48311
(313) 268-8100

11. Draw a rectangle on the Color layer, sized to match the reversed-out portion of the bitmap. Use guidelines to make fitting it easier. Position the rectangle on the Color layer beneath the bitmap by clicking and dragging the Color layer to a lower position in the **L**ayers Roll-Up (see fig. 13.15). Fill it with a spot color gradient from Pantone 187 (100-percent tint) at the top to Pantone 187 (0-percent tint) at the bottom. Although actual Pantone inks are not used, the Pantone 187 color closely approximates the appearance

of the DeskJet ink refill for visual purposes. The white areas of the 1-bit bitmap are transparent and allow the colored rectangle beneath it to show through.

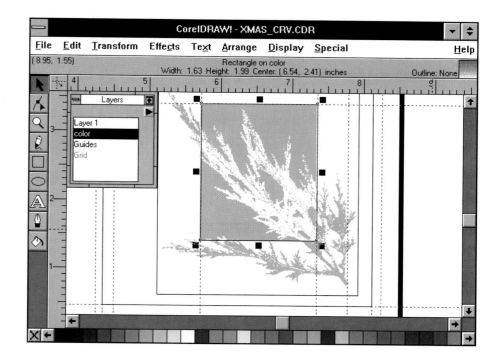

Figure 13.15:
*Use **L**ayers Roll-Up to position the rectangle on the Color layer beneath the bitmap.*

12. Duplicate the gradient-filled rectangle by pressing the + key (on the numeric keyboard) and dragging the duplicate below the original while pressing the Ctrl key (to constrain motion vertically). Fill the duplicate rectangle with a solid Pantone 187. Then position the duplicate so that it touches the page rectangle at the bottom and also coincides with the bottom of the reversed-out portion of the bitmap.

If a preview is done now, some small parts at the bottom of the bitmap are not dark enough. Draw several small rectangles and color them with Pantone 187 to make the small, lighter areas less obvious. **G**roup them with the larger, bottom rectangle for easier global color changes, if necessary (see fig. 13.16).

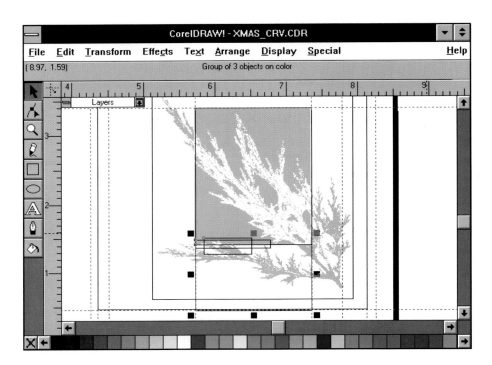

Figure 13.16:

Group objects of the same color together to make color changes easier.

13. Next, make a dotted-rule line, which is comprised of perfectly circular dots. Such a line is not a standard line in CorelDRAW, but one can be specified easily in the CORELDRW.DOT file.

Corel uses the CORELDRW.DOT file to store the settings for the various dashed or dotted lines that are shown in the Outline tool's Outline Pen dialog box.

Users might edit the CORELDRW.DOT file to modify existing dashed lines, or add additional dashed or dotted lines for use in the program. Using Notepad, open CORELDRW.DOT, and read the header at the top for instructions on how to modify the file. Create a dashed line of circular dots by specifying a zero dash length in the CORELDRW.DOT file, and calling for round end-caps in DRAW. In the following example, the code for the new dashed line (2 0 5) specifies a dashed line of two elements—the first one being a dot of zero width followed by a five unit wide space (see fig.13.17).

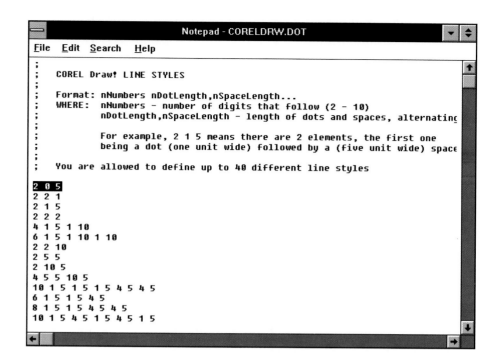

Figure 13.17:
Edit the CORELDRW.DOT file to add new dashed and dotted line styles.

In CorelDRAW, a line with zero length appears as a blank in the style field of the Outline Pen dialog box, but it still is selectable (see fig. 13.18). When round end-caps are selected in the Outline Tool's Outline Pen dialog box, the zero-length dashed line displays and prints as a perfect circle.

14. Add the remaining text and dotted lines (using the new dotted-line definition) to complete the illustration.

15. Time to print! I used ivory paper for the final output. The warm paper color enhanced the appearance of this piece. Make sure that everything to be printed black is on one layer and that everything to be printed dark red is on a separate color layer so that red objects don't print in black ink or vice versa.

To print the black alone, disable printing of the red layer by double-clicking on its layer name in **L**ayers Roll-Up and deselecting **P**rintable in Layer Options (see fig. 13.19). Print one copy to ensure that things are working. If everything is OK, print the remaining copies, plus a few extra copies for registration experiments that are detailed in the next steps.

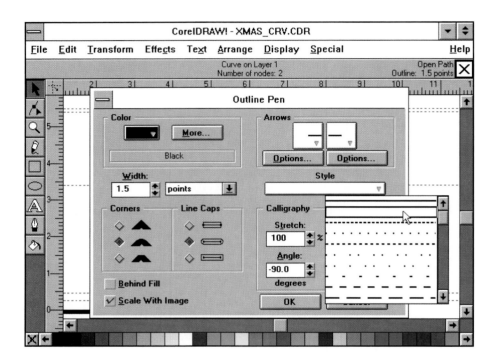

Figure 13.18:
The Outline Pen dialog box.

16. In the Layer Options dialog box, disable printing of the black layer, and enable printing of the color layer. This is an easy way to overprint the gradient on top of the bitmap and avoid some registration and trapping problems. Some designs won't work with overprinted colors, but in this case, the red prints over black with no adverse effect.

Another crucial step remains. If the printer is not a PostScript printer (and if you don't have a software PostScript emulator such as Freedom of Press), any attempt to print the red layer results in unwanted half-toning or dithering of the solid areas. This is because the printer is trying to simulate red by using a shade of gray.

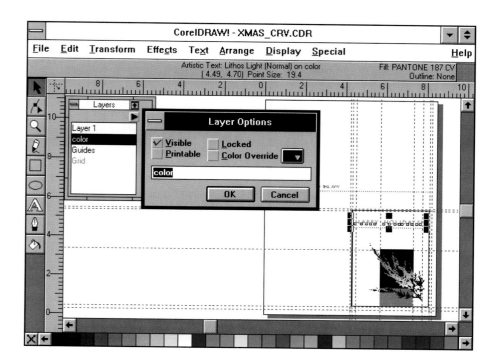

Figure 13.19:
Use the Layer Options dialog box to disable printing a layer.

To work around this problem, you must temporarily change the red objects to black, and the red-to-white gradient into a black-to-white gradient. Without the color separation capability of a PostScript printer, you cannot get solid color without an unwanted halftone pattern. PostScript allows printing of spot colors as solid areas when printing as color separations.

17. Place the previously printed pages in the paper tray of the DeskJet equipped with red ink, and print one sample to check registration.

18. In all probability, some misregistration exists. This is corrected easily by measuring the distance that the two colors are off with a scale and entering the measurements into the **M**ove dialog box found in the **T**ransform menu. If the red layer prints 1/16th (0.063)" too high, for instance, select all the red objects on the layer and enter a Move adjustment of 0.063" **V**ertical to compensate. Print another copy for a check, and if satisfactory, print a batch. Check periodically for creeping misregistration. You will be surprised at how well such a low-budget, two-color setup maintains accurate registration.

19. Fold the paper, and trim the edges with a paper cutter.

The finished image shown here is printed with process color on white paper, unlike the spot colors and ivory paper actually used. To simulate the appearance of the original card, the spot colors were changed to process colors, and an ivory background was added.

Because of its importance compared to the overall design, only the front of the card is reproduced here.

Figure 13.20 illustrates the completed design.

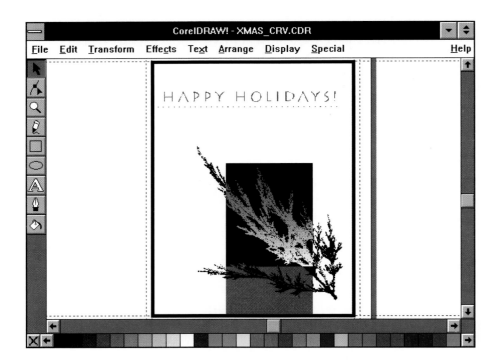

Figure 13.20:
The completed design.

Fantasy Effects

*"Most artists are surrealists…always dreaming something
and then they paint it."*

—*Dong Kingman*

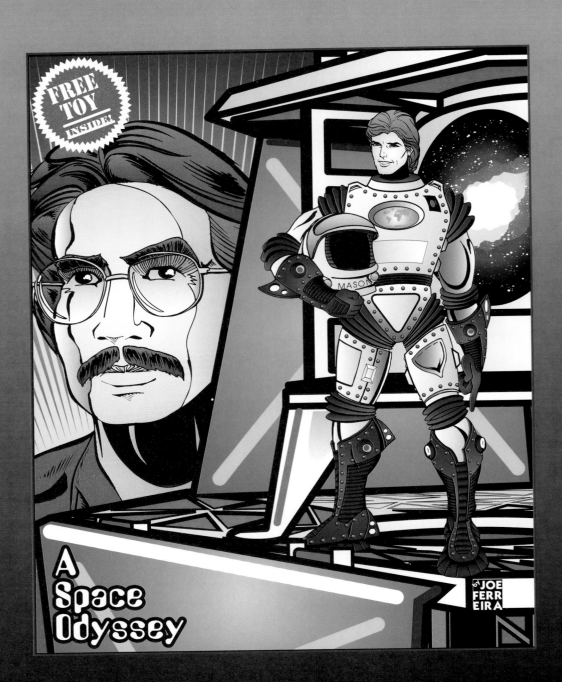

Major Matt Mason & Me

by Joe Ferreira

Pendragon Studios,
Redondo Beach, California

Equipment Used

386/33 Turbo Tower
8M of RAM
CD-ROM
The Complete Communicator, a bundled communications package

Output Equipment Used

IRIS Inkjet Printer

"That Joe Guy" is creative director of Pendragon Studios, a freelance toy design and packaging house in the Hollywood Riviera. He has been an enthusiastic CorelDRAW user for two years. Joe created this cover art to accompany an in-depth article that detailed his efforts to bring a favorite childhood toy back to life.

This is his most recently published piece.

This book provides step-by-step instructions on the construction of many different images, but don't overlook the big picture. That big picture is the art of visualizing an image before actually drawing it.

Jot down a thumbnail sketch to capture the essence of what you want to convey, for example. Then begin the process of bringing that sketch to life.

That process consists of the creation of each object separately, in its own CorelDRAW file. When you have completed each of the separate objects, those objects are imported (using the command **F**ile,**I**mport) one at a time and kept as unique groups and layers. Each group of objects then is sized and positioned to complete your interpretation of the original sketch.

Procedure

When you follow the techniques in this chapter, you will gradually build up a considerable clip art library of your own creations. You also will see just how much was accomplished (for this particular illustration) with existing files.

Because CorelDRAW works often consist of thousands of objects, this chapter describes the process that is used to generate them, instead of the literal creation of each object. In later chapters of this book, you learn more technical information, such as how many degrees to yank on a Bézier handlebar, or the optimum point size you should use for copyright symbols.

Each object that is used in a CorelDRAW work comes from either:

 Line art that is created by hand, and then scanned and autotraced with CorelTRACE.

 Vector art, which is actually created on-screen by using the Tool box.

 Clip art that is imported and then manipulated through the Tool box. Regardless of the origin as either CDR (CorelDRAW), EPS (PostScript), or PCX (scanned bitmap file), all clip art is imported, ungrouped, colored, and regrouped into a unique CorelDRAW file as a subset of the finished composition.

 Complex drawings such as the one in this lesson are much easier to create if you use groups and layers. Editing an object without the use of groups and layers would be difficult or impossible in a large drawing because of hundreds of objects.

1. For this image, a piece of clip art from an original logo design is used. This sunrise effect consists of a rectangle with a vertical fountain fill, which is overlapped by a

serrated burst that was created with the vector/connect-the-dots technique. This burst is given a faint outline (see fig. 14.1). The combined effect is similar to the airbrushed auras found on early fruit crate label art.

Your CorelDRAW package comes with a complete array of valuable images. You should frequently flip through the catalog to see what is available, as your eye probably will see only what you are in need of at any given moment. Remember that these images can be used "as is" or as a springboard for customization.

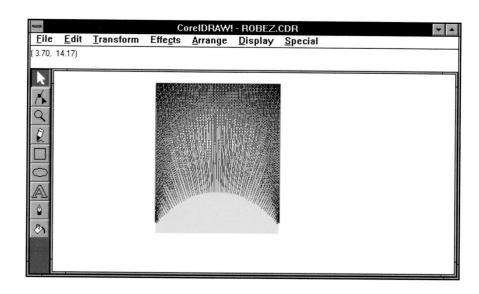

Figure 14.1:

Creating the air-brushed aura effect.

2. Another piece of clip art is dropped into position. This self-portrait was created using the "stained glass" technique discussed later (see fig. 14.2).

Creating Line Art

You can create line art in the traditional cartoonist or animator style by using the following steps:

1. Start with pencil sketches. You can execute black-and-white line art with a variety of pens and brushes, and then scan it with a scanner.

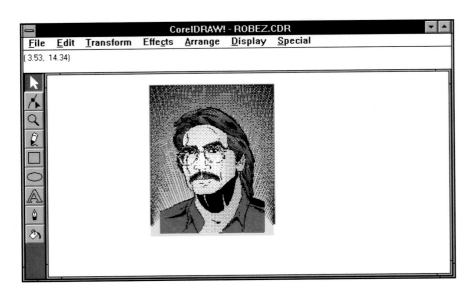

If you are utilizing a bitmap in the finished work, you can scan it at a full 600 dpi for maximum clarity. Because the actual cartoon panel is much smaller than the original art, you benefit from a 200 to 300 percent increase in resolution. Black-and-white art output from my Lasermaster 800 dpi printer is then camera-ready.

2. If you plan to autotrace the image, reduce the scanning resolution to 300 dpi. A custom setting is used in CorelTRACE to optimize the EPS file for CorelDRAW. Lines are converted to long curves. The object is made mostly of curves, and it follows the path tightly with fine sampling. This usually provides the best results for you to start coloring.

3. The EPS file now is imported into CorelDRAW and ungrouped. Each object or pocket within the perimeter of the outline now is individually colored, grouped, or combined, depending on what type of airbrush effect you want. Corel refers to this as a "Fountain Fill."

   If it is an object such as a man with his hand on his hip, this creates a window area between his arm and his body. These window areas require special treatment right up front so as to lend added realism when you import and layer other objects.

4. Choose the outline object and any number of windows in your object. Select N̲o Fill and N̲o Outline. Now **C**ombine them, assign a fill color, and send To **B**ack. Finish coloring the remainder of the group's objects.

You now have a real 3D object that enables you to see past (or through to) the next layer of illustration. Treat each object as a stained-glass artist would, separating each sliver or panel of color by the negative space of the outline object at the bottom of the stack. A final tuning or assigning of an outline to this bottom object finishes your piece.

5. On-screen vector art is created on the spot: rectangles of color to augment the color of the shirt and the window mask, keyline border to frame the image, and an I-beam/girder construct to lay the foundation for the space station.

Figure 14.3:
Vector art added to the clip art images.

For objects created on-screen, you can use a quick and dirty connect-the-dots process. Whether you are following a low-resolution scan template or "clicking from the hip," you can mark off the perimeter of the object with a polygon.

Then, where appropriate, curve sections of the polygon. Using the Node Edit tool, position the actual nodes or adjust the curves to give the final shape you desire. Colors are added, details are overlaid, and the objects are again grouped as a sub-set file.

Vector Art

1. Vector art is created on-the-fly. Perspective lines can be adjusted to the eye's satisfaction. Windows are combined with the platform's polygon to provide a view to the sub-ject's shirt and to create the illusion that the subject is standing behind this new structure.

Figure 14.4:

Perspective lines add depth.

2. If the illusion were complete, you would be building a six-sided polygon. I cheated with the help of a border mask. Going along with the illusion, cordon off the polygon into six imaginary sections with invisible, two-point lines. Then create (through dot-to-dot) a single, triangular depression. This shape is duplicated, and rotated and skewed until the first section of the platform is filled.

   All these items are grouped, and then the entire group is duplicated, scaled, and skewed to fit the other sections of the platform.

Figure 14.5:
The triangular pattern on the platform is copied and skewed.

3. A simple vector-art polygon with a radial fill provides the first solar panel framing the subject's face and the far edge of the space station's platform.

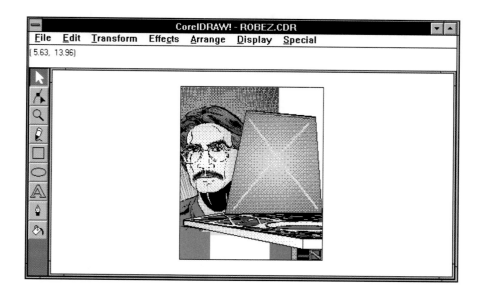

Figure 14.6:
The solar panel uses a radial fill.

4. Vector art utilizing both flat color, fountain fills, and windows provides another level of depth to the drawing.

The vector art added to the station (see fig. 14.7) provides a "fifth dimension" for the drawing. The order of these levels starting from the bottom of the stack is:

1. Aura burst

2. Self portrait

3. Solar panel

4. Girder platform

5. More solar panels, the toy, and text

The fifth level has just been started in step four.

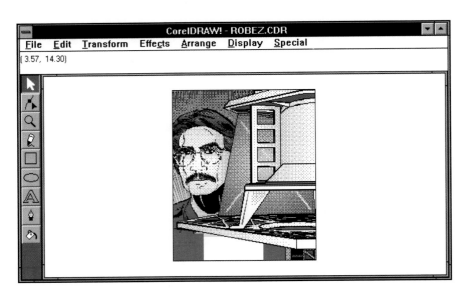

Figure 14.7:

More space station structure is added.

5. Clip art files, including my signature logo block and free toy burst, are dropped into position. An additional solar panel created through vector art is placed in the foreground of the drawing, and the copy line "A Space Odyssey" is set with the Text tool.

   Overlay a duplicate copy line with no outline on top of a line with a heavy outline to create the drop shadows. I get better results this way than by using an intermediate outline on a single copy line (see fig. 14.8).

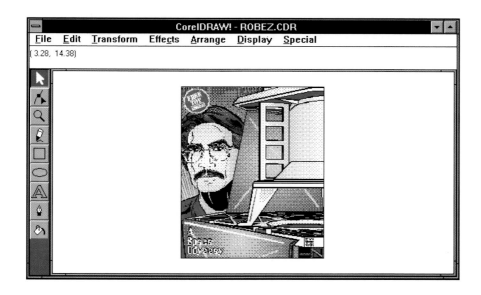

Figure 14.8:
Add text to the drawing.

6. This star field/map/chart is a piece of clip art taken from the Star Trek/Next Generation toy packaging that I developed last year. This is the burst that the toy figures are positioned against on their blister paks. By stretching the clip art horizontally a negative percentage (use the Edit tool's stretch and rotate bars) and placing it on the curved surface of the station's central cylinder, it appears to bend as well (see fig. 14.9).

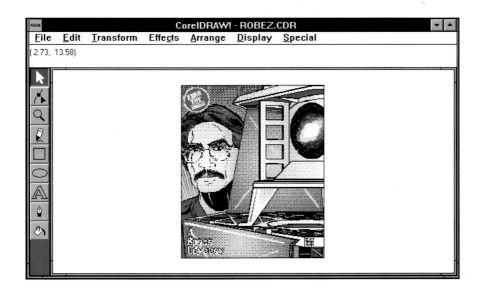

Figure 14.9:
The starfield stretched and rotated.

7. The final component (my friend, Major Matt Mason) is a clip art file for various situations. Whether it's a boy and his toy, or a man and his dream, this is Major Matt Mason and Me.

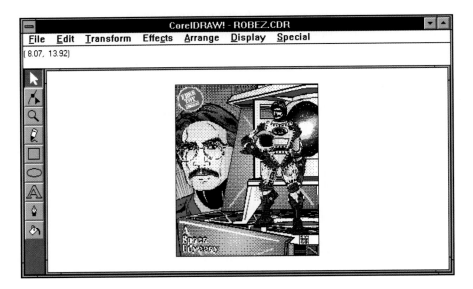

Fig. 14.10:
The completed design.

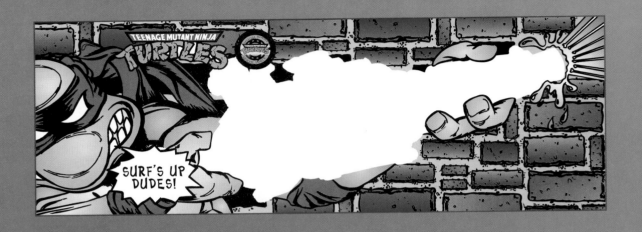

Sewer Shooter

by Joe Ferreira

Pendragon Studios
Redondo Beach, California

Equipment Used

IBM PS/2
1M of RAM

Output Equipment Used

FORCAST Inkjet Printer

"I love being a Turtle!" That's the battle cry of Joe Ferreira, creative director of Pendragon Studios, a freelance toy design and packaging house in the Hollywood Riviera. He designed and illustrated many of the Teenage Mutant Ninja Turtle (TMNT) packages. This was Joe's first published piece created in CorelDraw. It won the first place award in the CorelDRAW World Design Contest packaging category in November, 1991. It also won first place in Microtek's 1991 Design Contest and toured with the MacWorld Exhibit. "Cowabunga Dude!"

Procedure

Going from my very latest composition, Major Matt Mason & Me, to my very first, Sewer Shooter, is a good test of the techniques that I have previously outlined, including: the stained-glass effect, vector art, and clip art.

My previous Turtle packages were created with pen, ink, and markers. I used CorelDRAW for logo design and color separations, but this example was my first attempt at a completely self-contained electronic document. The following steps tell how I did it.

1. A solid gray rectangle provides both a full-bleed area for the composition and the negative space/mortar for a brick wall.

2. An opaque border mask is applied by creating two rectangles (one within the other), combining them, and assigning the color white. No keyline is added, as the printer still needs the freedom to crop at your discretion from the full-bleed image.

A single brick is hand-inked, traced, fountain filled, and then run through the gauntlet of tools: it is then stretched, compressed, rotated, and flipped (both horizontally and vertically) until a complete, yet varied, brick wall becomes a backdrop for the rest of the work (see fig. 14.11).

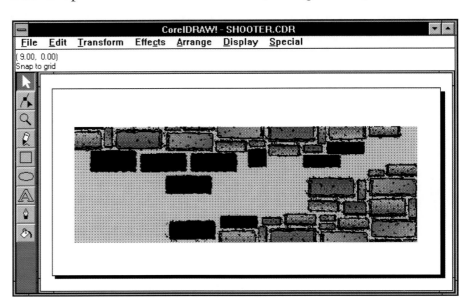

Figure 14.11:
Creating the brick wall.

3. The famous ninja headband, which was created separately (saved as an entire grouped entity), is imported whole (see fig. 14.12).

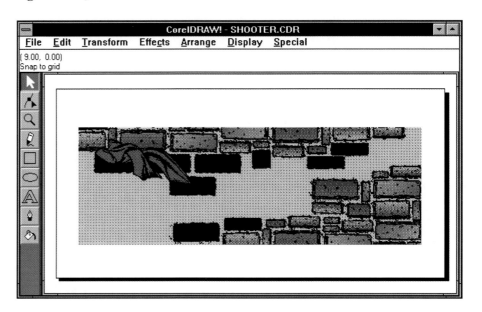

Figure 14.12:
The headband is imported.

4. The head and torso also are imported as a whole (see fig. 14.13).

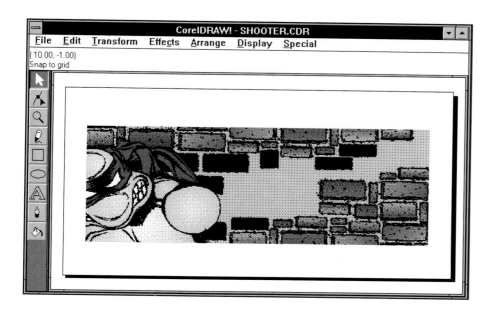

Figure 14.13:
Other separate entities added to the drawing.

5. Do the same for the floating elbow. Remember, you are creating a 3D space (see fig. 14.14).

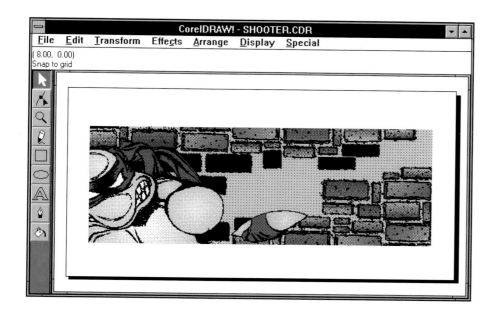

Figure 14.14:
Add the elbow next.

6. The final printed package displays a twist on the Roger Rabbit idea. Instead of populating a real world with cartoon characters and cartoon props, I created a cartoon world stocked with real-world toys. A prototype of the actual squirt gun is attached to a rod, then photographed at various angles in the studio. An image is selected from the proof sheet, and enlarged to fit the layout of the package.

The turtle is then sketched to fit the actual photograph. Next, the outline is traced, making a mask, or electronic frisket of the squirt gun. That mask is autotraced, imported, and scaled to the proper dimension. It now fits perfectly with the turtle and the brick backdrop. The printer now has an exact shape to use when the color photo of the toy is stripped into the image, eliminating the added hassle of overlays and mechanical masks (see fig. 14.15).

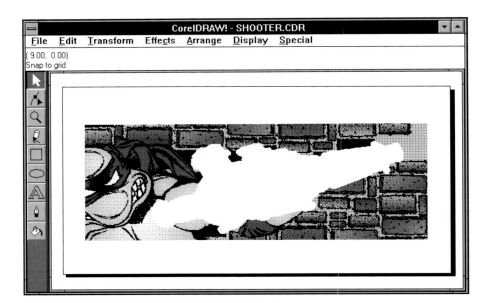

Figure 14.15:

The autotraced representation of the product.

7. The turtle's forearm is imported and scaled to match the gun's mask. You can start to see the dimensional quality of the pose (see fig. 14.16).

8. The squirting water is imported and positioned to illustrate the play pattern (see fig. 14.17). This technique also is used and stripped into all inset photos on the box, to show a live model playing with the toy.

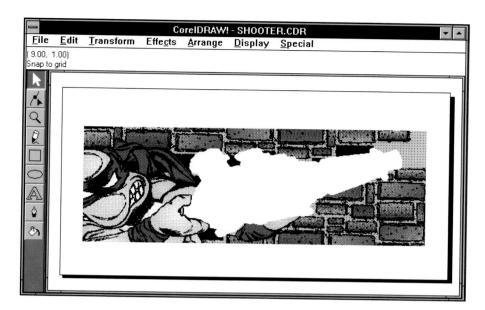

Figure 14.16:
Adding the forearm reveals the turtle's pose.

Figure 14.17:
Adding the squirt effect.

9. Stained glass thumb and fingers (don't ask which one is which...IT'S A TURTLE!!) are overlapped along the barrel of the squirt toy to finish the 3D effect (see fig. 14.18).

10. Clip art I drew of the famous Turtle logos is imported, along with the required trademark symbols. A talk bubble also is imported.

Figure 14.18:

The fingers added to the image round out the 3D effect.

I supplied several aftermarket fonts to Corel to protect the integrity of my contest submissions. As a pleasant surprise, all these comic style fonts were incorporated into the next release of CorelDraw under similar names. Now you can share them as well.

Although CorelDraw comes with hundreds of fonts, I use only these comic style fonts for all my work. Why? All my work revolves around the style of sequential art you're most familiar with as "comix." Plus, I think they're fun!

Figure 14.19 illustrates the completed design.

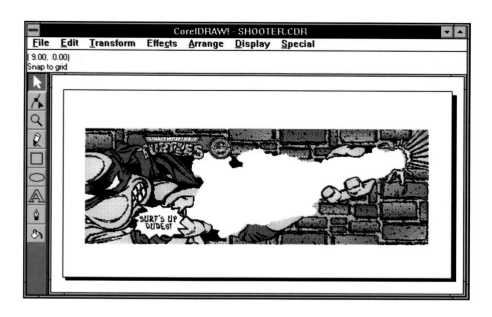

Figure 14.19:
The completed design.

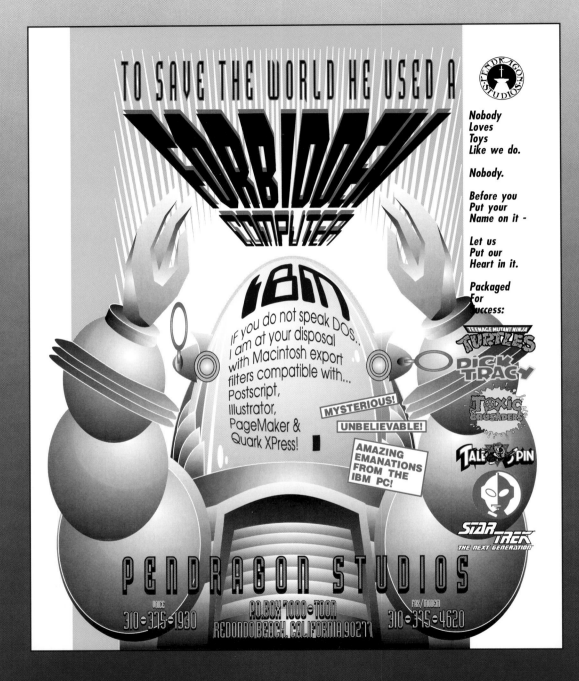

Forbidden Computer

by Joe Ferreira

Pendragon Studios,
Redondo Beach, California

Equipment Used

386/33 Turbo Tower
8M of RAM
The Complete Communicator,
a bundled communications package

Output Equipment Used

IRIS Inkjet Printer

Joe Ferreira, Creative Director of Pendragon Studios, a freelance toy design and packaging house in the Hollywood Riviera, designed this promo piece to combat the notion that only Macs are capable of producing effective art. As a collector of sensational B-movie posters from the '50's and '60's, Joe pays tribute with this homage to marketing genius.

"The summer that Disney's adaptation of Dave Stevens' 'Rocketeer' came out I was looking to do something in CorelDRAW that would be a complete departure from my usual heavily inked, graphic, cartoon style of work.

The finished piece would be used in a professional directory, which meant I also had to find a way to stand out from all the other Macintosh designers. At the same time I felt I needed to challenge the stigma that DOS systems have in the design field. The goal was a daunting task.

Dave Stevens' art deco, rocket retro movie poster really impressed me. Not only was its subject matter interesting, but also its subtle execution in airbrushed patterns without the support of heavy line art. My goal was to achieve the same effect using the CorelDRAW Tool box. I took inspiration from one of my favorite movies, 'Forbidden Planet'; it's mechanical marvel, Robby the Robot; and my archive of ridiculous and bitchin' movie posters. The result: 'To save the world he used a Forbidden Computer.'"

Procedure

With the exception of clip art logos imported at a later stage, the entire composition consists of simple vector art created on-the-fly, then fountain filled and overlapped. Again, with the exception of drop shadows on portions of the copy, no black line art exists anywhere in the illustration.

1. Clicking from the hip, start with a connect-the-dots approach to a simple triangle. Convert it to a curve by entering the Node Edit tool and stretching the triangle's upper point to create a very skinny shape. Then convert the left sloping edge to a curved segment, adjusting the Bézier control bars to achieve a tall, thin, fin.

What's a Bézier curve? It's wonderful! It's designing on a molecular level. With the Node Edit tool, your cursor gives you control over every node or point defining the edge of the object you're drawing. Each node has a pair of "handle bars" that you can pull, stretch, or spin to control the arc of each particular curve.

2. A metallic fountain fill is assigned. For a metallic blend, I chose a radial fountain fill from various shades of gray to white. This provides the dull gun-metal look. Then the finished fin is duplicated several times and overlapped in a gentle arc resulting in a set of mechanical lapels for my friend's metal suit (see fig. 14.20).

3. This group is mirrored horizontally and repositioned farther to the right, as shown in figure 14.21.

4. Use the technique you used in step 1 to create a rectangle. It's upper, horizontal edge is converted to a curved segment, duplicated, and overlapped vertically to create the metallic chest plates of Robby's torso (see fig. 14.22).

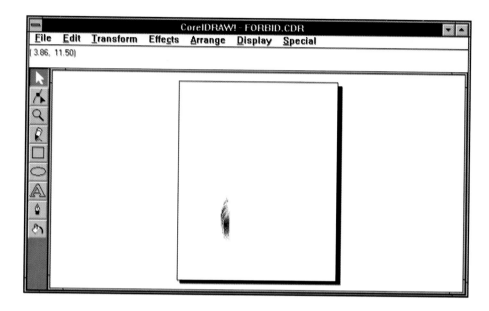

Figure 14.20:
Mechanical lapels for my friend's metal suit.

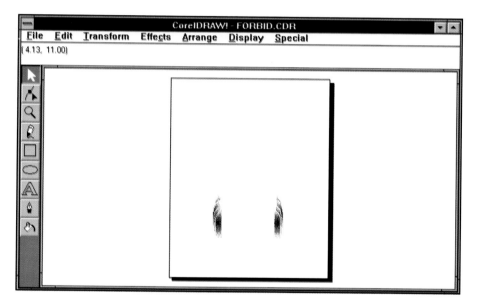

Figure 14.21:
Duplicating the lapels.

5. This group is duplicated and shrunk (eyeball it), leaving the original, and then both are aligned center to center. (The voice box is an exact duplicate of the torso plates with a color change.) This time the coloring is changed from a metallic radial fill to a hot pink blend to white, as shown in figure 14.24. Use the radial fountain fill tool in the Corel Paint box. This gives the great jukebox-like neon glow of his voice box.

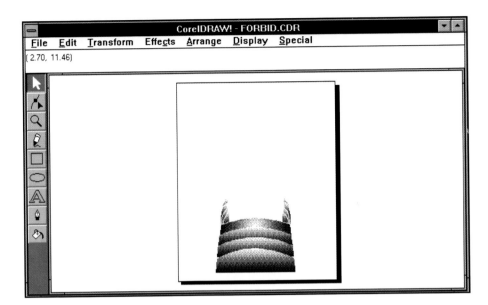

Figure 14.22:
Creating the metallic chest plates.

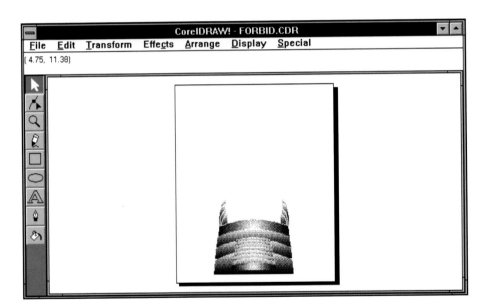

Figure 14.23:
Creating a neon glow.

6. The horizontal plate is pressed into service again. This time it is stretched severely upward by using the Node Edit tool. This creates a frame for the voice box and adds depth immediately to an early stage of the work (see fig. 14.24).

7. An ovoid (oval shaped) half ellipse is sent to the back to provide the rear of Robby's beloved dome (see fig. 14.25).

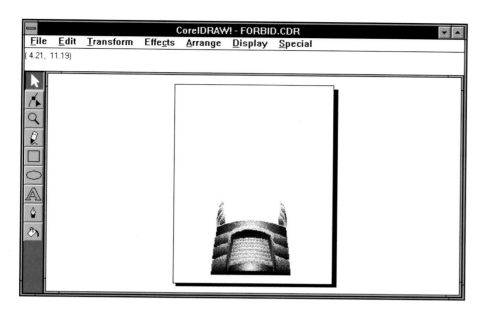

Figure 14.24:
Creating a frame for the voice box.

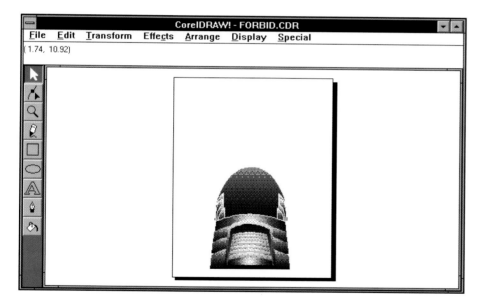

Figure 14.25:
Creating Robby's dome.

8. **D**uplicate this shape (leave the original), then elevate it one layer. Make sure the new ovoid shape stays "behind" the original "lapel fins." It is shrunk horizontally and stretched vertically (see fig. 14.26). The blend is as close as I could come to that light green window tint found on a '57 Chevy Bel Air Coupe. (Don't laugh! This is how I make my living.)

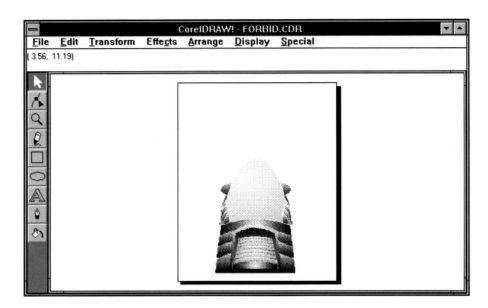

9. White ellipses and curves are added to give this windshield proper reflections, as shown in figure 14.27.

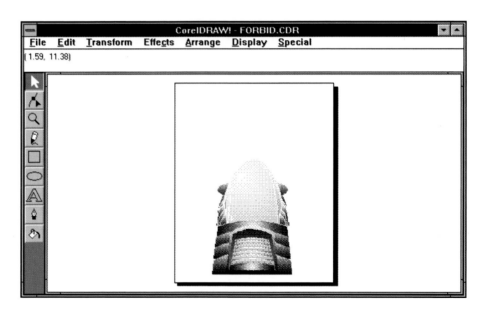

Figure 14.27:
Creating a reflection.

10. An ellipse and rectangle are given a metallic fountain fill, centered, and placed at the back of the composition (see fig. 14.29). These pieces will support more armature (additional mechanical devices) for Robby.

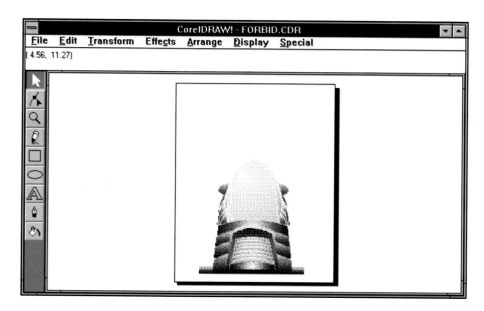

Figure 14.28:
The ellipse after positioning.

Pretend this is a cooking show on TV. Here's a complete arm assembly on the left (see fig. 14.29). Now I'll show you how I did it.

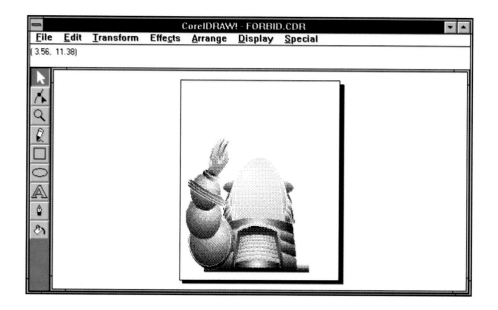

Figure 14.29:
The finished left arm assembly.

Use Robby's left arm displayed in figure 14.29 as a reference during the creation of Robby's right arm.

11. Two ellipses with an attached point outside of themselves are placed one on top of the other off-center. The floating point outside the ellipses (see the Tip) allows for an off-center radial fill that gives the impression of the surface of a sphere (see fig. 14.30). If you've ever seen Robby, you know he appears to be built of a series of metallic spheres. This is the shoulder unit.

How do you create a spherical effect for Robby's arm joints? Here is a method I found in the CorelDRAW manuals:

1. Draw an ellipse with the Ellipse tool.

2. Draw a point (single node) outside the ellipse with the Pen tool or Line tool.

3. Select both objects and **C**ombine them with the Arrange tool.

4. Apply radial fountain fill. The node will remain invisible but will change the center point of the fill.

Voilà!

12. Robby's elbow is simply a duplication of the top shoulder ellipse at a smaller size (leave the original). The new smaller ellipse is slipped upward and slightly to the right, as shown in figure 14.31.

13. Repeat step 11, moving the ellipse slightly to the left this time to create his forearm (see fig. 14.32).

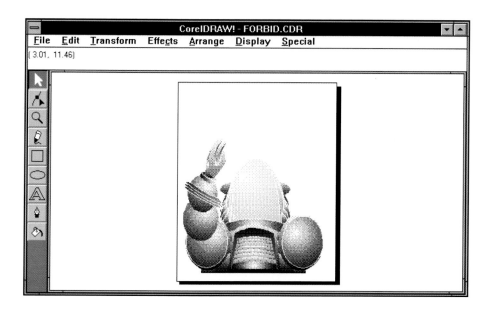

Figure 14.30:
Making the ellipses appear as spheres.

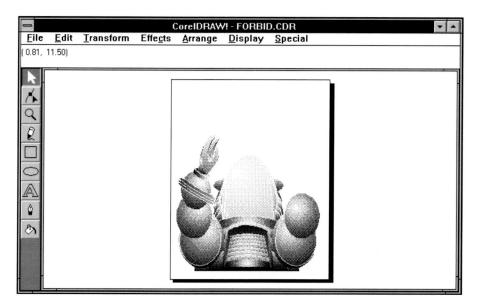

Figure 14.31:
Creating the elbow.

14. Now it's time for Robby's cuffs. Draw a severe horizontal ellipse, then convert it to a curve. Now use the Node Edit tool to add two additional points (see preceding Tip) to the top side of the ellipse. Convert this middle section to a curved segment, and use the Béziers to reverse the curve so that it appears slightly concave.

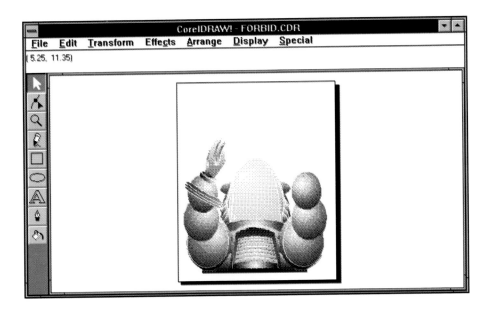

Figure 14.32:
Creating the forearm.

15. Apply radial metallic fountain fill and rotate the cuff and the fill. You now have your first Saturn-ring-like cuff. **D**uplicate the cuff and position it slightly above the first (see fig. 14.33). Do this one more time. Trust me, George Jetson has been wearing these things for years.

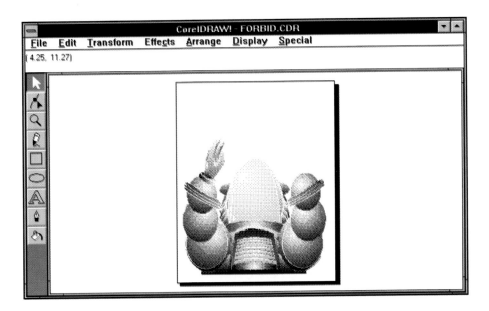

Figure 14.33:
Creating the space age cuff.

16. Draw a small ellipse, apply radial metallic fill, **D**uplicate (leaving the original), and reposition it slightly above the original. Rotate the same degree as wrist cuffs and position at upper edge of forearm. This completes the wrist (see fig. 14.34).

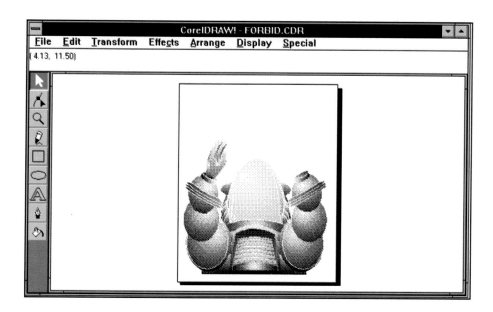

Figure 14.34:
Finishing the wrist.

17. The appropriately crude-looking claw hands are drawn dot-to-dot with the Pencil tool. The back of the hand is drawn the same way with straight, flat edges. Give the opposing facets of the hand reversed vertical fountain fills to increase contrast of the surfaces. Simply invert or reverse the compass degree variable in the Fill tool (that is, change a 90 variable to –90). All other groups of armor plates on the robot have their fills going in the same direction.

18. Rotate the claw to the same angle as the wrist and forearm, and center it on the wrist (use **A**rrange,**A**lign). Group everything from the shoulder to the claw, **D**uplicate horizontally (leaving the original), and slide it directly to the left by using the Ctrl key to make sure that it doesn't change alignment (see fig. 14.35).

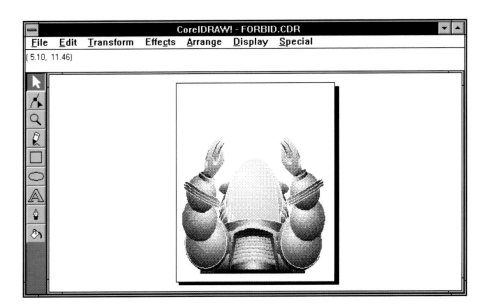

Figure 14.35:

Drawing the claw hands and duplicating the entire arm.

19. Concentric circles and ellipses are combined to form rings which make up the left antenna. Place the antenna at the edge of the upper ellipse you placed behind Robby's dome (see fig. 14.36).

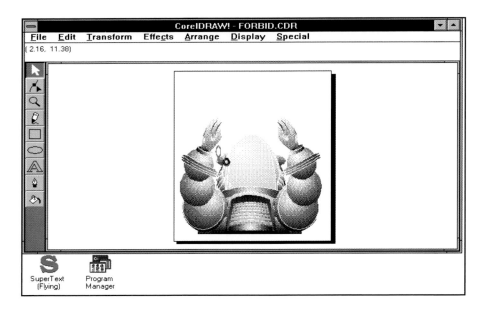

Figure 14.36:

Creating the left antenna.

20. **D**uplicate this group, rotate it 90 degrees, and place it at the right edge of the base ellipse (see fig. 14.37).

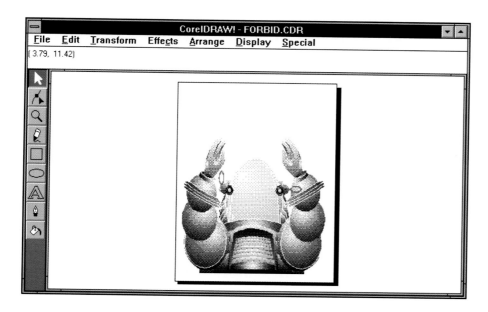

Figure 14.37:
See that little sideways antenna?

Robby doesn't mind if you put words in his mouth. In fact he's so transparent you can read his mind. This is your chance to get inside his head and program his speech yourself.

21. A single block of copy is formed from two separate text items that are stacked and aligned. The text is set in the Keypunch typeface and then stretched top and bottom by using the E**d**it Envelope tool from the Effe**c**ts menu. Adjust the Béziers until the copy block conforms to the curvature of Robby's dome (see fig. 14.38). The actual text is a play on words taken from his famous greeting in the MGM spectacular.

22. The background burst is a piece of dot-to-dot clip art (a vector graphic). It is imported, and sent to the back of the stack with the To **B**ack command in the **A**rrange menu. Then it is modified with the Node Edit tool to slide the left edge nodes even farther to the left by performing a marquee-select of those nodes only, depressing the Ctrl key and then dragging them to the left. The top, left, and bottom edges of this burst define the full-bleed trim lines of the finished ad (see fig. 14.39).

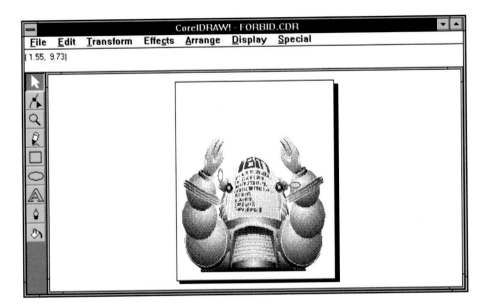

Figure 14.38:
Creating the text.

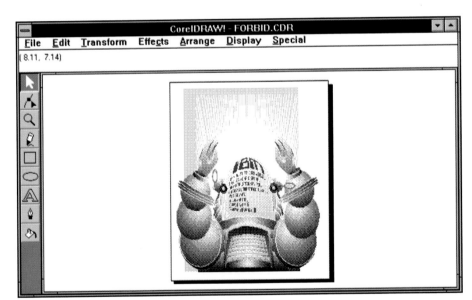

Figure 14.39:
Importing the clip art as the background.

23. The "Forbidden Computer" logo is simply set in the Motor typeface, converted to curves (see the following Tip), then skewed with the E**d**it Envelope tool from the Effe**c**ts menu.

How do you convert text to curves? Simple! Check this out:

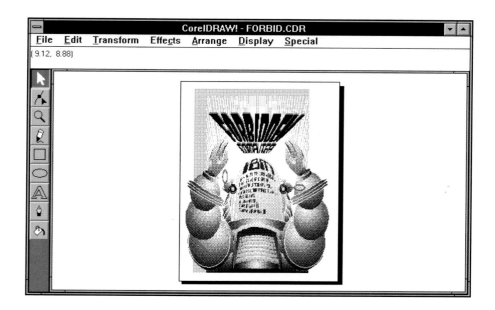

1. Set the type (type the text you want to modify).

2. Choose Con**v**ert To Curves from the **A**rrange menu.

3. Select the Pick tool, then double-click on the type. The skew and rotation handle bars will appear.

4. Eyeball the correct angles for the text.

24. Next, use the regular Node Edit tool to eliminate any curves on the original flat-edge characters. It is duplicated, sent back one, and repositioned slightly downward for the drop-shadow effect (see fig. 14.40).

Figure 14.40:

Setting the Forbidden Computer logo.

25. The headline is set in either the Architect or Bedrock typeface, then stretched and spaced to match the top edge of the "Forbidden Computer" logo (see fig. 14.41). To stretch and space the type, click on the Node Edit tool, then click on a piece or "string" of text. Drag the horizontal arrow handle bars. Your text string will now open the space between each character.

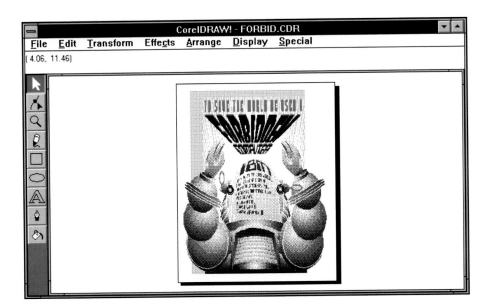

Figure 14.41:
Setting the headline.

26. **D**uplicate the introductory headline, and drop it straight down to the bottom of page (hold down the Ctrl key while you move the headline). Then edit the headline to reflect the name of the business.

    Below the headline, create and center three separate blocks of copy (use the same font) by choosing **A**rrange,**A**lign. These blocks of copy are voice phone, fax phone, and street address (see fig. 14.42).

27. Smaller paste-up style bursts (Amazing! and Mysterious!) are set and rotated filling the empty space of the lower right side of the robot's dome (see fig. 14.43).

28. The ad's main copy slug is set in Fujiyama Bold, flush left, and stacked (choose **A**rrange,**A**lign) along the right border of the green burst in the white column (see fig. 14.44).

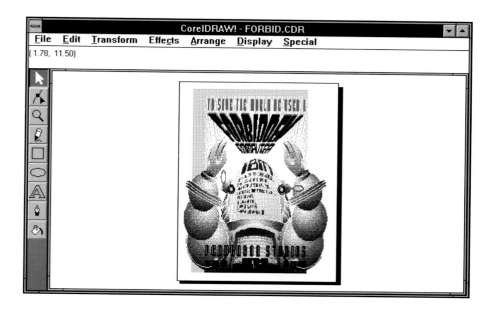

Figure 14.42:
Setting the company name and address.

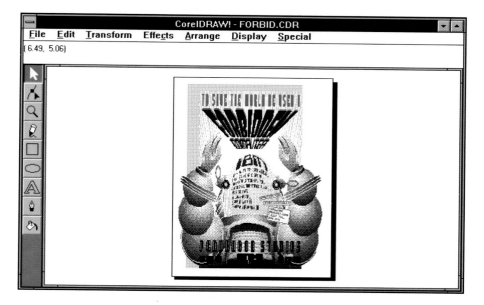

Figure 14.43:
Setting up the bursts.

29. Clip art logos are imported, stacked (choose **A**rrange,**A**lign), and center aligned to complete this visual resume for PENDRAGON STUDIOS—"Nobody Loves Toys Like We Do. Nobody." Figure 14.45 shows the completed drawing.

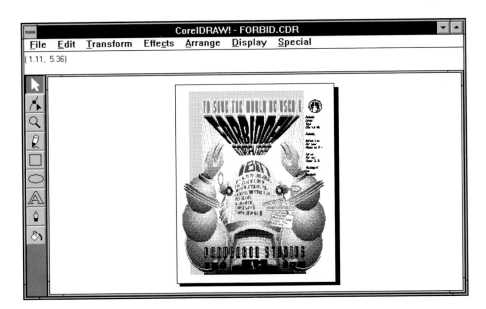

Figure 14.44:
Setting the main copy.

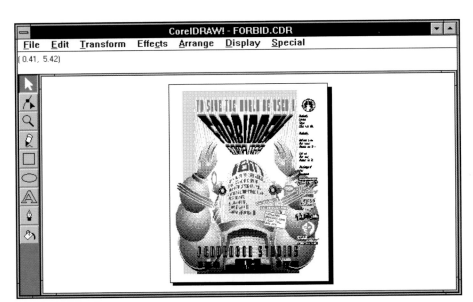

Figure 14.45:
The complete Forbidden Computer.

Technical Effects

"Drawing is like making an expressive gesture with the advantage of permanence."

—Henri Matisse

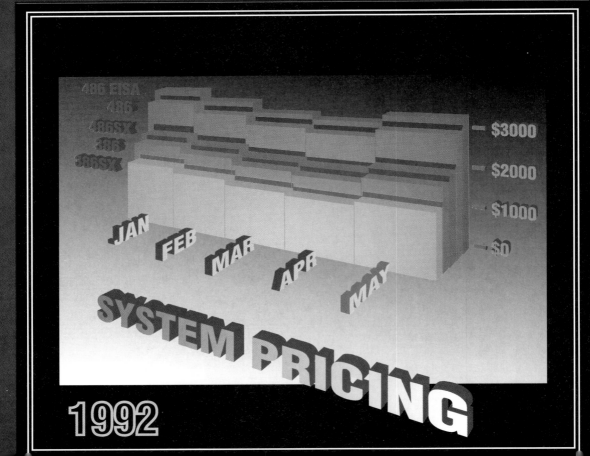

Charts

by David B. Libby

Doublegraph Inc.
Vincennes, Indiana

Equipment Used

Gateway 2000 486/33C with Matrox
1024 Impression true-color video card

Output Equipment Used

Film recorder

David Libby is the president and principal artist of Doublegraph Incorporated, a graphics design and illustration firm. This piece is the product of his work with ray-traced graphs.

Originally conceived as a ray-traced TIFF bitmap overlaid with text in CorelDRAW, this chart has been reworked as a vector-based illustration using the perspective and extrusion effects in CorelDRAW 3.0. The goal was to retain the original appearance of ray-tracing.

Procedure

1. Work in Wireframe mode, and set Nudge in the **P**references menu for 0.10".

2. Select Pa**g**e Setup from the **F**ile menu, then click on **A**dd Page Frame, and fill with black.

3. Place a 7.5" × 6.25" rectangle in the center of the page with a 0.14" white outline and no fill. Select Con**v**ert To Curves from the **A**rrange menu, and then **D**uplicate.

4. Select the top two nodes of the duplicate, press and hold down the Ctrl key, and move the nodes down 0.06". Select the bottom two nodes, again hold down the Ctrl key, and then move the nodes up 0.06".

    Follow this same procedure and select the nodes on each side and move them inward 0.06". You should now have a parallel rectangle inside the original. This serves as a decorative border.

5. With the inner rectangle selected, choose **D**uplicate. Change to No Outline. Fill with a linear fountain fill (F11) using the color spread black to white with an angle of 260 degrees.

6. Size this rectangle downward by holding down the Shift key and dragging a corner handle inward until it reaches 90 percent. Then hold down the Shift key, and drag the top middle handle downward until you reach 80 percent. This is a receding background for the illustration.

7. Because this is a 3D bar chart, start by drawing the back set of rectangles for the bars.

8. Draw a rectangle by placing your cursor at 8.0" horizontal and 5.5" vertical, then drag down and to the left to create a box approximately 0.9" wide and 2.4" tall. **D**uplicate this rectangle and move the duplicate to the left 0.9". Repeat this procedure until you have five rectangles in a row with no space between them (see fig. 15.1).

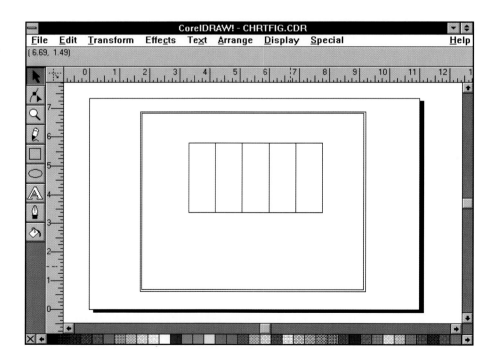

Figure 15.1:

The basic bars used to make the graph.

9. At this point, you need to size the height of each rectangle so that it matches the actual amount of whatever numbers you are graphing. One way to do this is to use a percentage basis, or perhaps by drawing a temporary scale to the side to adjust the height of each box in accordance with its value. For this example, just eyeball it.

10. After varying each rectangle's height, select all five rectangles and **C**ombine them. Choose No Outline.

To remove an object's outline, click on the "X" at the left end of the color palette.

11. **D**uplicate this five-rectangle object and nudge the duplicate down 0.10". At this point, you again would relate the height of each rectangle to its actual value. Because the rectangles are now combined into one object, you need to select the top nodes and, holding down the Ctrl key, resize vertically. For this example, simply select the object, grab the top middle handle, and size this object downward 85 percent.

12. Repeat the preceding step three more times to create five rows of rectangles.

13. Select each row object and nudge it to the left 0.10" from the one above and behind. Leave the back row in place.

14. In the **D**isplay menu, turn on Snap to **G**uidelines. Then pull a guideline down from the top ruler to the 6" mark. Pull another guideline from the left to the –6.75" mark. This will be your left hand vanishing point. You should adjust the page magnification so that your page and the vanishing point are both visible (see fig. 15.2).

15. Select a row object, and choose Edit Perspecti**v**e from the Effe**c**ts menu. Select the lower left hand node and, holding down the Ctrl key, move the node upward until the vanishing point crosshair comes into view (see fig. 15.3). Then click on the crosshair, and drag it onto the vanishing point you set up with the guidelines. Repeat this step with each row object.

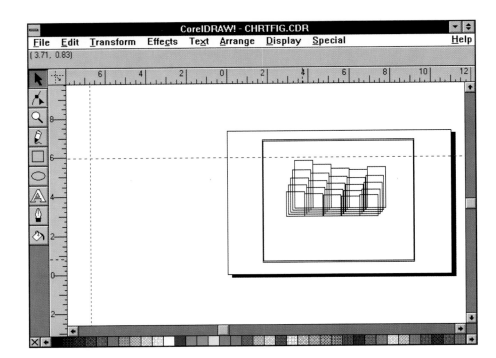

Figure 15.2:

Setting a vanishing point for the 3D chart.

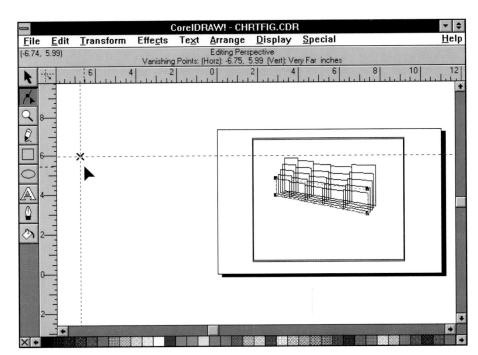

Figure 15.3:

Snapping the vanishing point to the guidelines.

Color each row. I sampled colors from the original ray-traced bitmap in Aldus Photostyler, and converted the 1-255 range of RGB values to 1-100 values to be used in CorelDRAW. You can use any light-to-dark ranges for the next step; the RGB values are used as an example.

16. Select the back (and upper) row object, and be sure there is no outline. Select fountain fill in the flyout menu. Select Radial, and enter RGB values (by clicking on More) 064, 006, and 006 for From, and 084, 022, and 022 for To (again by clicking on More). For the back row, use no offset. Repeat for each row object, using the following values:

Row	RGB From Values	RGB To Values	Offset Value
4	062, 012, 029	090, 032, 051	−10 vertical offset
3	058, 011, 042	066, 007, 047	−20 vertical offset
2	074, 012, 074	100, 042, 100	−45 vertical offset
1	075, 035, 058	100, 074, 093	−75 vertical offset

17. At this point, you might want to Preview (F9) and see how the effect is taking shape. When you are done, go back to Wireframe mode.

18. Choose E**x**trude Roll-Up from the Effe**c**ts menu. Starting with the back row, select a row object, and set Depth to 2, H to 12.00, and V to 8.00. Check the Perspective box. Then activate the color wheel icon, select Solid Fill, and choose Apply. Repeat for each row object.

19. Now you should have the 3D bars for the graph. All that remains is to add the text.

20. Start by adding the text string "SYSTEM PRICING" centered beneath the shaded background. This could be 55-point Switzerland Condensed Black (or a similar typeface, such as Helvetica Condensed Bold).

21. Fill this text with a linear fountain fill of white to twilight blue (R040, G040, B080) at an angle of 160 degrees. Use no outline.

22. Repeat the procedure used to add perspective to the rectangular bars. Choose Edit Perspective from the Effects menu. Press and hold down the Ctrl key, and move the lower left hand node upward until the vanishing point crosshair comes into view. Then click and drag the crosshair until it snaps to the vanishing point created with the guidelines.

23. Apply the same extrusion used for the bars—Depth=2, H=12.00, V=8.00, and solid fill. This time I used a darker blue fill for added contrast.

24. Using the same steps used for the text "SYSTEM PRICING," add the vertically stepped price guides to the right of the bars and the system labels to the left. I used slightly different shades of blue for each to increase readability and contrast. I also used a slightly smaller point size. If you need to adjust the placement of the text strings after adding perspective to them, be sure to check to see if the vanishing point crosshair has moved from the guidelines. Readjust the crosshair if necessary.

25. The text strings identifying the months are added in the same manner; only the vanishing points are reversed. In other words, the guidelines are set to 12" horizontal and 8" vertical, and the perspective crosshairs are snapped to these coordinates. The extrusion points then are set to –6.75" horizontal and 6" vertical, and a lesser depth of 1 is used. Figure 15.4 shows the results.

26. An interesting way to add the 3D tube pointers for the price levels is to draw a small circle, extrude it to a depth of about 1, and then rotate the result 180 degrees. After duplicating and placing the copies in their appropriate positions, another trick can be used to align them with the proper perspective: Use the Pencil tool, and click on the left-hand vanishing point, then click a little to the right of one of the tubes. Zoom in on the tube, then rotate it until the top line of the tube aligns with the line drawn from the vanishing point. Use the Node Edit tool and click on the right hand point of the alignment line to swing it close enough to each tube to use it as a guideline for rotation.

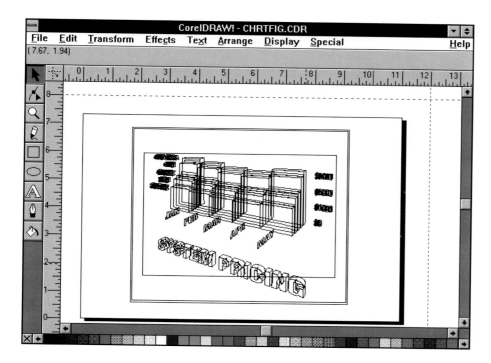

Figure 15.4:
Wireframe view showing perspective text.

27. The last elements to be added are shadows. This drawing has been constructed as though it were lit from the front and slightly below center. If this were the case, then each bar would cast a shadow onto the face of the bar behind it. An approximation of that shadow can be drawn by tracing along the top back edge of the bar, and then moving up a small distance and retracing back along the same path.

For clarity, figure 15.5 shows the shapes with a black fill. It helps to visualize the drawing in 3D as you draw the shadows. You might even want to turn off **D**isplay, **E**dit Wireframe so that you can see the actual surfaces on which the shadow rests. This might require that you also fill the rectangles with a solid fill temporarily to avoid waiting for the radial fill to redraw. When finished, the shadows can be filled with a darker shade of the color used to fill the underlying bar.

28. After placing all the elements, you might want to adjust their size for a better overall composition within the framing rectangles. The only caution is to be sure that all elements are drawn and placed in their final position relative to each other. Resizing will move the vanishing points and make any readjustments more difficult.

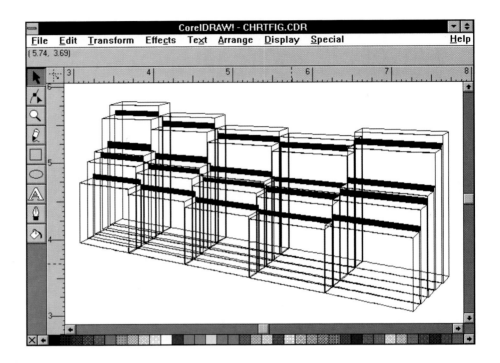

Figure 15.5:

Filling the shapes with black.

29. Finally, place the text "1992" with a 0.024" powder blue outline and no fill in the lower left corner inside the frame. The drawing is finished!

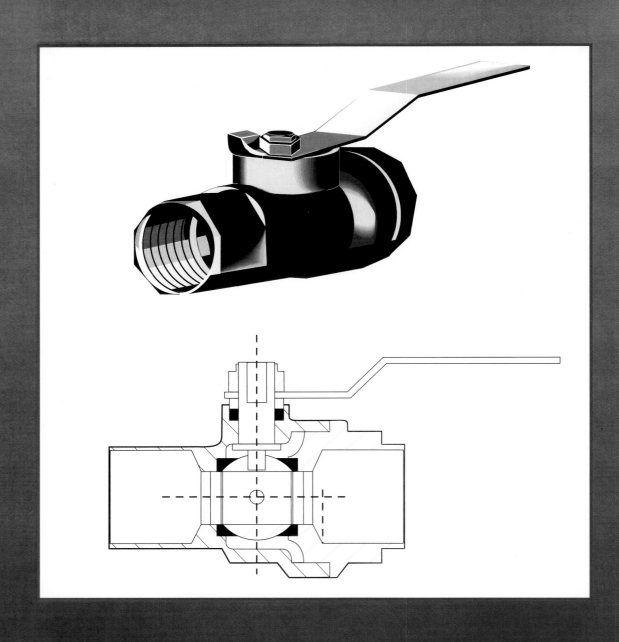

Ball Valve

by Deborah Miller

Miller Graphic Consulting, Ltd.

Mesa, Arizona

Equipment Used

386DX-33 home-built clone
8M of RAM

Output Equipment Used

Panasonic KX-P4450 Laser Partner at 300 dpi

Deborah Miller is co-owner, with her husband Mike, of Miller Graphic Consulting, Ltd. in Mesa, Arizona. She has been a professional graphics artist for over 25 years and has been using CorelDRAW since 1989.

Deborah created this piece of award-winning art to prove a point to a Macintosh software developer. The developer was skeptical that a PC-illustration package, and CorelDRAW in particular, could produce technical illustrations equal to, or better than those produced on a Macintosh.

Procedure

The rendered portion of the drawing consists of five parts: main body, back flange, top flange, handle, and threaded coupling (see fig. 15.6). The blueprint view and the text complete the final drawing.

Tackling a technical illustration that has photo-realistic qualities requires some planning. It is important to consider your light source, reflected light, an artificial horizon, and the space you want your finished drawing to occupy. It is sometimes helpful if you draw these on-screen before starting, and use them as a guideline throughout your drawing.

In addition, you should set up a 1/8" grid on-screen by selecting Gri̲d Setup from the **D**isplay menu. This provides another visual reference to guide your drawing (see fig.15. 7).

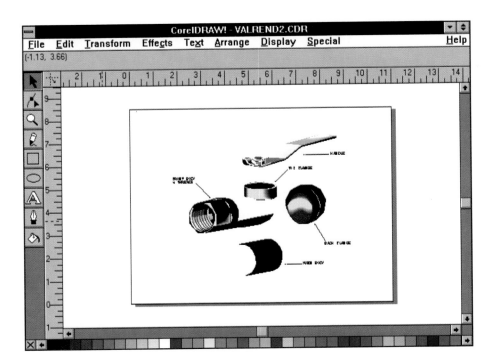

Figure 15.6:
Main parts of the ball valve.

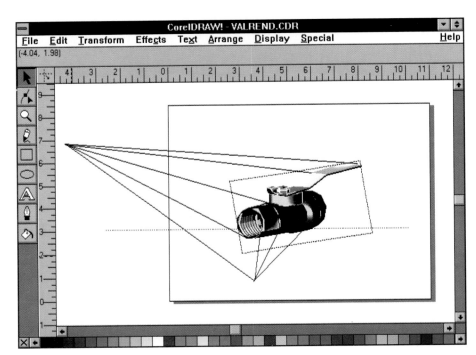

Figure 15.7:
Guidelines and light sources.

The Main Body

1. Using the Ellipse tool, create a 1.63" × 1.88" ellipse. Rotate the ellipse 10 degrees, and convert it to curves.

2. Using the Shape tool, click on the ellipse. Double-click on the node on the left side of the ellipse. Select **B**reak from the Node Edit dialog box.

3. Use the Shape tool to marquee-select the two nodes created in the preceding step. Delete the selected nodes by double-clicking on the nodes and selecting **D**elete from the Node Edit dialog box, or by pressing the Del key (see fig. 15.8).

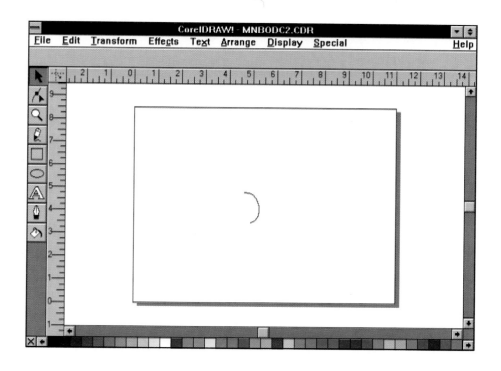

Figure 15.8:
Creating the front arc.

4. Select the arc created in step 3, and choose **M**ove from the **T**ransform menu. Turn on Leave Original, set Horizontal to 1.1" and Vertical to .2" (see fig. 15.9).

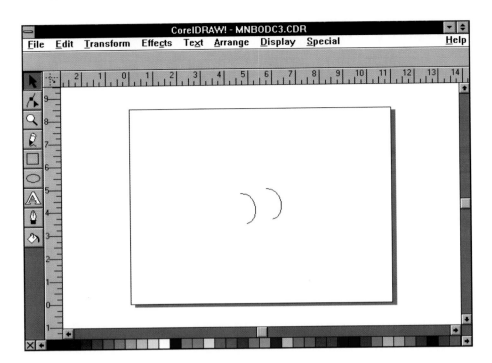

Figure 15.9:

Creating the back arc of the main body.

5. Turn on Snap To Ob**j**ect from the **D**isplay menu. Use the Pencil tool to draw a line from the upper portion of one of the arcs to the other. Repeat this process for the lower portions of the arcs.

6. Using the Pick tool, marquee-select all the objects, and **C**ombine them.

7. Using the Shape tool, marquee-select a pair of nodes at one corner. Double-click on the selected nodes, and select **J**oin from the Node Edit dialog box. Repeat this process for the other corners.

8. Fill the resulting object with black (see fig. 15.10).

The Top Flange

1. Draw a rectangle the length of the top portion of the main body and 1/3 as high. Select Con**v**ert To Curves from the **A**rrange menu.

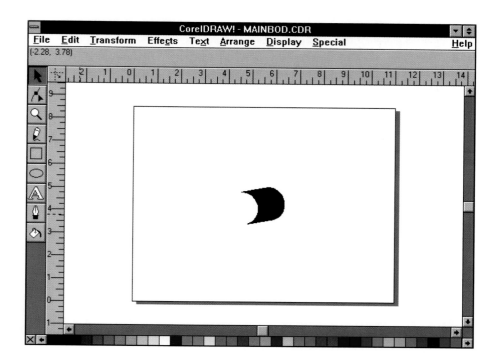

Figure 15.10:
Filling the main body with black.

2. Using the Shape tool, double-click on the bottom line of the rectangle and select **t**oCurve. Repeat this process for the top line.

3. Use the Shape tool to modify the bottom curve to conform to the shape of the main body.

4. Using the Shape tool, select the top curve of the modified rectangle, and pull the handles to change the shape of the top line to an ovoid curve.

5. Fill the resulting shape black with a .003" white outline (see fig. 15.11).

6. Select **D**uplicate from the **E**dit menu.

Pressing the + key on the numeric keypad drops a duplicate behind the selected object.

7. Fill the duplicated shape with 10-percent black.

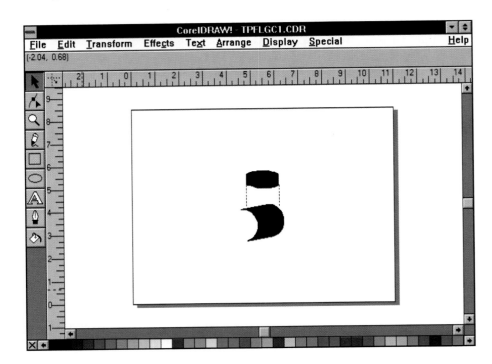

Figure 15.11:
Filling the shape with a white outline.

8. Using the Shape tool, double-click on the right hand, vertical line of the duplicated shape, and select **t**oCurve from the Node Edit dialog box.

9. Use the Shape tool to modify the duplicated shape until it looks like the gray shape in figure 15.12.

10. Using the Pick tool, click on the black shape. Then, holding the Shift key, click on the gray shape.

11. Select **B**lend Roll-Up from the Effe**c**ts menu.

12. In the Blend Roll-Up dialog box, set Steps to 20, and click on Apply.

13. Using the Ellipse tool, draw an ellipse to match the top of the flange.

Place a vertical guideline at the left and right edges of the flange, and select Snap To **G**uidelines from the **D**isplay menu. Then anchor the Ellipse tool on one of the guidelines, and drag to the other guideline. This procedure guarantees that the ellipse will be the correct width.

14. Fill the ellipse 10-percent black and no outline (see fig. 15.13).

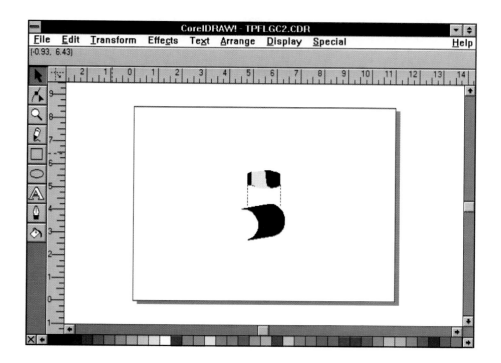

Figure 15.12:
Modifying the shape to create the top flange highlight.

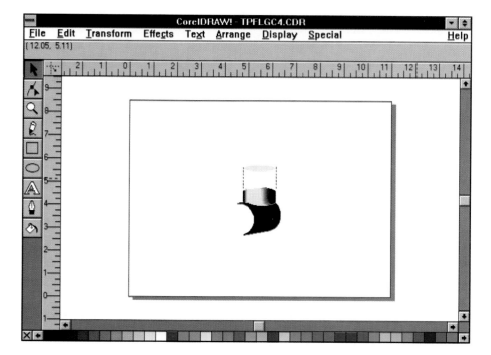

Figure 15.13:
Filling the ellipse.

15. Select **S**tretch & Mirror from the **T**ransform menu. Set Stretch Horizontal to 90 percent and Vertical to 100 percent. Select Leave Original, and click on OK.

16. Using the Pick tool, fill the duplicated ellipse 100-percent black (see fig. 15.14). Move the ellipse until it snaps to the left guideline. Alternately, select both the 10-percent black and the 100-percent black ellipses, and select **A**lign from the **A**rrange menu. Select the vertical-left option in the Align dialog box, and click on OK.

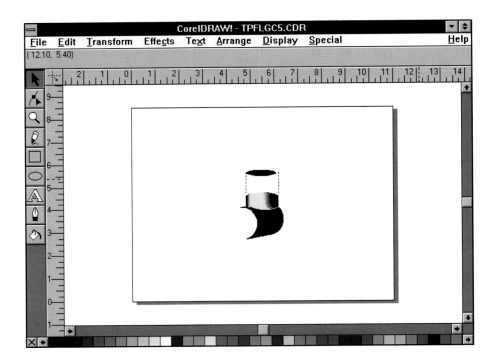

Figure 15.14

The shadowed ellipse.

17. **G**roup the two ellipses. Holding down the Ctrl key to constrain the movement in one direction, drag the grouped ellipses on top of the flange body.

18. **G**roup the flange parts. Hold down the Ctrl key, and drag the grouped flange onto the main body (see fig. 15.15).

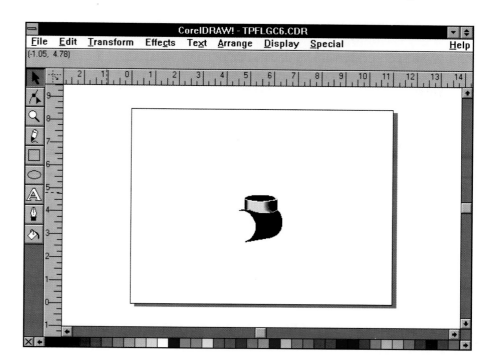

Figure 15.15:
Finished main body with top flange.

The Handle

1. Draw a 2" × 1/2" rectangle.

2. Select Convert To Curves from the **A**rrange menu.

3. Use the Shape tool to adjust the rectangle so that it appears to be viewed from an oblique angle. Fill this rectangle with 40-percent black and no outline (see fig. 15.16).

4. Select **D**uplicate from the **E**dit menu.

5. Move the duplicate rectangle so that the right edge of the second rectangle butts up against the left edge of the first rectangle, as shown in figure 15.16.

6. **D**uplicate this rectangle, and move it off to the side for use as the third part of the handle.

7. Make sure that the nodes on the right edge of the second rectangle align with the left corners of the first rectangle.

8. Marquee-select the nodes on the left edge of the second rectangle.

9. Click on one of the selected nodes, and, holding down the Ctrl key, drag the node so that the second rectangle is shortened with a 20-degree downward angle. Fill this rectangle with 10-percent black and no outline.

10. Use the Pick tool to click on the third rectangle, and drag it until its right edge butts up against the left edge of the second rectangle. Fill this rectangle with 50-percent black and no outline. (See fig. 15.16; for reference, these rectangles are labeled A, B, and C.)

11. **D**uplicate rectangle A. Hold down the Shift key, and click-and-drag one of the corner handles until the resulting rectangle is approximately one half the size of the original in both dimensions. Align the smaller rectangle with the top corner of rectangle A. Leave the fill at 40-percent black and no outline.

It is important to hold down the Shift key to constrain the angles, preventing them from becoming skewed out of shape.

12. **D**uplicate the smaller rectangle. Select the bottom node. Delete this node to create a triangle. Fill the triangle with white and no outline.

13. Select both the triangle and the small rectangle below it. Then select **B**lend Roll-Up from the Effects menu, set the Steps to 20, and click on Apply. See figure 15.17.

14. Select rectangle B, and **D**uplicate it. Holding down the Shift key, click-and-drag one of the side handles reducing it to one half the width of the original rectangle. Align the resulting rectangle, as shown in fig. 15.16, and fill with 5-percent black and no outline.

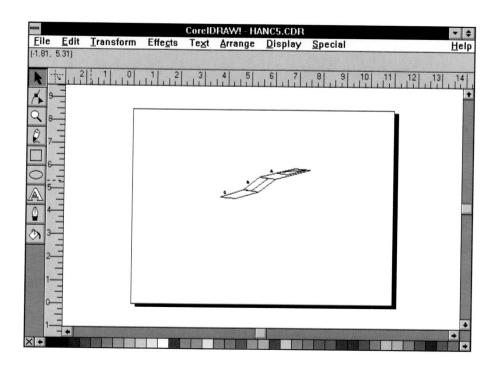

Figure 15.16:
Basic handle objects in Wireframe mode.

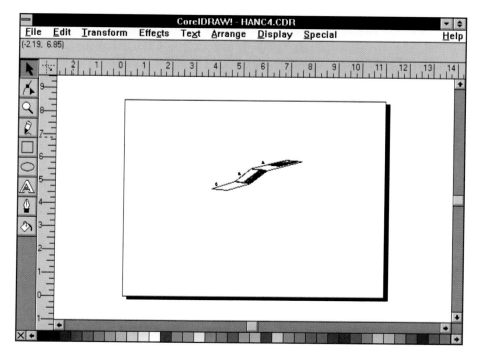

Figure 15.17:
Handle blends in Wireframe mode.

15. Select the small rectangle, hold down the Shift key, and click on rectangle B, to select both rectangles. Select **B**lend Roll-Up from the Effe**c**ts menu, set the Steps for 20, and click on Apply (see fig. 15.17).

16. To create the bottom shadow of the handle, select rectangles A, B, and C, **D**uplicate them, and **G**roup them. Place this group behind the original handle by selecting Back O**n**e (PgDn) from the **A**rrange menu. Fill the grouped object with 100-percent black.

17. Select **M**ove from the **T**ransform menu, and move the grouped object –.04" vertically.

Select Pr**e**ferences from the **S**pecial menu and preset Nudge to .01". Then you can move the group by pressing the down arrow key four times.

18. Select Snap To Obj**e**cts from the **D**isplay menu. Draw a .014" black line around the bottom portion of the shadow by clicking on the far left corner of the shadow and double-clicking on each corner as you go around the shape. This gives the shadow a 3D effect.

19. Draw a .007" white line at the lower edge of the grouped object to highlight the shape (see fig. 15.18).

20. The stop on the front of the handle is created of free-form shapes. Consider your light source, and fill the resulting shapes with 10-percent black for the highlight, 50-percent black for the medium tones, and 100-percent black for the shadowed pieces. **G**roup the resulting shapes, give them no outline, and align on the handle, as shown in figure 15.19.

21. The nut on the top of the handle is drawn in four basic sections comprised of a series of free-form shapes. The shapes are filled with white for the highlight, 50-percent black for the medium tones, and 100-percent black for the shadowed pieces.

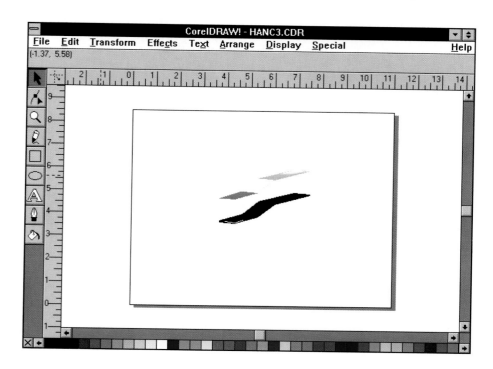

Figure 15.18:
Highlighting the shape.

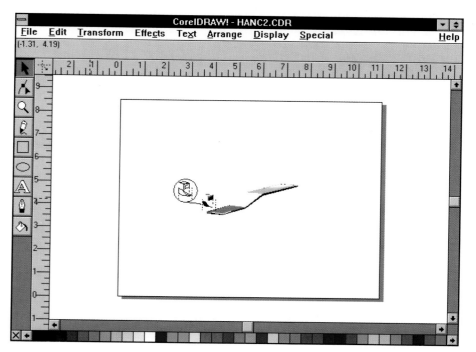

Figure 15.19:
Grouping the shapes and aligning them.

22. Create the bottom section of the nut first, and fill it as indicated in step 21. Then select the four pieces, and **G**roup them. Apply a .003" white outline to the grouped object. With Snap To Ob**j**ects turned on, draw a .003" black line at the front and bottom edge of the nut base. Using the Pencil tool, draw a slightly curved .003" white line at the top of the front edge of the grouped object. **G**roup the lines with the bottom section of the nut (see fig. 15.20).

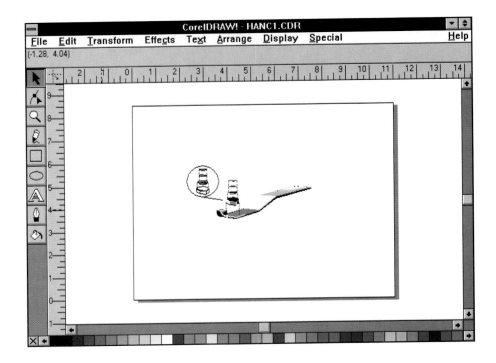

Figure 15.20:
Grouping the lines.

23. Select **S**tretch & Mirror from the **T**ransform menu, and set the horizontal stretch to 80 percent and the vertical stretch to 50 percent. Select **L**eave Original, and click on OK. Select **M**ove from the **T**ransform menu, set the vertical option for .1", and click on OK.

24. Draw an ellipse approximately 75 percent of the width and 5 percent of the height of the smaller nut section. Fill the ellipse with 100-percent black, and give it a .007", 50-percent black outline.

25. **D**uplicate the ellipse, and **M**ove the ellipse vertically .002".

26. Align the parts as indicated in figure 15.21 to complete the handle.

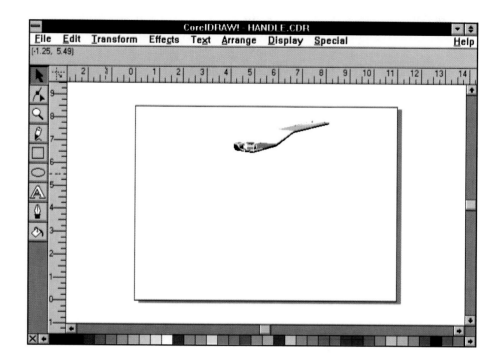

Figure 15.21:
Aligning the parts to finish the handle.

The Back Flange

1. Draw a 1-1/2" × 1-3/4" ellipse. Select **R**otate & Skew from the **T**ransform menu, set the rotation for 10 degrees, then click on OK (see fig. 15.22). Fill the ellipse with 10-percent black with a .03", 100-percent black outline.

For purposes of clarity, the handle is not depicted in this section's figures.

2. Select **P**references from the **S**pecial menu, and set the Place Duplicate **H**orizontal option to 0.0" and the **V**ertical option to 0.0".

3. **D**uplicate the ellipse, and fill it 100-percent black. Convert the ellipse to curves by selecting Con**v**ert To Curves from the **A**rrange menu.

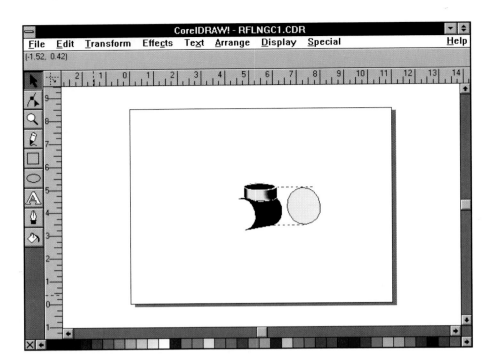

Figure 15.22:
Rotated ellipse for back flange.

4. Using the Shape tool, double-click on the left node to bring up the Node Edit dialog box, and select **B**reak. Marquee-select the resulting two nodes. Then create an arc by deleting the two nodes.

5. Select **M**ove from the **T**ransform menu, and set the Horizontal value to .20" and the Vertical value to .10". Then select Leave Original, and click on OK.

6. Select the two arcs, and then click on **C**ombine from the **A**rrange menu.

7. Use the Shape tool to select the top two nodes. Double-click to bring up the Node Edit dialog box, and select **J**oin. Repeat this process for the bottom two nodes.

8. Add nodes at the points indicated on figure 15.18. Marquee-select the nodes, and double-click on one of them to bring up the Node Edit dialog box. Select **t**oLine (see fig. 15.23).

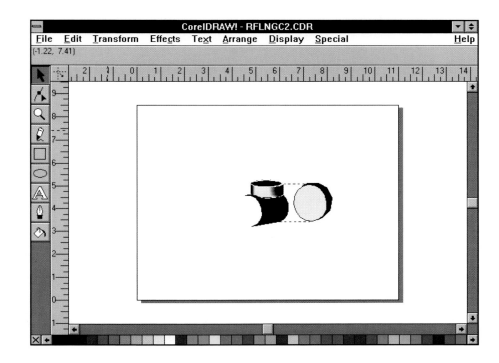

Figure 15.23:
Back flange outer shell.

9. Using the Pick tool, duplicate the 10-percent black filled ellipse, and nudge, or move it vertically –.04". Fill the ellipse with 100-percent black (see fig. 15.24.).

10. Select the black ellipse, and choose **S**tretch & Mirror from the **T**ransform menu. Set the horizontal option for 80 percent and the vertical option for 90 percent. Choose **L**eave Original, and click on OK. Fill the resulting ellipse with 80-percent black and no outline.

11. Select the 80-percent and 100-percent black ellipses, and click on **A**lign from the **A**rrange menu. Set the options for Horizontal/Left, Vertical/Bottom, and click on OK (see fig. 15.25).

12. **D**uplicate the 80-percent ellipse, and click on Con**v**ert To Curves from the **A**rrange menu. Leave the fill as 80-percent black.

13. Using the Shape tool, marquee-select the four nodes of the resulting object. Double-click on one of the nodes to bring down the Node Edit dialog box, and select **C**usp.

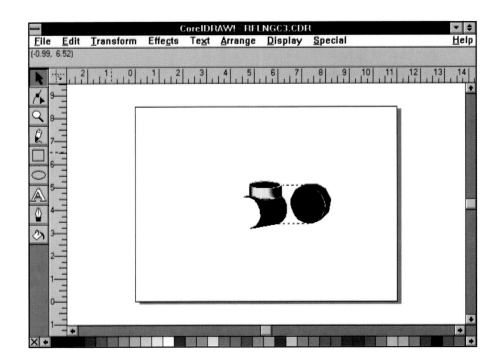

Figure 15.24:

Back flange outer shell with edge highlight.

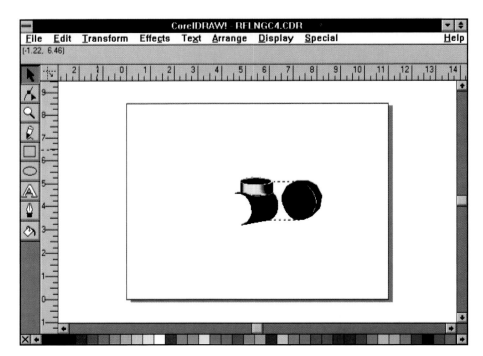

Figure 15.25:

Aligning the ellipses.

Selecting **C**usp enables you to move one handle without symmetrically moving the opposite handle of a given node.

14. Use the Node Edit tool to adjust the nodes.

To make manipulating the nodes easier in Color Preview mode, temporarily give the object a contrasting outline. After the object is shaped, eliminate the outline.

15. Duplicate the modified object, and fill the new object with 10-percent black and no outline. Modify the object with the Shape tool as indicated in figure 15.26.

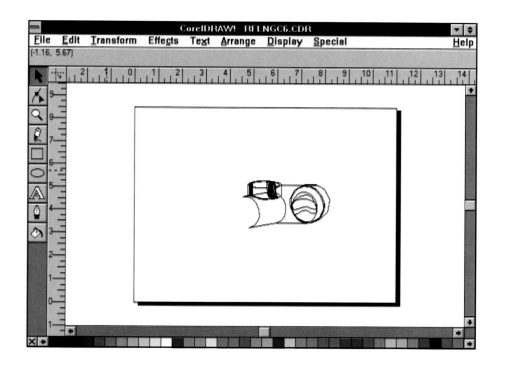

Figure 15.26:
Back flange shapes shown in Wireframe mode.

16. Select the two modified objects, and click on **B**lend Roll-Up from the Effe**c**ts menu. Set Steps to 20, and click on OK (see fig. 15.27).

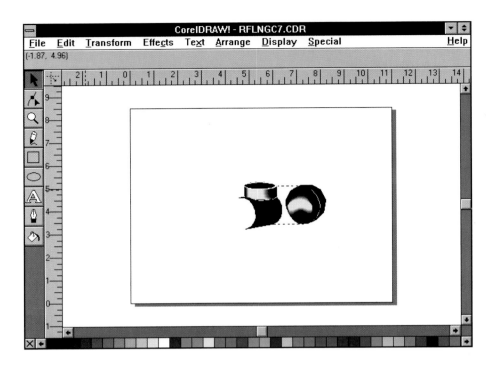

Figure 15.27:

Blended view of back flange.

17. Select all of the back flange parts, and **G**roup them. Place the grouped object behind the main body as indicated in figure 15.28.

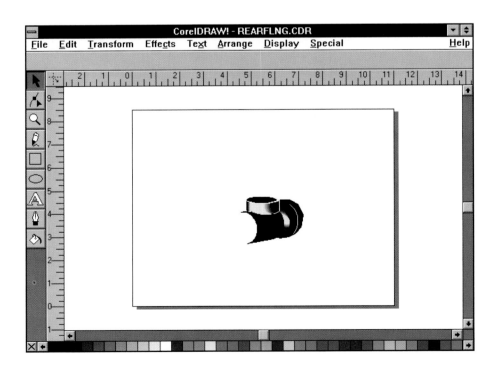

Figure 15.28:

Main body showing back flange alignment.

The Threaded Coupling

1. Draw an ellipse approximately 1" × 1-1/4". Give the ellipse no fill and .007", 100-percent black outline. Select **R**otate & Skew from the **T**ransform menu, set the rotation for 10 degrees, and click on OK (see fig. 15.29).

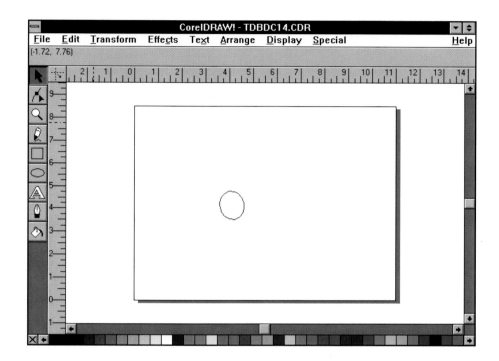

Figure 15.29:
Rotated ellipse for threaded coupling.

2. A step and repeat technique is used to create the threads of the coupling. Select the ellipse, and select **M**ove from the **T**ransform menu. Set the horizontal value at 0.06" and the vertical value at 0.01". Choose Leave Original, and click on OK.

3. Select **R**epeat from the **E**dit menu to repeat the move eight times (see fig. 15.30).

Press Ctrl-R to repeat a command.

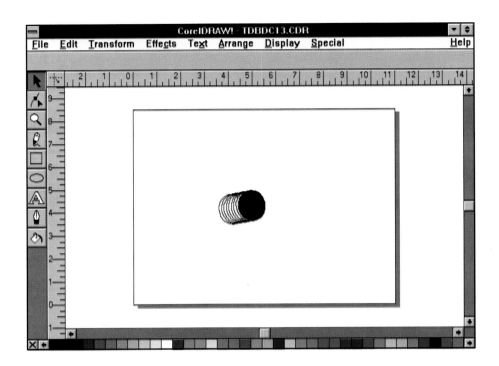

4. Select the seventh ellipse from the left, and fill it with 10-percent black. Select the eighth ellipse, and fill it with 100-percent black.

5. Draw a rectangle at the bottom of the threads to add a black shadow. Then select the rectangle, and click on Convert To Cur**v**es from the **A**rrange menu. Use the Shape tool to modify the nodes as indicated in figure 15.31. Fill the object with 100-percent black and no outline.

6. Use the Pencil tool to freehand draw the bottom of the body. The object should be approximately 3" long. Use the threads as a guideline for the angle (see fig. 15.32).

7. Fill the object with 100-percent black and no outline, and place as indicated in figure 15.33.

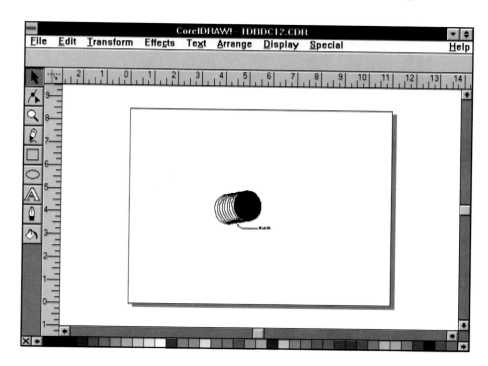

Figure 15.31:
Modifying the nodes and filling with black.

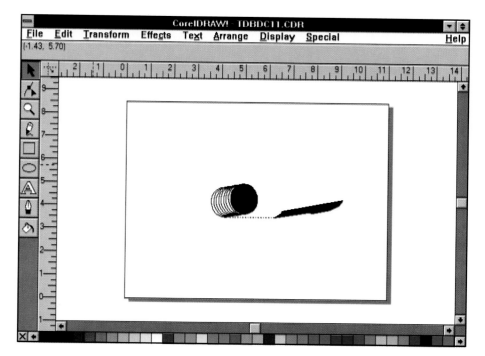

Figure 15.32:
Creating the bottom of the body.

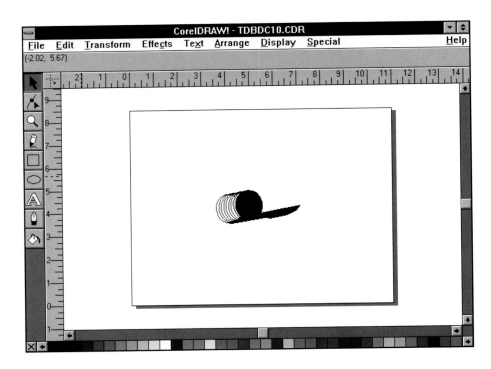

Figure 15.33:
Placing the bottom of the body.

8. Create a barrel shape using the procedure described in the Main Body section. The original ellipse should be 1" × 1-1/4". Place the object as shown in figure 15.34.

 Turn on Snap To Objects from the **D**isplay menu to place the barrel shape more easily.

9. Use the Rectangle tool to draw the shadows for the threads. Convert each rectangle to curves. Select **T**o Back from the **A**rrange menu, and place and fill each shadow as indicated in figure 15.35. Use the Shape tool to adjust the nodes to conform to the shape of the threads.

10. Use the Ellipse tool to create the arcs. Draw an ellipse approximately 1/2" × 1/4", then select Con**v**ert To Curves from the **A**rrange menu.

11. Using the Shape tool, select and delete the bottom node of the ellipse. Double-click on the bottom line of the ellipse, and select **t**oLine. Fill the object with 10-percent black.

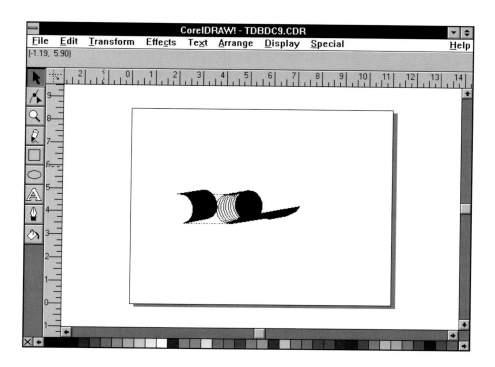

Figure 15.34:
Placing the barrel shape.

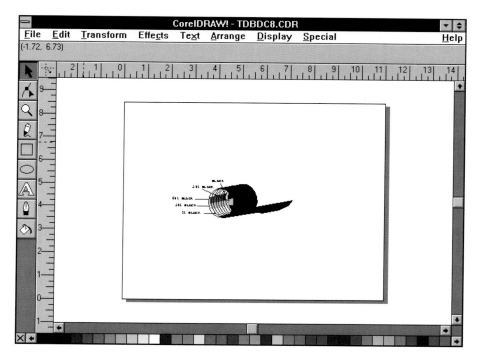

Figure 15.35:
Placing and filling the shadows.

12. Select **R**otate & Skew from the **T**ransform menu. Set the rotation for –60 degrees, choose **L**eave Original, and click on OK.

13. Select **R**otate & Skew again. Set the rotation for –30 degrees, choose **L**eave Original, and click on OK.

14. Place the three arcs as shown in figure 15.36.

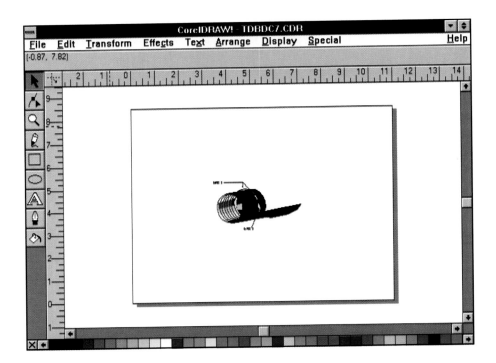

Figure 15.36:
Placing the arcs.

15. Draw a rectangle for the top of the barrel shape. Fill the rectangle with 100-percent black and no outline. Double-click on the rectangle with the Pick tool to show the skew and rotation handles. Click-and-drag the top handle until the side angles match the angle of the top of the barrel. Place the skewed rectangle as shown in figure 15.34.

16. Draw a second rectangle for the side of the barrel, and skew it to match the angle of the bottom of the barrel shape. Fill the rectangle with 10-percent black and a .003", 100-percent black outline.

17. To create the highlight on the side piece, **D**uplicate the rectangle, and select Con**v**ert To Curves from the **A**rrange menu. Fill the rectangle with 100-percent black.

18. Using the Shape tool, select the bottom right node, and delete it. Double-click on the diagonal line of the triangle to bring up the Node Edit dialog box. Select **t**oCurve, then marquee-select all three nodes of the triangle. Double-click on one of the nodes and select **C**usp from the Node Edit dialog box. Click on the diagonal line to show the handles, and adjust the handles to produce the shape shown in figure 15.37.

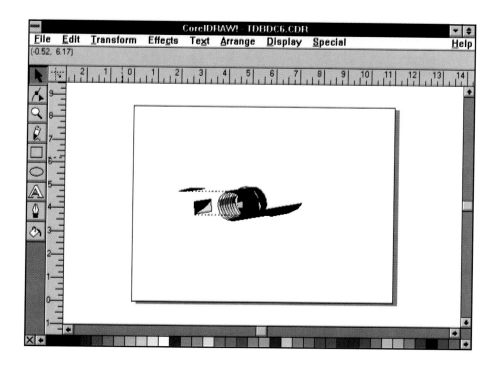

Figure 15.37:
Barrel shape detail.

19. Select the rectangle and the overlying triangle. Click on **B**lend Roll-Up from the **E**ffects menu, set Steps to 20, and click on Apply.

20. Marquee-select the resulting blend group and control objects, and click on **G**roup from the **A**rrange menu. Then align the left edge of the grouped object with the left edge of the barrel.

21. Draw another ellipse measuring 1" x 1-1/4". Select **R**otate & Skew from the **T**ransform menu, set the rotation for 10 degrees, and click on OK. Fill the ellipse with 100-percent black and a .003", 100-percent black outline.

22. Select **M**ove from the **T**ransform menu. Set the horizontal value to –.01", choose Leave Original, and click on OK. Fill the new ellipse with white, leaving the outline the same.

23. Using the Pick tool, select the white ellipse, and click on Con**v**ert To Curves from the **A**rrange menu.

24. Add nodes at the points indicated in figure 15.38. Marquee-select the points on the left side and bottom of the ellipse, and double-click on one of them. Choose **t**oLine from the Node Edit dialog box to create the squared-off portions of the object.

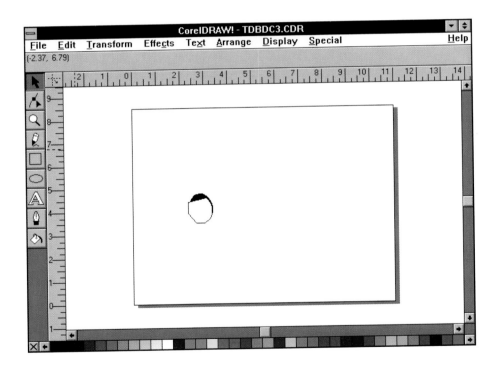

Figure 15.38:
Front ellipse detail.

25. Using the Pick tool, select both the modified ellipse and the underlying black ellipse. Click on **C**ombine from the **A**rrange menu to create a mask.

26. Select the mask and the left thread ellipse. Using the ellipse as your alignment guide, place the mask. Select **A**lign from the **A**rrange menu, set the horizontal and vertical alignment options to center, and click on OK (see fig. 15.39).

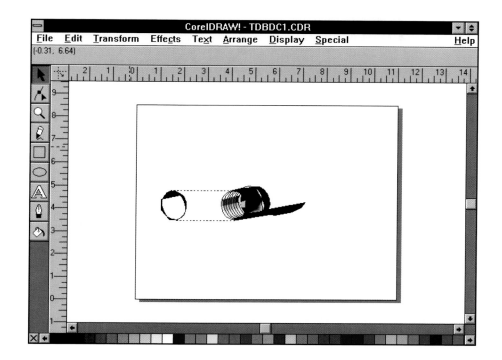

Figure 15.39:
Aligning the front mask.

27. Draw a small rectangle, and select Con**v**ert To Curves from the **A**rrange menu. Adjust the nodes on the rectangle appropriately to create one of the skewed rectangular faces. Fill the rectangle with 100-percent black for dark tones, 50-percent black for medium tones, and 10-percent black for light tones with no outline, as shown in figure 15.35. Repeat the procedure to create the other skewed rectangles.

To save time, **D**uplicate the first modified rectangle, alter the fill, and adjust the nodes.

28. Select the rectangles, and **G**roup them. Then select the grouped object and the mask. Click on **A**lign from the **A**rrange menu, and select Horizontal/Left, Vertical/Center. Click on OK to place the highlight group (see fig. 15.40).

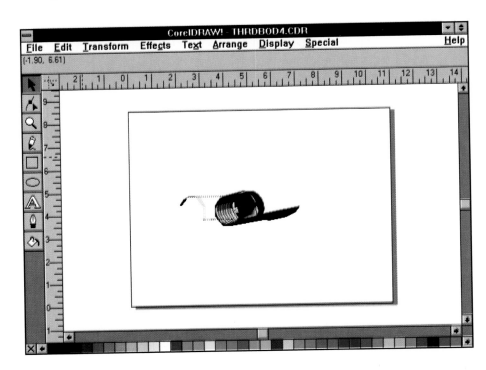

Figure 15.40:

Placing the highlight group.

29. The additional highlights on the threaded portion of the coupling are drawn freehand. Fill and place them as indicated in figure 15.41.

The Blueprint View

Once upon a time, back in the days of drawing boards, drawing a blueprint was a tedious exercise in laying individual lines and applying hatching. Drawing a blueprint required that you visualize the image and organize your thoughts from back to front. Working primarily with pen and ink, this often became a time-consuming process.

1. Using CorelDRAW, the blueprint for the valve is created in minutes. Although it still is a good idea to visualize things from back to front, it is not as critical. The blueprint is created by using filled objects to cover areas that are not to be seen.

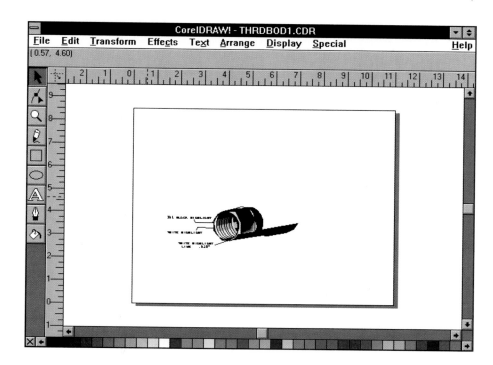

Figure 15.41:
Final highlights on thread coupling.

2. Custom fills are created to vary the hatching. To create a custom fill, draw a 1" square on the workspace. Then select Snap To Objects from the **D**isplay menu, and draw a single diagonal line in the desired direction. Eliminate the outline on the square so that it does not become a part of the fill (see fig. 15.42).

3. Select **C**reate Pattern from the **S**pecial menu, and set the options for Two Color and High Resolution. Click on OK and the cursor changes to crosshairs. Move the crosshairs to one corner of the image, and click-and-drag the crosshairs diagonally to the opposite corner. Now the custom fill is ready to select from the Fill tool flyout menu. Repeat the procedure to create the other fill.

Text

Most technical drawings and schematics require text describing the application of the subject of the drawing. In this case, the text was taken from the Uniform Plumbing Code, and as such, is accurate regarding the application and installation specifications.

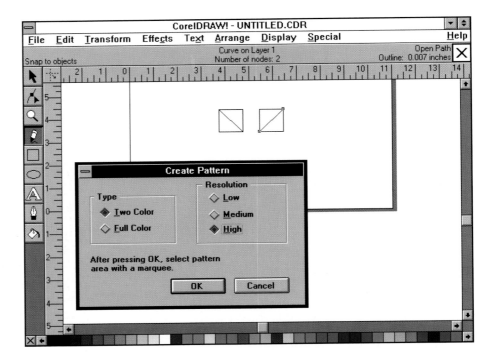

Figure 15.42:

Custom fill creation example.

A couple of things are missing from this drawing, however, that generally are required of a technical illustration with a cut-away blueprint. I omitted the inclusion of dimensioning and the scale legend for aesthetic reasons.

Black-and-White Effects

"Drawing is the honesty of art. There is no possibility of cheating. It is either good or bad."

—*Salvador Dali*

Fish Fry Logo

by Kevin Marshall

Fishers, Indiana

Equipment Used

Gateway 2000 386/25
Logitech Scanman 256 hand-held scanner
4M of RAM

Output Equipment Used

HP Laserjet II

Kevin Marshall is a 3D animation and paintbox artist for a local video production company in Indianapolis, Indiana. He has been a CorelDRAW user for four years.

He developed this award-winning piece of art in response to a client's need for a logo celebrating one of Indianapolis' longest-running fish frys. The logo needed to be one color so that it could easily be printed on such items as T-shirts and signs.

Procedure

1. I always start with a fully developed idea that is sketched out. For this particular design, I wanted to keep the rough "woodcut" look of the fish from the sketched drawing, and create the type, ellipses, and checkerboard pattern on the computer.

    I sketched the fish first, leaving out a section so that the top half of the fish would be above the oval and the tail would be beneath the oval. Then I enlarged the sketch on a photocopier.

    I sketched the fish to keep the look of a hand-drawn picture. Many drawings created on the computer tend to look perfect.

2. Enlarge the drawing of the fish to the maximum size that the scanning device allows. Scan the image at 300 dpi, and make it black and white (as opposed to grayscale).

3. You can save the scanned image as a TIFF or a PCX file.

I prefer to use the TIFF format because it is widely accepted across several desktop publishing platforms.

4. Open a new Corel file, and import the TIFF bitmap image for manual tracing.

You could use CorelTRACE at this point, but for this particular logo I want to selectively choose which parts to convert to vector form. Choosing the parts selectively helps to eliminate the possibility of scanning stray elements, such as dirt or dust.

5. Zoom in on the image so that it fills the entire screen. Now you are ready to trace.

6. Make sure the bitmap is selected, and use the Pencil tool to autotrace the outside edge of the fish's body (see fig. 16.1).

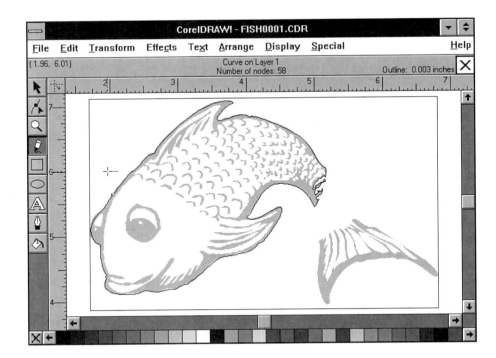

Figure 16.1:
The bitmapped image with outline.

7. Place the Pencil tool on the inside of the fish's body and to the right of the leftmost eyeball. Then, trace the inside outline.

8. These images are two separate lines. To create the desired thick outline, the two objects must be combined into one. To combine the lines, use the Pick tool and hold down the Shift key to select both lines. Then choose **C**ombine from the **A**rrange menu (see fig. 16.2).

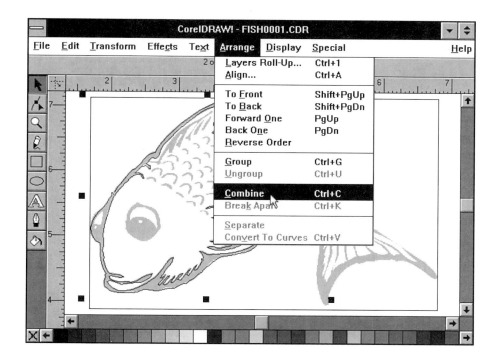

Figure 16.2:
*Use **C**ombine to combine the two lines into one line.*

9. Fill this outline with 100-percent black and no outline (see fig. 16.3).

10. Select the original bitmap image again, and use the Pencil tool to resume tracing.

11. Zoom in on the fish's rightmost eyeball, and trace each section: the inside, the outside, and the highlight inside the pupil. You should have three curves—the eyeball's outline, the pupil, and the highlight in the pupil (see fig. 16.4).

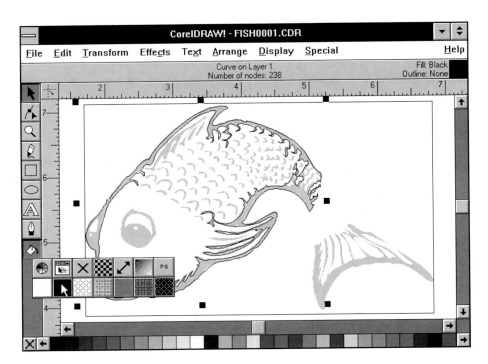

Figure 16.3:

*Filling the outline
with solid black.*

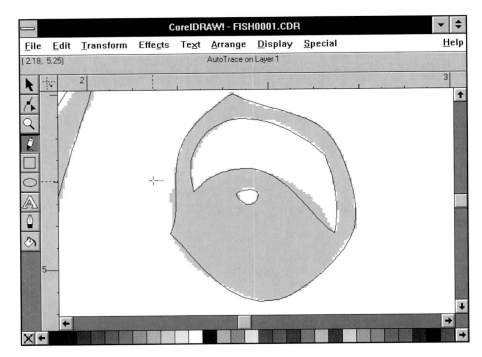

Figure 16.4:

*Close-up of the
autotraced eyeball.*

Remember that this is supposed to look like a woodcut. Don't worry if the traced outline does not follow the edge of the original. This helps to add to the effect.

12. Select all three curves. To select the curves, hold down the Shift key and select each curve with the Pick tool, or use the Pick tool to marquee-select the three curves.

13. Choose **C**ombine from the **A**rrange menu to combine the three curves into one.

14. Fill the eye with 100-percent black and no outline.

15. Select the original bitmapped image again, and finish tracing the rest of the fish's body by using the Pencil tool. You might have to zoom in and out to get every detail. Do not trace the tail yet.

16. After everything but the tail is traced, use the Pick tool to marquee-select all the traced pieces (see fig. 16.5).

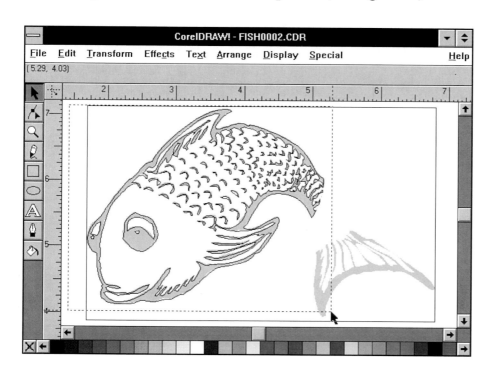

Figure 16.5:
Marquee-select the traced pieces.

17. **C**ombine all of the individual pieces into one. Everything now should be filled with 100-percent black and no outline. If everything is not filled with black, do so now.

18. Now, trace the tail. **C**ombine all of the elements of the tail into one element, and fill that element with 100-percent black and no outline.

19. Now delete the original bitmapped image. You are left with two pieces that comprise the fish (see fig. 16.6).

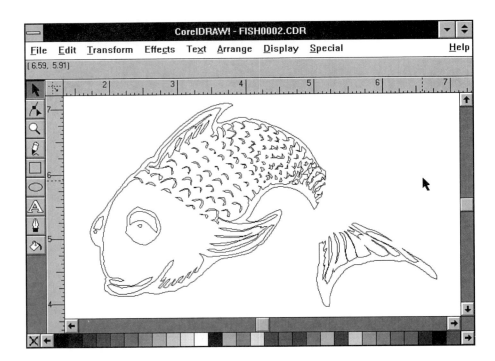

Figure 16.6:
The two traced pieces.

20. Using the Pencil tool, draw an outline inside the main thick outline that makes up the fish's body. You may have to zoom in and out to get the line between the main outlines (see fig. 16.7).

21. Fill the new outline with 100-percent white and no outline, and place it behind the fish by selecting the To **B**ack command from the **A**rrange menu. This provides a solid fill for the fish so that any pattern behind it does not show through.

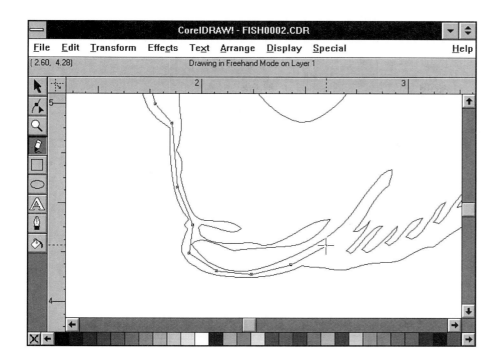

Figure 16.7:
Detail of the line.

22. Select all of the pieces you have created, and drag them off to the side for now.

23. Select **S**nap To Grid from the **D**isplay menu. Then choose Grid Setup.

24. In the Grid Setup dialog box, set the grid frequency to 4 per inch horizontally and vertically (see fig. 16.8).

25. Draw a checkerboard pattern using alternating squares .25" × .25". (The pattern needs to taper at the top and bottom. Refer to figure 16.9.)

26. **C**ombine all of the squares into one, and fill them with 20-percent black and no outline. Then send them to the back, and move them off to the side.

27. Turn off **S**nap To Grid.

28. Use the Ellipse tool and hold down the Ctrl key to draw a circle. Make the circle 4.13" in diameter.

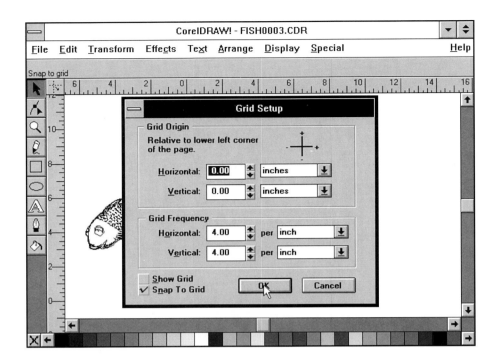

Figure 16.8:

Set the grid frequency in the Grid Setup dialog box.

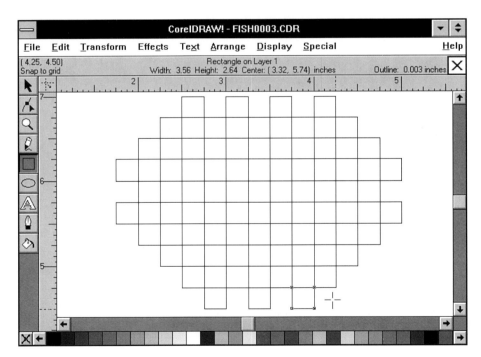

Figure 16.9:

The checkerboard.

Hold down the Ctrl key while using the Ellipse tool to create a perfect circle. If you do not hold down the Ctrl key, you will create an ellipse.

29. Scale vertically by 82 percent. The circle created in step 28 now is an ellipse.

It is easier to draw a circle and scale it to get the desired ellipse than to draw an ellipse.

30. Make a duplicate of the ellipse, and scale it down proportionally by 69 percent.

31. Select both ellipses, and align them to the center of the page by using the **A**rrange menu's **A**lign command (see fig. 16.10).

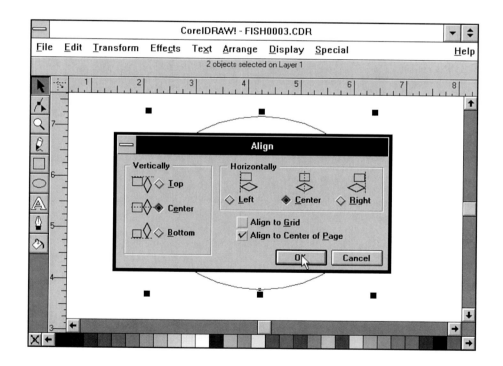

Figure 16.10:
Use the Align dialog box to align the ellipses.

32. With both ellipses still selected, **C**ombine them into one, and fill them with 60-percent black and 100-percent black outline.

33. Click on the Pen Nib icon in the Outline flyout menu to set the width to .056", and select Scale With Image. This keeps the outline in proper proportion should the logo need to be scaled later (see fig. 16.11).

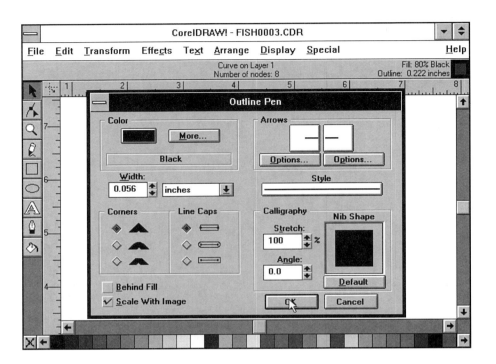

Figure 16.11:

Use the Outline Pen dialog box to set the width.

34. Select all three parts of the fish, and drag them into position over the ellipse.

35. Send the fish's body and solid white piece to the front. Send the fish tail to the back (see fig. 16.12).

36. Use the Pencil tool to draw two separate pieces for the chef's hat. Fill both with 100-percent white and no outline.

37. Use the Pencil tool to add shadows to the hat by drawing two shadow pieces and three shadow crease lines (see fig. 16.13).

38. Fill the two shadow pieces with 20-percent black and no outline. Send the bottom shadow piece back one layer.

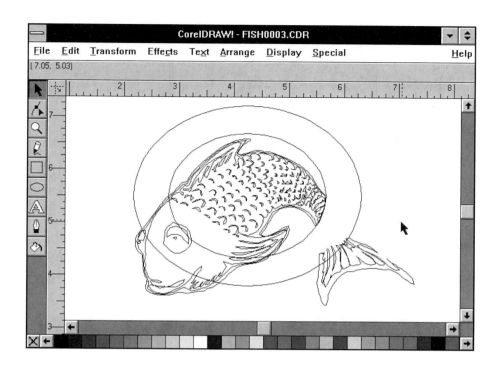

Figure 16.12:
The finished ellipses and the fish.

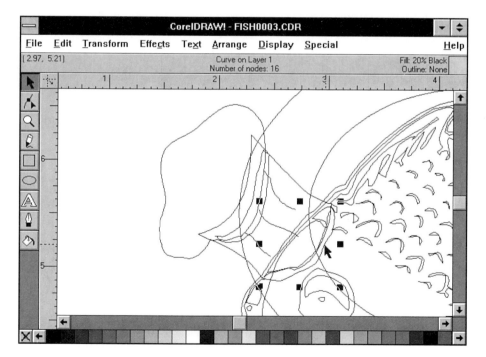

Figure 16.13:
Detail of a chef's hat.

39. The three shadow crease lines should be set to 20-percent black with a line width of .028". In the Outline Pen dialog box, set the Nib Shape to a 62-percent Stretch and a –30-degree Angle. Also, select Scale With Image.

40. Bring the top portion of the hat to the front, and draw two concentric outlines to simulate one thick outline. **C**ombine the two outlines, and fill with 100-percent black and no outline. Do the same for the base of the hat making sure that the top portion of the hat stays on the top layer along with its outlines.

41. Draw a circle with a diameter of 3.48", scale it vertically by 82 percent, and align it to the center of the page. Make sure the circle does not have a fill or an outline (see fig. 16.14).

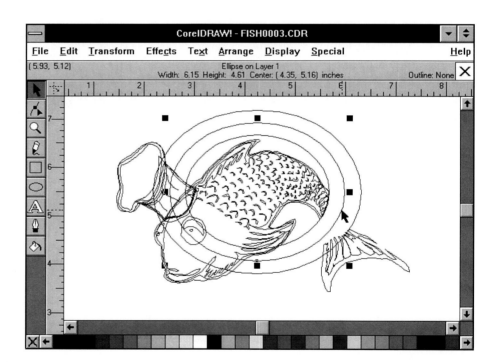

Figure 16.14:

The vertically scaled ellipse.

42. Use the Con**v**ert To Curves command from the **A**rrange menu to convert the center ellipse to a curve.

43. Using the Node Edit tool, add nodes to the chef's hat and directly underneath the fish's bottom fin. Break these

nodes, and delete the line segments that run through the head of the fish (see fig. 16.15).

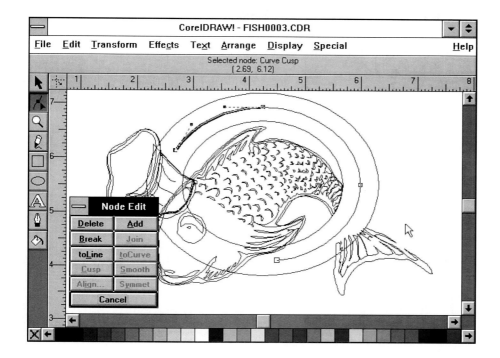

Figure 16.15:
Use the Node Edit dialog box to edit nodes.

44. Use 32.5-point Bodnoff normal text with a 19-percent intercharacter spacing for the word "Fairview." Fill the text with 100-percent white and no outline.

45. Set the words "Fish Fry" to 32.6-point Bodnoff normal text with a 57-percent intercharacter spacing and 344-percent interword spacing. Fill with 100-percent white and no outline.

46. Select the word "Fairview" and the inner curve, and choose Fit **T**ext To Path from the **T**ext menu. Use the settings shown in figure 16.16. Click on Apply.

If Fit **T**ext To Path places the text on the wrong end of the curve, change the setting for Place On Other Side and reapply.

47. Select the words "Fish Fry" and the same inner curve as before. Change the settings to match figure 16.17, and click on Apply.

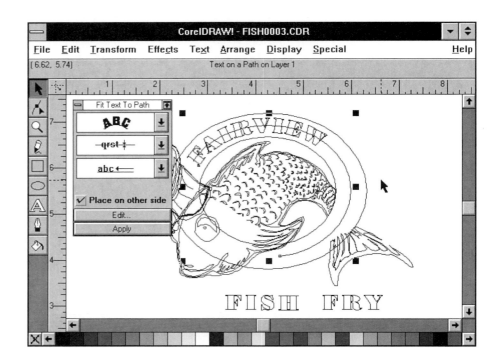

Figure 16.16:

Fitting the upper text to a path.

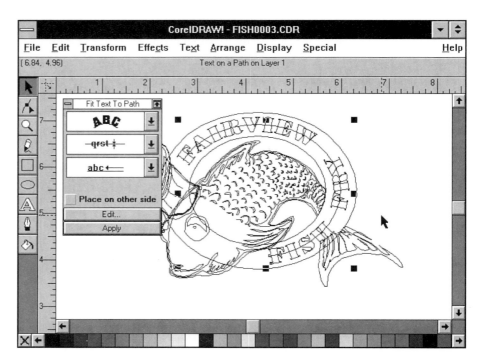

Figure 16.17:

Fitting the lower text to a path.

48. Select the checkerboard pattern you created earlier, and
align it to the center of the page. You now have a completed logo that looks like figure 16.18.

Figure 16.18:
The completed artwork.

Celebrate Cole Porter's
100th anniversary
at the American Music
Theater Festival's
ninth annual gala
featuring Cole Porter's
first Broadway hit

**FIFTY MILLION
FRENCHMEN**

Enjoy special selections from this
sassy and sophisticated tale of
Americans set loose in 1929 Paris
featuring "You Do Something To
Me", "You've Got That Thing"
and many more.

**Saturday
September 14, 1991**

The Ballroom of
Hotel Atop the Bellevue
Broad & Walnut Streets
Philadelphia, Pennsylvania

7:00 p.m.
Cocktails

8:00 p.m.
Dinner, Show, and Dancing
to the Jack Keller Orchestra
The fifth annual Stephen Sondheim
Award presentation

Black Tie

CURTAIN RAISERS

Mr. & Mrs. Joel N. Bloom
Mr. & Mrs. William A. Callanan
Ellen and Neil Carver
Gary A. Clinton
Mr. & Mrs. Gerard J. Davies
Judith A. Dooling
Mr. & Mrs. Robert M. Elder
Mr. & Mrs. Matthew Garfield

Mr. & Mrs. James B. Ginty
Lisa A. Granozio
Mr. & Mrs. Daniel J. Haley, Jr.
William J. Harry
Mr. & Mrs. Leslie C. High
Elsie Hossack
Peter F. Iacovoni
Mr. & Mrs. Michael J. Joyce
Albert Konrad, Jr.
Craig J. Klofach
Dr. & Mrs. Leonard M. Lodish
Mr. & Mrs. James Marks
Donald M. Millinger, Esq.
Mr. & Mrs. Edward A. Montgomery, Jr.
Mr. & Mrs. James J. Morley
James P. O'Brien
Mr. & Mrs. Harold W. Pote
Frank J. Powell
Myron and Phoebe Resnick
Eric B. Rymshaw, AIA
Mrs. M. Yetter Schoch
Mrs. John J. Shaw, Jr.
Joseph and Janet Shein
Mr. & Mrs. Richard Sherman
D. Michael Stroud, Esq.
Drs. Mona and Alton Sutnick
Mr. & Mrs. Andrew J. Talone
Mr. & Mrs. A. Thomas Tebbens, Jr.
Robert and Barbara Tiffany
Richard C. Torbert
Dr. & Mrs. R. Robert Tyson
Mr. & Mrs. Peter Vaira, Jr.
Mr. & Mrs. Robert G. Wilder

American Style Invitation

by Dora Modly

Ten On Twelve Studio
Philadelphia, Pennsylvania

Equipment Used

386AT
DFI Handy Scanner
4M of RAM

Output Equipment Used

High-resolution linotronic

Dora Modly, a freelance designer in Philadelphia, has been a CorelDRAW user for five years. This invitation was designed for a client's annual gala event. The client wanted something upbeat and festive to express the musical theme of the event—Cole Porter's 100th Anniversary. The three-panel invitation uses simple illustrations and icons related to the copy running down the right margin.

Procedure

1. Select Page Setup from the File menu, and assign a custom size of 17" × 10" portrait to accommodate the open invitation size of 16.5" × 8.5".

2. Using the Rectangle tool, create a 16.5" × 8.5" frame for the layout. Use the Pencil tool to draw two straight horizontal lines that divide the main frame into three equal-sized panels measuring 5.5" × 8.5". Set the line attributes to None because they will be used as guidelines only.

3. Using the Rectangle Tool, start in the upper right corner and drag your cursor down the length of the frame, creating a wide band measuring 17" × 3.5". Assign the rectangle a fill of 100-percent black (see fig. 16.19).

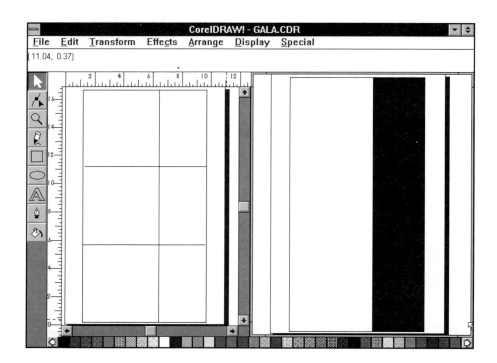

Figure 16.19:

Setting up the invitation frame and black text.

4. The copy for the invitation will appear within the black band on the right that you just created. To begin, click on the Text tool and, in the Text dialog box, select Prose Antique for the typeface with a centered alignment. Type the lines of text in the text entry window. The headings and subheadings will be typed in individual text strings. Set the point size and spacing requirements while in the Text dialog box. Move the text strings into position with the Pick tool, and assign all text with white fills (see fig. 16.20).

5. For the long list of names in the lower half of the invitation, use a block of paragraph text instead of individual text strings. To do this, click on the Text tool, position your cursor where the text should begin, and drag it down to where the bottom right margin of the paragraph should be. A dotted rectangle follows the cursor and defines the space for your paragraph (see fig. 16.21).

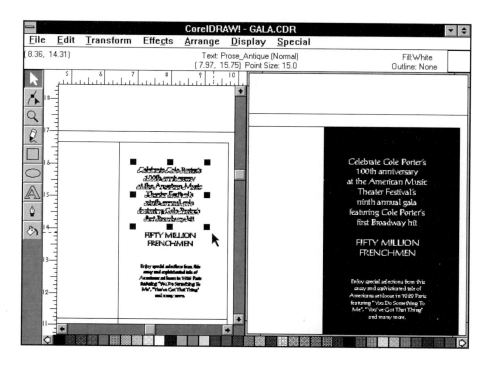

Figure 16.20:
Adding the text.

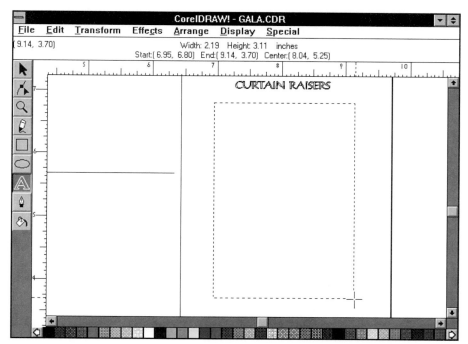

Figure 16.21:
*Adding a block of
paragraph text.*

6. Type your text, and set the desired point size and interline spacing while in the Text dialog box. Return to your editing screen, and assign a white fill to this text as well.

7. After you have compiled or created the artwork to be incorporated in the design (such as musical notes, dancing couples, party favor curls, pieces of confetti and streamers) scan the images from clean, black-and-white copies, and save them as PCX files in a scanning program. Import the files by selecting **I**mport from the **F**ile menu.

If you don't have a scanner, find a friend who does or purchase a simple hand-held scanner. New grayscale, hand-held scanners are under $200. If finding a scanner is too difficult, look on CompuServe, GEnie, America Online, and other on-line and BBS systems for clip art and bitmaps. CorelDRAW also includes a sizable clip-art library that comes with the program.

8. Trace the PCX files in CorelTRACE, and import the pictures into your CorelDRAW file. Do not clean up the edges of the images. The rough, unfinished quality creates a desired effect and is part of the overall design concept (see fig. 16.22).

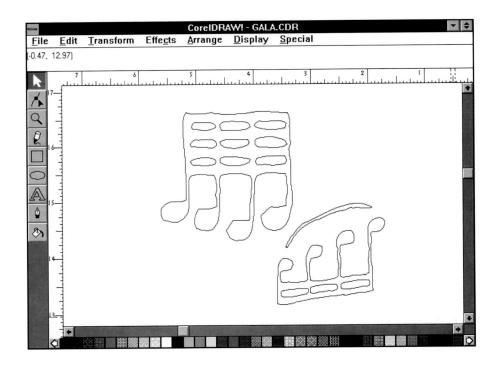

Figure 16.22:

Leave the edges of imported graphics rough.

9. To create the background shapes for the illustrations, use the Pencil tool to draw three irregular rectangles with black fills. Output these from a laser printer and scan them. Import the traced shapes into your CorelDRAW file, again leaving the edges rough so that they are consistent with the other graphics.

10. Position each box in one of the three panels to the left of the text. Size each with the Pick tool by dragging one of the highlighted corners until it fits proportionately within the allotted space (see fig. 16.23).

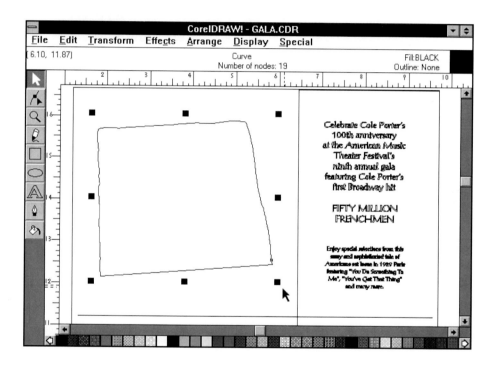

Figure 16.23:
Fitting the black boxes in panels.

11. Fill the musical notes and the party favor graphics with white. **U**ngroup the dancing couple, and fill the dress, glove, shirt, and flower with white. Assign a 1.5-point white outline to the curves defining the woman's head, the flounce of the dress, and the man's head and body (no fills), then regroup.

12. Position and size each graphic within one of the black rectangular shapes in the following order: notes in top panel, dancers in middle panel, and party favor in lower panel.

The graphics should be sized large enough so that certain edges bleed off the black box into the white background, as shown in figures 16.24 through 16.26.

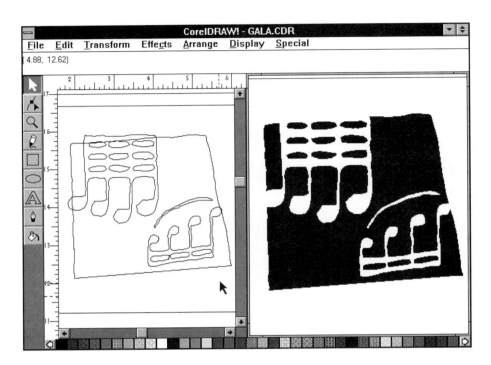

Figure 16.24:
Placement of the first graphic.

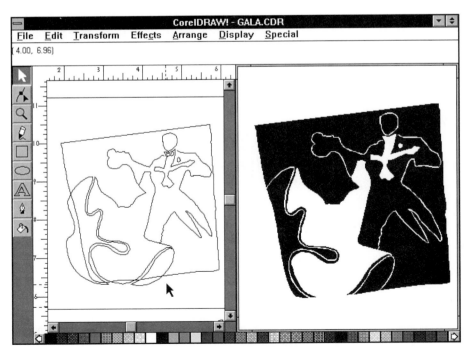

Figure 16.25:
Placement of the second graphic.

Figure 16.26:

Placement of the third graphic.

13. Select the confetti shapes that were scanned (or drawn), and **D**uplicate them until there are enough for the background.

14. Position the confetti throughout the background and within the "picture boxes." Assign black fills to the confetti pieces on the white background; assign white fills to the confetti pieces in the black boxes (see fig. 16.27).

15. Finally, stretch the streamer vertically by clicking on it and dragging it with your cursor, or by choosing **S**tretch & Mirror from the **T**ransform menu. Because my imported graphic was 7", I stretched it 225 percent so that it extended the length of the invitation.

16. Assign a fill of white and position the streamer to the right of the text (see fig. 16.28).

Figure 16.29 shows the completed invitation.

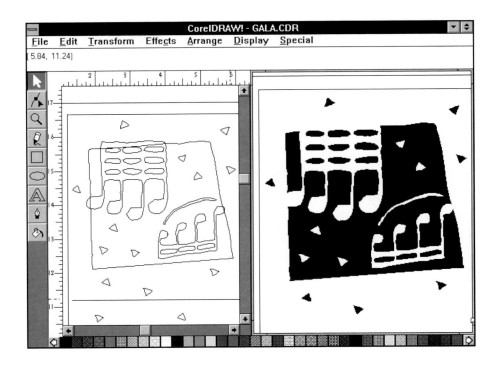

Figure 16.27:

Assign white fills to the confetti pieces within the black box.

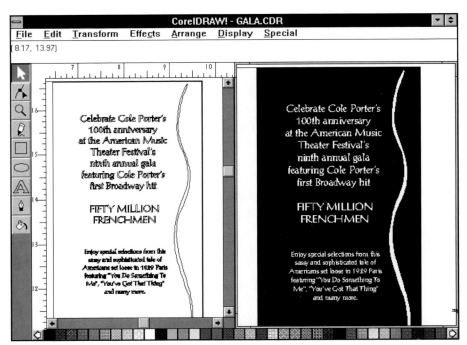

Figure 16.28:

Placement of streamer to right of text.

Celebrate Cole Porter's
100th anniversary
at the American Music
Theater Festival's
ninth annual gala
featuring Cole Porter's
first Broadway hit

**FIFTY MILLION
FRENCHMEN**

Enjoy special selections from this
sassy and sophisticated tale of
Americans set loose in 1929 Paris
featuring "You Do Something To
Me", "You've Got That Thing"
and many more.

**Saturday
September 14, 1991**

The Ballroom of
Hotel Atop the Bellevue
Broad & Walnut Streets
Philadelphia, Pennsylvania

7:00 p.m.
Cocktails

8:00 p.m.
Dinner, Show, and Dancing
to the Jack Keller Orchestra
The fifth annual Stephen Sondheim
Award presentation

Black Tie

CURTAIN RAISERS

Mr. & Mrs. Joel N. Bloom
Mr. & Mrs. William A. Callanan
Ellen and Neil Carver
Gary A. Clinton
Mr. & Mrs. Gerard J. Davies
Judith A. Dooling
Mr. & Mrs. Robert M. Elder
Mr. & Mrs. Matthew Garfield

Mr. & Mrs. James B. Ginty
Lisa A. Granozio
Mr. & Mrs. Daniel J. Haley, Jr.
William J. Harry
Mr. & Mrs. Leslie C. High
Elsie Hossack
Peter F. Iacovoni
Mr. & Mrs. Michael J. Joyce
Albert Konrad, Jr.
Craig J. Klofach
Dr. & Mrs. Leonard M. Lodish
Mr. & Mrs. James Marks
Donald M. Millinger, Esq.
Mr. & Mrs. Edward A. Montgomery, Jr.
Mr. & Mrs. James J. Morley
James P. O'Brien
Mr. & Mrs. Harold W. Pote
Frank J. Powell
Myron and Phoebe Resnick
Eric B. Rymshaw, AIA
Mrs. M. Yetter Schoch
Mrs. John J. Shaw, Jr.
Joseph and Janet Shein
Mr. & Mrs. Richard Sherman
D. Michael Stroud, Esq.
Drs. Mona and Alton Sutnick
Mr. & Mrs. Andrew J. Talone
Mr. & Mrs. A. Thomas Tebbens, Jr.
Robert and Barbara Tiffany
Richard C. Torbert
Dr. & Mrs. R. Robert Tyson
Mr. & Mrs. Peter Vaira, Jr.
Mr. & Mrs. Robert G. Wilder

Figure 16.29:
The completed design.

INDEX

INDEX

INDEX

INDEX

I N D E X

INDEX

INDEX

I N D E X

CorelDRAW! Special Effects
REGISTRATION CARD

Fill out this card to receive information about future CorelDRAW! books and other New Riders titles!

Name _____ **Title** _____

Company _____

Address _____

City/State/ZIP _____

I bought this book because _____

_____

I purchased this book from:
☐ A bookstore (Name _____)
☐ A software or electronics store (Name _____)
☐ A mail order (Name of Catalog _____)

I purchase this many computer books each year:
☐ 1–5   ☐ 5 or more

I currently use these applications: _____

_____

_____

_____

I found these chapters to be the most informative: _____

_____

I found these chapters to be the least informative: _____

_____

Additional comments: _____

_____

☐ I would like to see my name in print! You may use my name and quote me in future New Riders products and promotions. My daytime phone number is:_____

New Riders Publishing 11711 North College Avenue • P.O. Box 90 • Carmel, Indiana 46032 USA

Fold Here

PLACE
STAMP
HERE

New Riders Publishing
11711 North College Avenue
P.O. Box 90
Carmel, Indiana 46032
USA